Putting Skeptics in Their Place

THE NATURE OF SKEPTICAL ARGUMENTS AND THEIR ROLE IN PHILOSOPHICAL INQUIRY

John Greco
Fordham University

CAMBRIDGE UNIVERSITY PRESS
Cambridge, New York, Melbourne, Madrid, Cape Town, Singapore, São Paulo

Cambridge University Press
The Edinburgh Building, Cambridge CB2 8RU, UK

Published in the United States of America by Cambridge University Press, New York

www.cambridge.org
Information on this title: www.cambridge.org/9780521772631

© John Greco 2000

This publication is in copyright. Subject to statutory exception
and to the provisions of relevant collective licensing agreements,
no reproduction of any part may take place without the written
permission of Cambridge University Press.

First published 2000
This digitally printed version 2007

A catalogue record for this publication is available from the British Library

Library of Congress Cataloguing in Publication data
Greco, John
Putting skeptics in their place : the nature of skeptical arguments and their role in
philosophical inquiry / John Greco
p. cm. – (Cambridge studies in philosophy)
Includes bibliographical references and index
ISBN 0-521-77263-X (hardcover)
1. Skepticism. I. Title. II. Series.
B837 .G74 2000
149'.73–dc21
99-042103

ISBN 978-0-521-77263-1 hardback
ISBN 978-0-521-04553-7 paperback

Putting Skeptics in Their Place

This book is about the nature of skeptical arguments and their role in philosophical inquiry. John Greco defends three theses: that a number of historically prominent skeptical arguments make no obvious mistake and therefore cannot be easily dismissed; that the analysis of skeptical arguments is philosophically useful and important and should therefore have a central place in the methodology of philosophy; and that taking skeptical arguments seriously requires us to adopt an externalist, reliabilist epistemology.

Greco argues that the importance of skeptical arguments is methodological. Specifically, skeptical arguments act as heuristic devices for highlighting plausible but mistaken assumptions about the nature of knowledge, thereby requiring us to replace these assumptions with something better. Consequently, the analysis of skeptical arguments drives positive epistemology. It is further argued that taking skeptical arguments seriously requires us to adopt a version of "virtue epistemology," or a theory of knowledge that makes intellectual virtue central in the analysis of knowledge. This methodology has consequences for moral and religious epistemology; in particular, a theory of moral perception is defended.

This book will be of interest to professionals and graduate students in epistemology and moral philosophy.

John Greco is Associate Professor of Philosophy at Fordham University.

CAMBRIDGE STUDIES IN PHILOSOPHY

General editor   ERNEST SOSA (Brown University)

Advisory editors:
JONATHAN DANCY (University of Reading)
JOHN HALDANE (University of St. Andrews)
GILBERT HARMAN (Princeton University)
FRANK JACKSON (Australian National University)
WILLIAM G. LYCAN (University of North Carolina at Chapel Hill)
SYDNEY SHOEMAKER (Cornell University)
JUDITH J. THOMSON (Massachusetts Institute of Technology)

RECENT TITLES:

LYNNE RUDDER BAKER   *Explaining Attitudes*
ROBERT A. WILSON   *Cartesian Psychology and Physical Minds*
BARRY MAUND   *Colours*
MICHAEL DEVITT   *Coming to Our Senses*
MICHAEL ZIMMERMAN   *The Concept of Moral Obligation*
MICHAEL STOCKER with ELIZABETH HEGEMAN   *Valuing Emotions*
SYDNEY SHOEMAKER   *The First-Person Perspective and Other Essays*
NORTON NELKIN   *Consciousness and the Origins of Thought*
MARK LANCE and JOHN O'LEARY HAWTHORNE   *The Grammar of Meaning*
D. M. ARMSTRONG   *A World of States of Affairs*
PIERRE JACOB   *What Minds Can Do*
ANDRÉ GALLOIS   *The World Without the Mind Within*
FRED FELDMAN   *Utilitarianism, Hedonism, and Desert*
LAURENCE BONJOUR   *In Defense of Pure Reason*
DAVID LEWIS   *Papers in Philosophical Logic*
WAYNE DAVIS   *Implicature*
DAVID COCKBURN   *Other Times*
DAVID LEWIS   *Papers on Metaphysics and Epistemology*
RAYMOND MARTIN   *Self-Concern*
ANNETTE BARNES   *Seeing through Self-Deception*
MICHAEL BRATMAN   *Faces of Intention*
AMIE THOMASSON   *Fiction and Metaphysics*
DAVID LEWIS   *Papers on Ethics and Social Philosophy*
FRED DRETSKE   *Perception, Knowledge, and Belief*
LYNNE RUDDER BAKER   *Persons and Bodies*

To Lizabeth and Sofia

Contents

Preface		*page* xiii
1	The Nature of Skeptical Arguments and Their Role in Philosophical Inquiry	1
	1. The Three Theses	2
	2. Strategy and Outline of the Book	6
	3. Three Criteria for an Adequate Theory of Knowledge	15
2	Skepticism about the World: Part One – Reconstructions	25
	1. An Argument from Hume	25
	2. An Argument from Descartes	34
	3. Need the Skeptic Challenge All of Our Knowledge at Once?	39
	4. Two More Ways Not to Understand Descartes' Argument	51
	5. Discriminating Evidence	54
	6. Supporting Evidence	58
3	Skepticism about the World: Part Two – Dismissive Responses	61
	1. Charges of Self-Refutation	61
	2. Pragmatic and Rhetorical Responses	64
	3. More Dismissive Responses	69
	4. Transcendental Arguments	71
4	Skepticism about the World: Part Three – Dualism, Realism, and Representationalism	77
	I. What Is Necessary for Skepticism about the World	83
	1. The Modern Ontology and Skepticism	83
	2. Realism and Skepticism	88
	3. Representationalism and Skepticism	90

ix

	II.	What Is Sufficient for Skepticism about the World	94
	1.	The Big Mistake	95
	2.	The Modern Ontology Again	102
	3.	Representationalism Again	103
	4.	Conclusions	106
5	The Argument from an Infinite Regress of Reasons	108
	1.	The Regress Argument and Strong Particularism	108
	2.	Foundationalism	118
	3.	Contextualism	121
	4.	Coherentism	126
	5.	The Objection to Traditional Coherence Theories	128
	6.	The Objection to Nontraditional Coherence Theories	130
	7.	The Role of Sensory Appearances	134
	8.	Conclusions	135
6	Hume's Skepticism about Unobserved Matters of Fact	137
	I.	*Hume's Arguments and Dismissive Responses*	138
	1.	The Arguments in Sections IV and VII of the *Enquiry*	138
	2.	Objection (a): Hume Relies on an Inadequate Theory of Ideas	141
	3.	Objection (b): Hume Requires Absolute Certainty for Knowledge	145
	II.	*The Standard Objection against Hume*	146
	1.	The Objection	147
	2.	Deductive, Inductive, and Nonsupportive Inferences	149
	3.	An Objection Considered (against Our Interpretation of Hume)	155
	4.	The Lesson of Hume's Skeptical Argument	159
7	Agent Reliabilism	164
	I.	*Simple Reliabilism*	165
	1.	Simple Reliabilism: The Big Idea	165
	2.	Why Skeptical Arguments Go Wrong	167
	3.	From Processes to Virtues	174
	II.	*Agent Reliabilism and the Question of Subjective Justification*	180
	1.	Knowing That One Knows	181
	2.	Understanding That One Knows	184
	3.	Sosa's Perspectivism	187
	4.	From Perspectives to Dispositions	190
	5.	The Place of Epistemic Norms	192
	6.	The Place of Epistemic Responsibility	200
	7.	Conclusions	202

8	Agent Reliabilism and the Relevant Sense of "Relevant Possibility"	204
	1. Two Tasks for Working out This Approach	205
	2. The Relevant Sense of "Relevant Possibility"	207
	3. A Theory of Virtues and a Virtue Theory of Knowledge	211
	4. Agent Reliabilism and Relevant Possibilities	217
9	Moral and Religious Epistemology	220
	I. Religious Epistemology	221
	1. Plantinga's Rejection of the Evidentialist Objection to Religious Belief	222
	2. Alston's Defense of Religious Perception	226
	II. Moral Epistemology	231
	1. Three Kinds of Moral Epistemology	232
	2. A Theory of Empirical Perception	235
	3. A Theory of Moral Perception	241
	4. Some Traditional Objections to Moral Perception	244
	III. General Conclusions	248

Bibliography	255
Index	261

Preface

This book is largely the result of snide remarks from my colleagues at Fordham University. I arrived there very interested in skeptical problems, and people like Vincent Colapietro and Merold Westphal would wonder, out loud, why. One time, after I had presented a paper to the department on Humean skepticism, Chris Gowans bluntly asked me why anyone should find this sort of thing interesting. On another occasion, I was asked why I had my heart set on raising the dead – Hume had already been refuted, so why bother doing it again? Remarks like this were only half serious, but they were frequent enough to set me thinking about why I was so interested in skeptical arguments. It certainly was not because I thought that skepticism might be true. In fact, in this sense I was far less skeptical than most of my colleagues. Rather, I came to realize that my interest in skepticism was methodological. Along with a great many other epistemologists, I was interested in skeptical arguments because I thought that they could teach substantive lessons about the nature of knowledge and evidence. It was part of my methodology, in fact, to *assume* that skepticism is false, and that skeptical arguments must go wrong somewhere. The trick was to say where, and to learn the philosophical lesson contained therein.

A second thing that set me thinking was an observation about the profession: it seemed to me that nearly all philosophers have a story about why skepticism is wrong. Even people who are not interested in epistemology usually have a neat refutation of skepticism that they take for granted and think closes the case. None of these stories seemed even remotely plausible to me, but many nevertheless seemed to have the status of philosophical lore, with different lore existing in different circles. Finally, I was impressed that so many philosophers found the recent reliabilist trend in analytic philosophy to be entirely counterintuitive, almost a nonstarter. I became convinced that all of these things were related. It was partly because people thought that they had an easy answer to skepticism that they dismissed it as a non-problem. And it was partly because they thought skepticism to be a non-problem that they could not see the motivations for reliabilism. Finally, only a methodology that took skeptical arguments seriously could drive home either of these points. You need to take the arguments seriously to see that they cannot be easily refuted. And it is only after seeing this that you can appreciate the necessity of adopting some form of reliabilism in the theory of knowledge.

I take it that the views about skepticism just described have wide currency in philosophy. As I have already said, nearly everyone in philosophy has a story about skepticism that is incompatible with the one I am telling in this book. Accordingly, I take myself to be writing for a broad philosophical audience, including philosophers from a wide range of traditions, and including philosophers who are not particularly interested in epistemology. Finally, I hope also to have said some things that will be of interest to epistemologists, in particular. Specifically, the current trend toward reliabilist theories is not ubiquitous in analytic epistemology. On the contrary, a variety of objections have been directed against externalism in general and reliabilism in particular. By defending a version of reliabilism that is also a version of virtue epistemology, I hope to show how a reliabilist epistemology can be developed to meet the most powerful of those objections. For example, a virtue account allows us to see how knowledge is subjectively appropriate as well as objectively reliable. At the same time, developing the position as a version of virtue epistemology places it in a historical context going back at least to Aristotle, which helps to further address the counterintuitiveness of the position.

Acknowledgments

I am indebted to many people for my thinking in this book. The most influential of these were my teachers in epistemology at Brown University: Roderick Chisholm, Ernest Sosa, and James Van Cleve. My continuing debt to Sosa will be obvious to anyone who is familiar with the territory. Indeed, the extent of this debt is sometimes embarrassing, but I decided early on that it was better to be right than original, and so that is what I have tried to do. In graduate school I considered a number of people to be my teachers in books and essays. These were William Alston, Robert Audi, Laurence BonJour, Alvin Goldman, Alvin Plantinga, John Pollock, and Barry Stroud.

I am indebted to many more people for their comments on the manuscript or on relevant material. Keith Lehrer, Frederick Schmitt, and Michael Williams read all of the manuscript and provided me with many valuable comments, as did an anonymous referee. I thank all four for helping me to think through the relevant issues and to improve the manuscript on the basis of their careful criticisms. Robert Audi, Matthias Steup, Ernest Sosa, James Van Cleve, Margaret Walker, and Linda Zagzebski all read parts of the manuscript and also provided me with countless valuable suggestions and criticisms. I am sure that I have not adequately addressed all of the concerns that they have raised; I can only promise that I will try to think more about these issues in days to come.

So many other people have also read or heard relevant material and have provided me with all sorts of comments, ranging from useful advice to insightful criticisms. These include William Alston, José Bermudez, Judith Bradford, Lizabeth Byrne, Norris Clarke S. J., Stewart Cohen, Vincent Colapietro, Terence Cuneo, Brian Davies, Wayne Davis, Michael DePaul, Keith DeRose, Chris Gowans, Stephen Grimm, Christopher Hookway, Terence Horgan, John Jenkins, Jude Jones, Jaegwon Kim, Hilary Kornblith, Joseph Koterski S. J., Matthew Kuenning, James Marsh, David Martens, Richard McCombs, Robert Meyers, Dennis Monokroussos, Ralf Muller, Hilde Nelson, Carmen Pace, George Pappas, Rob Philp, Alvin Plantinga, Vincent Potter S. J., Curt Purcell, Alan Rhoda, Bob Roth S. J., Michael Sharkey, John Stolt, Dennis Sweet, Daryl Tress, John Van Buren, Merold Westphal, Michael Williams, Nicole Williams, Nicholas Wolterstorff, John Zeis, and Michael Zimmerman. I am sure there are more who should have been mentioned.

In what follows I draw from a number of my previously published essays. Chapter 4 expands on material from "Modern Ontology and the Problems of Epistemology," *American Philosophical Quarterly* 32 (1995), while Chapter 6 expands on material from "The Force of Hume's Skepticism about Unobserved Matters of Fact," *Journal of Philosophical Research* 23 (1998). Chapter 8 draws quite heavily from "Virtue Epistemology and the Relevant Sense of 'Relevant Possibility,' " *Southern Journal of Philosophy* 32 (1994). Finally, Chapter 9 expands on material from "Perception as Interpretation," in Michael Baur, ed., *Texts and*

Their Interpretation, Proceedings of the American Catholic Philosophical Association (New York: American Catholic Philosophical Association, 1999). I would like to thank the editors of these publications for their permission to use the relevant material.

1

The Nature of Skeptical Arguments and Their Role in Philosophical Inquiry

This book has three major theses: (1) that a number of historically prominent skeptical arguments make no obvious mistake and therefore cannot be easily dismissed; (2) that the analysis of skeptical arguments is philosophically useful and important and should therefore have a central place in the methodology of philosophy, particularly in the methodology of epistemology; and (3) that taking skeptical arguments seriously requires us to adopt an externalist, reliabilist epistemology. More specifically, it motivates a position that I call "agent reliabilism," which is an externalist version of virtue epistemology.

If these theses are correct, then many philosophers have misunderstood the nature of skeptical arguments and their role in philosophical inquiry. For example, many philosophers think that skepticism poses no philosophically interesting problem. According to this view, skeptical arguments rest on some obvious mistake, such as a quest for absolute certainty or a demand for immutable foundations, and can therefore easily be dismissed. Others think that skepticism rests on a substantive philosophical mistake, but that skeptical arguments teach no epistemological lessons. For example, many philosophers think that skepticism is rooted in a bad ontology. On this view skeptical arguments assume an ontological dualism between knowing mind and material object of knowledge and can therefore be rejected by rejecting the offending dualism. Others have thought that skepticism is rooted in representationalism, and still others that it is rooted in realism. Finally, some philosophers have appreciated that skepticism is indeed an epistemological problem, but have tried to solve it by remaining within a traditional, internalist epistemology. Against all of these positions, I argue that the recent externalist revolution in epistemology is necessary for a quite traditional reason: to adequately address a range of well-known skeptical arguments.[1]

1. THE THREE THESES

My first thesis is that a number of historically prominent skeptical arguments make no obvious mistake. On the contrary, such arguments begin with assumptions about knowledge and evidence that seem eminently plausible, outside the context of philosophical inquiry. Often they are assumptions that we ourselves accept either explicitly or implicitly. But by reasoning that is seemingly cogent, such arguments "prove" a conclusion that is outrageously implausible, even incredible in the literal sense. Accordingly, skeptical arguments are powerful in the following sense: it is not at all easy to see where they go wrong, and rejecting them requires one to adopt substantive and controversial theses about the nature of knowledge and evidence. This is not to say that they are powerful in a psychological sense – that they have the power to persuade. In this respect skeptical arguments are like arguments for God's existence: it is doubtful that any has ever produced a convert.

My second thesis is methodological and is closely tied to the first. Specifically, I argue that the analysis of skeptical arguments is philosophically useful and important. This is not because skepticism might be true and we need to assure ourselves that we know what we think we know. Neither is it because we need to persuade some other poor soul out of her skepticism. Rather, skeptical arguments are useful and important

---

[1] Some philosophers do take skeptical arguments seriously, giving them pride of place in their own methodology. For recent discussions that endorse my first two theses, see Peter Klein, *Certainty: A Refutation of Scepticism* (Minneapolis: University of Minnesota Press, 1981); Barry Stroud, *The Significance of Philosophical Scepticism* (Oxford: Clarendon Press, 1984); Robert Fogelin, *Pyrrhonian Reflections on Knowledge and Justification* (Oxford: Oxford University Press, 1994); and Michael Williams, *Unnatural Doubts* (Princeton: Princeton University Press, 1996). None of these authors endorses my third thesis, however. Williams argues that skeptical arguments mistakenly assume a thesis he calls "epistemic realism," while Klein argues for a defeasibility theory of knowledge. Stroud and Fogelin suggest that certain skeptical arguments cannot be answered in any satisfactory manner. In the context of the more usual attitudes regarding the nature and usefulness of skeptical arguments, however, my disagreements with these authors come fairly late in the day. Much of what I say in the book, in fact, overlaps with one or another of them. Finally, a good number of analytic epistemologists – reliabilists and externalists among them – engage in the analysis of skeptical arguments episodically as part of their methodology, and it is fairly clear that their own accounts of knowledge and evidence are motivated by this. In what follows I try to give this common practice an explicit articulation and systematic defense. I also recommend a more consistent application of it.

because they drive progress in philosophy. They do this by highlighting plausible but mistaken assumptions about knowledge and evidence, and by showing us that those assumptions have consequences that are unacceptable. As a result we are forced to develop substantive and controversial positions in their place. On this view skeptical arguments are important not because they might show that we do not have knowledge, but because they drive us to a better understanding of the knowledge we do have. There is another side to this coin: the price of ignoring skeptical arguments, or of rejecting them for the wrong reasons, is that we miss the lessons that the arguments can teach us.

Again, if these two theses are correct, then philosophers from a wide range of traditions have badly misconceived the nature and place of skeptical arguments. As we have already noted, many philosophers think that skeptical arguments make some obvious mistake and may therefore be easily dismissed. One example of this position is the view that skeptical arguments require some high level of certainty for knowledge — perhaps infallible premises, or incorrigible ones. Another is the view that skeptical arguments allow only deductive inferences. According to these diagnoses, to reject skepticism we need only reject its implausible standards for knowledge. Yet another widely held view is that skepticism is self-refuting, either because the skeptic makes incompatible claims (she knows that no one knows), or because skepticism cannot be lived and so the skeptic is caught in a "performative" contradiction.

If any one of these diagnoses were correct, then the analysis of skeptical arguments would not be philosophically useful or important. Such easy refutations would teach no lesson at all, or perhaps only one learned long ago — that rationalism is false. But against these views I argue that historically prominent skeptical arguments — for example, ones from Aristotle, Descartes, and Hume — make no obvious mistake and therefore cannot be easily dismissed. These skeptical arguments can be interpreted so that they involve no contradiction, performative or otherwise. Moreover, a close investigation of such arguments reveals that they run on assumptions much more dear to us than infallibilism or deductivism. Their lesson is not that some vestige of rationalism is false, but that something much more plausible will have to be given up.

There is another view of skepticism that is widely popular among philosophers, and that is incompatible with the one I am defending here. Philosophers from a surprising range of traditions claim that skeptical arguments presuppose a Cartesian ontology of internal subjects and external objects. Once the offending dualism is given up, these philosophers claim, skeptical arguments cannot even get off the ground. A strong version of this diagnosis implicates not only skepticism but epistemology as well. The idea is that epistemology is essentially the activity of constructing solutions to skeptical problems. But if skeptical problems cannot arise in a post-modern world, then epistemology is robbed of its purpose, and therefore of its existence.

Other philosophers think that skepticism is grounded not in a bad ontology but in a bad philosophy of mind. These philosophers make representationalism the root of all skeptical arguments. Still other philosophers think that a bad theory of reference is the problem, and still others think that the skeptic makes some kind of linguistic mistake. Against all of these positions I want to argue that skeptical arguments run on mistaken assumptions about the nature of knowledge and evidence. A close analysis of skeptical arguments drives positive epistemology, not ontology, or philosophy of mind, or philosophy of language.

My third thesis is that taking skeptical arguments seriously pushes us in a particular direction in epistemology. Specifically, it pushes us toward externalism and reliabilism. Even more specifically, it pushes us toward agent reliabilism. The idea is this: reconstructed in their most plausible form, a number of skeptical arguments show, quite correctly, that there is no necessary relation between our beliefs and their evidential grounds. It is now a commonplace to recognize that there is no such deductive relation. The more interesting point, however, is that there is no necessary inductive relation either; it is not a necessary truth that the grounds for our beliefs make them even probable. For many philosophers this contention would be enough to entail skepticism. If there is no logical or quasi-logical relation between our evidence and our beliefs, as some would require for our cognition to be "within the logical space of reasons," then a fundamental condition of knowledge goes unfulfilled.

There is in fact no such relation, however. This is one of the most important lessons that skeptical arguments teach us. A necessary condition for avoiding skepticism, therefore, is to rethink what it is for the grounds of our beliefs to be good evidence. Put another way, it is necessary to rethink what it is to be within the space of reasons. As it turns out, that space is neither logical nor quasi-logical. It is at most a contingent fact that the grounds for our beliefs are reliable indications of their truth, and any adequate epistemology must account for this.

The relevance of all of this to reliabilism is now easy to see. Taking skeptical arguments seriously provides a powerful motivation for reliabilism in epistemology, insofar as reliabilism can explain why evidence need not be logical or quasi-logical. According to reliabilism, a belief has positive epistemic status (roughly) just in case it is in fact reliably formed. Put in terms of evidence, the grounds on which a person forms her belief amount to good evidence (again roughly) just in case those grounds are in fact a reliable indication that the belief is true. There is no requirement that the person know that her grounds are reliable, or even that she could know this on reflection. The latter requirements are plausibly fulfilled if we think that evidential relations are necessary. In that case, one might expect a kind of *a priori* insight into the fact that one's evidence indicates the truth of one's belief, either by entailing it or by necessarily making it probable. But there is no possibility of fulfilling such a requirement if the relation between our evidence and our beliefs is merely contingent. On the contrary, a requirement in that direction leads straight into skepticism. Reliabilism makes no such requirement and gives us a general approach to knowledge and evidence that explains why none is needed.

There are serious problems with generic reliabilism, however – serious enough to cause some philosophers to reject the position out of hand. One problem is that beliefs can be reliably formed by accident – for example, by arbitrarily adopting a method which, unknown to the believer, happens to be reliable. This would seem to violate a "no accident" condition on knowledge. A second problem is that beliefs can be reliably formed and yet subjectively inappropriate. This seemingly violates a "subjective justification" condition on knowledge, and reliabilism has been widely criticized on this point. Agent reliabilism addresses both problems by drawing on the resources of virtue theory. The main idea is to define knowledge in terms of virtuous cognitive character, and to define virtuous character in terms of proper motivation and reliable success. This takes care of the "no accident" condition on knowledge, in that true belief which is formed through an agent's reliable character is not an accident in any relevant sense. It takes care of the "subjective justification" condition as well, since there is proper motivation, and, as Aristotle would say, "the moving principle is within the agent." Roughly, a belief is both subjectively and objectively justified, in the sense required for knowledge, when it is produced by a properly motivated, reliable cognitive character.

Agent reliabilism is therefore a kind of virtue epistemology, in the sense that it makes cognitive or intellectual virtue central in the analysis of important epistemic concepts. As such, it is an improvement over previous versions of reliabilism, including process reliabilism, method reliabilism, and evidence reliabilism. All of these are subject to one or both of the two problems that I have mentioned, precisely because they fail to ground knowledge in the virtuous character of the knower. In defending agent reliabilism I do not pretend to offer a position that is either wholly original or fully worked out in its details. Rather, I am defending a general direction in epistemology. This direction has been taken by others, both historically and more recently. I am arguing that it is necessary in the context of well-known but underappreciated skeptical considerations.[2]

2. STRATEGY AND OUTLINE OF THE BOOK

So I have three major theses: one about the structure and content of skeptical arguments, one about their methodological role in philosophical inquiry, and one about where this methodology leads us. My strategy for establishing these is to engage in five tasks.

One thing I will have to do is to consider and reject dismissive responses to skepticism. I define a "dismissive response" as one that either (a) does not engage skeptical arguments at all or (b) engages them only superficially. Such responses are "dismissive" because they reject the skeptical conclusion without seriously considering the reasoning that leads to it. I include charges of self-refutation under "type-a" dismissive responses. Type-a responses do not consider skeptical arguments at all but rather react to the implausibility of the skeptical conclusion. But skepticism is not self-refuting in any philosophically interesting sense. To think that it is blinds one to the more subtle mistakes that skeptical arguments make, and that many non-skeptical philosophers make as well.

Under type-b dismissive responses I include the charges that skepticism assumes infallibilism or deductivism. We will see that these responses depend on uncharitable readings of the skeptical arguments and so are rightly classified as dismissive responses; if they engage the arguments at all, they do so only superficially.

My second task is to consider and reject non-epistemological diag-

---

[2] Agent reliabilism has its historical roots in Aristotle, Aquinas, and Thomas Reid, among others. More recently, versions of the position have been defended by Ernest Sosa, *Knowledge in Perspective* (Cambridge: Cambridge University Press, 1991); Alvin Goldman, *Liaisons: Philosophy Meets the Cognitive and Social Sciences* (Cambridge, MA: MIT Press, 1992) and Alvin Plantinga, *Warrant and Proper Function* (Oxford: Oxford University Press, 1993).

noses of skepticism. These diagnoses often engage skeptical arguments quite seriously ultimately fail to understand them correctly. For example, skeptical arguments can be reconstructed so that they do not presuppose a modern ontology. Neither do such arguments depend on representationalism, or some version of a traditional theory of ideas. Neither do they depend on realism. Again, the lessons that skeptical arguments teach are about the nature of knowledge and evidence, rather than ontology or the philosophy of mind.

These first two tasks constitute indirect defenses of my thesis about the nature of skeptical arguments – the thesis that such arguments run on plausible assumptions about the nature of knowledge and evidence. My third task is to make good on this claim by analyzing some historically prominent skeptical arguments, and by showing exactly what epistemological mistakes they do in fact make. Here I focus on four arguments in particular: the argument from an infinite regress of reasons, from Aristotle's *Posterior Analytics*; the argument for skepticism about the world, from Descartes' *Meditations on First Philosophy*; the argument for skepticism about the world, from Section XII of Hume's *Enquiry concerning Human Understanding*; and the argument for skepticism about unobserved matters of fact, from Section IV of the same work.

The task here is to look at these arguments as they actually appear in their texts, but also to reconstruct them so as to bring out their real force. The methodology I defend instructs us to put the arguments in their most powerful form rather than rely on historical particularities to score hollow victories. For example, Descartes begins his skeptical inquiry by doubting the validity of all of his knowledge at once. But is there anything essential in Descartes' reasoning that requires him to present it that way? I argue that there is not, and so rejecting it on that basis does not give us insight into the real force of Descartes' skeptical considerations. Likewise, Hume's skeptical arguments are couched in terms of his empiricist theory of ideas. But his reasoning does not essentially depend on that theory, and therefore Hume's arguments cannot be rejected on that basis.

This puts me in position to undertake a fourth task. Having identified several plausible but mistaken assumptions about the nature of knowledge and evidence, I offer a theory that shows why these are mistakes. The idea is that a theory of knowledge and evidence that explains why important skeptical arguments go wrong, and that therefore preserves our common sense intuitions about what we do and do not know, is made plausible by virtue of having those features. This makes good on my second thesis: that the analysis of skeptical arguments is philosophically useful because it drives positive epistemology.

My fifth task is to argue that the methodology I defend can be extended to moral and religious epistemology. In this way I continue to defend the thesis that skeptical arguments repay analysis, now by driving us to deeper understanding of moral and religious knowledge. Here the methodology can be extended in two ways. First, it can be extended directly, by applying it exactly as we do in the investigation of empirical knowledge. When doing empirical epistemology, we assume that we have knowledge, and we use skeptical arguments to root out assumptions that entail that we do not. In this way we uncover mistaken assumptions about the nature of empirical knowledge and evidence. This same methodology can be applied in moral and religious epistemology as well. For example, we can start with the assumption that we do have moral knowledge. We can then use skeptical arguments that conclude otherwise as heuristic devices for rooting out mistaken assumptions about the epistemology of moral beliefs. The methodology is as legitimate here as it is in the empirical realm. It is implausible to claim that I do not know that here is a hand, and any argument that concludes that I do not is almost certainly mistaken somewhere. But it is equally implausible to claim that I do not know that killing innocent children is wrong. If a moral epistemology entails that I do not, then we have good reason to think that there is something wrong with that moral epistemology.

The methodology can also be extended indirectly. In this case we do not assume that we have moral or religious knowledge, or even that some of these beliefs are more reasonable than others. Rather, we examine arguments for moral and religious skepticism, and we look for assumptions that, if true, entail that there is no empirical knowledge. If an argument for skepticism in the moral or religious realm can be shown to involve such an assumption, then we are warranted in rejecting it for that reason. Some arguments against the rationality of religious belief have exactly this character. Such arguments are meant to show that rational religious belief is impossible. But if these same arguments entail that I am not rational in believing that here is a hand, then something in them is almost certainly wrong. Accordingly, they do not have force against the rationality of religious belief. Some arguments against moral perception have an analogous character: if they were correct, they would show that moral perception is impossible, but they would also show that empirical perception is impossible. Since the latter claim is implausible, we have reason for rejecting the relevant objection to moral perception.

That is my five-point strategy for defending the three major theses of the book. The outline of the book is as follows: In Chapter 2 I look closely at two important arguments for skepticism about the world, one from Descartes and the other from Hume. The purpose here is to reconstruct the arguments in their most powerful forms. I conclude that the strongest version of Descartes' argument is an inarticulate version of Hume's. The main idea is that there is no good inference (deductive or inductive) from the way things appear to the way things are. Put another way, there is no good argument, not even an inductive one, from appearance to reality. Far from relying on implausibly high standards for knowledge, this argument offers powerful considerations for the conclusion that we lack even inductive knowledge of the world.

Another version of Descartes' argument, less powerful but still formidable, trades on the plausible assumption that knowledge must discriminate truth from alternative possibilities. For example, it is claimed that I cannot know that I am sitting by the fire if I cannot discriminate this state of affairs from the possibility that I am a disembodied spirit deceived by an evil demon. I suggest that a "relevant possibilities" approach is promising here. The central idea is that, intuitively, knowledge requires only that we can discriminate among some possibilities, while others can be ignored as irrelevant. But such a response requires development. We would like a principled account of what makes some possibilities relevant and others irrelevant. Such development is undertaken in Chapter 8.

In Chapter 3, I consider and reject several dismissive responses to the reconstructed arguments from Chapter 2. These include charges of self-refutation, as well as several other responses based on pragmatic and rhetorical considerations. I claim that all of these responses miss the mark, since the skeptical arguments retain their force even if there are no skeptics to put the arguments forward. What gives skeptical arguments their force is not that some *other* person is willing to defend them. Rather, it is that they begin from premises that *we* are inclined to accept, and that seemingly entail conclusions that we do not accept. If this is right, then skeptical arguments are a problem for us, and whether or not there are any "real" skeptics to defend them. Pragmatic and rhetorical considerations are therefore irrelevant for adequately answering skeptical arguments. They would be relevant if the problem of skepticism involved some *skeptic*, at whom such considerations could be directed. But if the problem of skepticism is the problem of analyzing skeptical *arguments*, such considerations are simply irrelevant.

Another kind of dismissive response considered in Chapter 3 charges that the standards for knowledge assumed by skeptical arguments are too high, requiring, for example, deduction from evidence or absolute certainty for premises. Here I argue that the arguments reconstructed from Hume and Descartes require no such thing, and that a close analysis of the arguments reveals this. Finally, several versions of transcendental arguments are considered as dismissive responses to skepticism, and all are rejected as inadequate.

In Chapter 4, I consider some non-epistemological responses to "no good inference arguments" for skepticism about the world. These include the diagnosis that skepticism requires a dualism between knowing mind and material object of knowledge. Alternatively, some philosophers see representationalism as the driving force behind skeptical arguments, while others claim that realism is the problem. I reject all of these diagnoses, arguing that "no good inference" arguments can be reconstructed without dualism, representationalism, or realism. In fact, even Berkeley's radical idealism is consistent with a charitable reconstruction of the skeptical argument.

These various non-epistemological diagnoses of skepticism are rejected in favor of an epistemological one. Specifically, I contend that "no good inference arguments" misunderstand the way that sensory appearances act as evidence for beliefs about the world. What these arguments assume, and what many non-skeptical philosophers assume with them, is that all evidential relations are inferential relations. In other words, they assume that sensory appearances can act as evidence for beliefs about the world only if the latter are inferred from the former. But since no such inference is forthcoming, the arguments conclude that appearances cannot give rise to knowledge of the world. My position is that skeptical arguments are correct in claiming that there is no good inference from appearance to reality and are therefore wrong in claiming that beliefs about the world must be inferred from sensory appearances. The latter is the plausible but ultimately disastrous assumption that many skeptical arguments and many non-skeptics mistakenly share.

In Chapter 5, I consider the ancient skeptical argument from an infinite regress of reasons. This argument contends that all knowledge requires justification by adequate evidence, and that all such justification involves inference from good reasons. But since all good reasons require further reasons for their evidence, knowledge requires an infinite regress of justifying reasons, and therefore no knowledge is possible. I begin by revisiting some dismissive responses to skepticism and showing that these miss the mark against the regress argument as badly as they do against Cartesian and Humean arguments. For example, the argument does not trade on a requirement for infallible reasons, or irrevisable ones. Second, I look at the three most popular non-dismissive responses to the regress argument: foundationalism, coherentism, and contextualism. Here I argue that coherentism is psychologically implausible, and that plausible versions of contextualism reduce to foundationalism. Accordingly, I defend a contextualist version of foundationalism – one that is not open to the usual objections to the foundationalist position.

"Contextualist foundationalism" might sound like an oxymoron, but only because insufficient attention has been given to what foundationalism requires. Here again a close analysis of skeptical arguments proves instructive, in this case showing what foundationalism does and does not require to stop the infinite regress of justifying reasons. For example, it does *not* require that foundational beliefs be infallible, incorrigible, devoid of contextual or social features, or even irrevisable. What it does require is, once again, that not all evidential relations are inferential. Perhaps all knowledge must be grounded in evidence, but some knowledge is not inferred from other beliefs. This is the defining characteristic of foundationalism and is what is needed to answer the age-old infinite regress argument.

In Chapter 6 I consider Hume's skeptical arguments regarding unobserved matters of fact. Here I distinguish two arguments – one from Section IV of the *Enquiry* and one from Section VII. I argue that the former is the most powerful and is immune to dismissive responses that are, at best, effective only against the latter. For example, the argument is in no respect dependent on Hume's empiricist theory of ideas. I also argue against the most popular interpretation of Hume, namely, that he is a deductivist regarding knowledge of the unobserved. On my interpretation Hume's claim is that our beliefs about unobserved matters of fact are not even inductively supported by past observations. On this view Hume does not require that our evidence be deductive, but that there be some necessary inductive relationship between our evidence and our conclusions. This makes Hume's argument far more powerful than is usually supposed. No one thinks nowadays that all evidence must be deductive, and if Hume's argument ran on that assumption, then it could be easily refuted. But it is seemingly obvious that evidence must be at least inductively relevant to give rise to knowledge. This is in fact false and is the real lesson of Hume's skepticism about unobserved matters of fact. It is also a good illustration of the claim that skeptical arguments drive positive epistemology. If we did not see its skeptical consequences, we would hardly be inclined to reject such a commonplace, seemingly innocent assumption. But once focused on the real force of Hume's argument, we see that the assumption must go in favor of some better understanding of the nature of evidence.

Chapters 4 through 6 constitute a kind of negative epistemology: rather than saying what knowledge is, negative epistemology largely restricts itself to saying what knowledge is not. This is a worthwhile activity, in that it disabuses us of plausible but mistaken assumptions about the nature of knowledge and evidence. But the ultimate goal of the methodology I defend is to construct a positive epistemology, or a positive account of what knowledge is and how evidence works. This happens when we construct a theory of knowledge that *explains* the largely negative conclusions drawn from our analyses of skeptical arguments. This project is undertaken in Chapter 7.

Notice that the progress from negative to positive epistemology corresponds to three degrees of success we might have in refuting a skeptical argument. The first and least satisfying degree of success is to find an assumption in the argument that we need not accept. If we see that an assumption leads to unacceptable consequences, and if there is no overwhelming reason to accept the assumption, then we are warranted in giving it up as mistaken. For example, suppose we identify as disastrous the assumption that knowledge of objects must be inferred, deductively or inductively, from knowledge of how objects appear. This assumption is something we need not accept, and so we should give it up once we see where it leads.

In the next degree of success we arrive at some reason why the skeptical assumption is mistaken. For example, we conclude that not all evidential relations are inferential, and that this explains why sensory appearances can be evidence for a belief even if the latter is not inferred from the former. This seems to be a plausible position, and we might look for further confirmations of it in cases unrelated to the skeptical argument at hand. But even at this second degree we do not have an explanation of a particular sort. What we really want is to have a theory of knowledge that explains why the skeptical assumption is false. In other words, we want an account that tells us what knowledge is and how evidence works, and which thereby provides a theoretical explanation of why the assumption in question is mistaken.

In Chapter 7, I defend a virtue theory of knowledge that does just this. Again, by a "virtue theory" I mean one that makes the cognitive faculties and habits of persons central in the analysis of important epistemic concepts. As we saw, the theory is a version of reliabilism, in that a stable disposition of a person counts as a virtue only if it is reliably successful in achieving its end. In the case of the cognitive virtues, this means that the faculty or habit makes the person reliable in forming true beliefs of the kind relevant to the virtue in question. Agent reliabilism explains *why* the skeptical assumptions rejected in earlier chapters are false. Namely, it explains (a) why not all evidence is inferential, (b) how sensory appearances can function as evidence without functioning as premises in an inference, (c) how some knowledge can be foundational, and (d) how propositional evidence that is neither logical nor quasi-logical can give rise to knowledge.

We saw earlier that one of Descartes' skeptical arguments trades on our inability to discriminate among various alternative possibilities. For example, if one's evidence does not discriminate between being in front of the fire and being a disembodied spirit deceived by an evil demon, then one cannot know that one is sitting in front of the fire. A promising strategy in response to this kind of skeptical reasoning is to distinguish between relevant and irrelevant alternative possibilities, and to claim that knowledge requires only that we discriminate among the relevant ones. The problem, then, is to give a theoretical account of what makes an alternative possibility relevant or irrelevant. In Chapter 8, I argue that agent reliabilism can do just this.

The main idea is that virtues in general are abilities to achieve some result, and abilities in general are functions of success in relevantly close possible worlds. In other words, to say that someone has an ability to achieve X is to say that she would be successful in achieving X in a range of situations relevantly similar to those in which she typically finds herself. But then possibilities that do not occur in typical situations are irrelevant for determining whether a person has an ability in question. For example, it does not count against Babe Ruth's ability to hit baseballs that he cannot hit them in the dark. Likewise, it does not count against our perceptual abilities that we cannot discriminate real tables and fires from demon-induced hallucinations. But then our inability to rule out hypothetical demon scenarios is irrelevant to whether we have knowledge, and the skeptical scenario is not a relevant possibility in that sense. This account of "relevant possibility" confirms the plausibility of agent reliabilism and deepens our understanding of what we must mean by a cognitive virtue or ability.

Finally, in Chapter 9, I argue that the methodology I am defending can be extended to religious and moral epistemology. Many arguments against the rationality of religious belief trade on assumptions about knowledge and evidence that, if true, would count against rational belief and knowledge in the empirical realm. By exposing such assumptions and rejecting objections to religious belief on that basis, the epistemology of religious belief is advanced. In the first part of Chapter 9 I endorse recent work by Alvin Plantinga and William Alston as instances of exactly this methodology, and I offer some suggestions about how their views might be further defended along this line.

In the second part of the chapter I consider the possibility of moral perception. Here I argue that recent work in the epistemology and psychology of empirical perception opens up possibilities for moral perception. Specifically, to avoid skepticism about the natural world we must understand empirical perception as a non-inferential cognitive faculty, but one that is nevertheless influenced by background beliefs, special training, and the like. Second, we must have an account of how complex, dispositional properties can be objects of empirical perception. Accounts of how these features are possible for empirical perception suggest promising extensions to moral perception as well. For example, recent theory concerning the roles of personae and scripts in empirical perception suggests interesting applications to moral perception.

Chapters 4 through 8 suggest a moderate foundationalism. The main idea is that knowledge and justified belief arise from the cognitive abilities of reliable believers, and that some of those abilities must be characterized as non-inferential. The combined results of Chapter 9 suggest that the foundations of knowledge are broad as well. In other words, they suggest that there exists a wide variety of non-inferential sources of evidence, including evidence for moral and religious beliefs. What emerges is a broad and moderate foundationalism in which much evidence is non-inferential, and where even inferential evidence is seldom deductive or inductive in a sense that is commonly supposed. What matters for knowledge and justified belief is not the infallibility or incorrigibility of our premises, nor even the logical or quasi-logical relations among our premises and conclusions. Rather, knowledge and justified belief arise from virtuous belief formation, where the notion of "virtue" must be understood in terms of the contingent causal and motivational features of our cognition, rather than the necessary or intrinsic features of propositions, evidential relations, or the like.

3. THREE CRITERIA FOR AN ADEQUATE THEORY OF KNOWLEDGE

Before closing this first chapter I want to talk about one more methodological issue. Specifically, I want to suggest three criteria for an adequate theory of knowledge, and to talk about how they are related to the methodology for epistemology that I have been proposing.

First, an adequate theory of knowledge should do a good job of organizing our pre-theoretical intuitions about what cases count as knowledge. In other words, the theory should count as knowledge those cases that intuitively seem to be knowledge, and it should count as not knowledge those cases that intuitively seem not to be. "But whose intuitions count as the right ones?", our suspicious friends will ask. The answer is the intuitions of us all in our non-philosophical lives. An adequate theory of knowledge should explain why normal people, not people caught in the grip of a philosophical theory, count particular cases as knowledge and other cases as not. "Normal people" includes most non-philosophers, and most philosophers when they are not philosophizing. Among such people there is in fact very wide agreement about which cases do and do not count as knowledge.

Moreover, universal agreement is not required for the methodology being proposed. What is necessary is that there is a wide range of cases that most people would find intuitively obvious. If a theory of knowledge does a good job with these, then that is a strong consideration in its favor. However, vague and contested cases are important as well; a good theory of knowledge should explain *why* certain cases are vague and why certain ones are contested. Consider vagueness first. There will be cases where we are not sure what to say — where we have no strong intuition about whether the case is one of knowledge or not. If our theory can identify some aspect of the case that is vague as described and can tell us that just this aspect is important for knowledge, then that will count in favor of the theory. For example, we saw that agent reliabilism requires that knowers be reliable in forming true beliefs and avoiding error in a relevant domain of inquiry. But how reliable must one be to have knowledge? This might be left vague by the theory, or might be left vague in the description of a particular case. Either way, this could account for the vagueness of an intuition.

Finally, a good theory of knowledge should account for *disagreement* among intuitions as well. For example, if knowledge requires reliability, and if we disagree over whether someone is reliable in a particular case, then we might disagree over whether the case is one of knowledge. To say that a theory of knowledge should account for our intuitions, then, does not require that our intuitions lack vagueness or enjoy unanimity. A good theory should account for agreement where we agree, disagreement where we disagree, and should explain why vagueness arises when it does.

The second criterion for an adequate theory of knowledge is that it be immune to skeptical arguments. This criterion is related to the first, because our pre-theoretical intuitions are overwhelmingly non-skeptical. Any theory that entails that there is no knowledge of objects in the world, or no knowledge of unobserved facts, or no moral knowledge does a horrible job with our pre-theoretical intuitions about what cases count as knowledge. This is so for *all* of us, since none of us are skeptics in our everyday lives.

For this reason, a theory that has radically skeptical consequences does not capture the concept of knowledge that is actually in use – or at least there is a very strong presumption that it does not. It is, we may suppose, possible in principle that our ordinary concept of knowledge has widely unrecognized skeptical consequences. But if there are competitor accounts that do not have such consequences, then that is an almost insurmountable advantage of those accounts. Again, this follows from the first criterion of an adequate epistemology: that it capture our pre-theoretical intuitions about which cases count as knowledge.

We must take the qualification of the previous paragraph seriously, however, in light of a sophisticated version of skepticism recently suggested by Robert Fogelin.[3] Sophisticated skepticism claims that it *can* explain our non-skeptical intuitions, by virtue of certain aspects of our linguistic practices. The idea is that practical purposes make it appropriate to assert knowledge-claims in a wide range of cases, and that this linguistic fact is behind our pre-reflective intuitions that such claims are true. However, at least many of our knowledge-claims are literally false. Moreover, in contexts where practical considerations are put aside and

---

3 See Fogelin, *Pyrrhonian Reflections on Knowledge and Justification*.

our level of scrutiny regarding knowledge-claims is raised, our intuitions become skeptical, as when skeptical arguments are made or skeptical considerations pushed. In light of this Fogelin-type sophisticated skepticism, we cannot claim that skeptical arguments, by their very nature, cannot account for our pre-theoretical intuitions about which cases count as knowledge. Rather, we have to put emphasis on the claim that a non-skeptical theory of knowledge is strongly preferable, other things being roughly equal. That is, if a non-skeptical theory of knowledge is available that explains why the majority of our intuitions are true, this will be preferable to a skeptical theory, and even if that theory comes with an explanation as to why what seems obviously true is in fact false.[4]

One reason that the non-skeptical theory will be preferable, other things being equal, is that it does not need the extra explanation. Another reason is that our non-skeptical intuitions are both strong and persistent. Fogelin is correct that our intuitions are to some extent unstable – that under the pressure of skeptical arguments it can seem to us that we do not know such things as that here is a hand or this is a pencil. But these fleeting moments of doubt should not be overemphasized. On the other side are the persistent and overwhelming intuitions of common sense, even among those philosophers who are convinced by skeptical arguments in the study.

For example, consider G. E. Moore's famous statement that he knows that here is a hand, made when his hand was held up in clear view. Any theory that entails that I do not know such a thing, even with an explanation of why it seems obvious that I do know, has its work cut out for it. In this respect, any skeptical theory will be in the position Russell's was in when Moore wrote the following:

> What I want, however, finally to emphasize is this: Russell's view that I do not know for certain that this is a pencil or that you are conscious rests, if I am right, on no less than four distinct assumptions. . . . And what I can't help asking myself is this: Is it, in fact, as certain that all these four assumptions are true, as that I *do* know that this is a pencil and that you are conscious?[5]

---

4 I say "Fogelin-type" skepticism because Fogelin's Pyrrhonian principles do not allow him to actually endorse any philosophical theory, including skepticism with respect to ordinary knowledge claims. Therefore, the skeptical position I have just described is not literally Fogelin's, although his discussion strongly suggests it as a possible alternative to non-skeptical theories.

5 G. E. Moore, "Four Forms of Scepticism," in *Philosophical Papers* (London: Allen and Unwin, 1959), p. 222.

The more radical the skeptical consequences of a position are, the more strongly this point will hold.[6]

The third criterion for an adequate epistemology is that it be psychologically plausible. What I mean by this is that an adequate theory of knowledge ought to be consistent with our common sense judgments about our own cognitive abilities, and with our best cognitive science as well. This too is related to the first two criteria, because an account that is not psychologically plausible will generate skeptical arguments. We can see this if we look at the most basic structure that any skeptical argument must have.

Although skeptical arguments come in many shapes and sizes, all of them can be boiled down to two essential premises: one stating that knowledge requires that some condition or set of conditions be fulfilled, and one stating that these conditions are in fact not fulfilled. More formally, we have the following skeptical argument structure:

(SAS) 1. $K \Rightarrow C$.
       2. Not-C.
       3. Therefore, not-K.

Any theory of knowledge that is psychologically implausible will generate an argument with this structure. First, any theory of knowledge whatsoever will entail premises corresponding to premise (1) of (SAS), since any such theory posits conditions that must be fulfilled in order to have knowledge. But the fact that a theory is psychologically implausible guarantees that it will generate a premise corresponding to (2): that is, a premise stating that conditions laid down by the theory in question are not satisfied by beings with our psychology. Accordingly, we will have a skeptical argument amounting to a *reductio ad absurdum* of the theory in question.

This points to an elaboration of the methodology I am defending. Specifically, we are not restricted to the use of historically prominent skeptical arguments and their reconstructions. We can make up new arguments to demonstrate the mistaken assumptions of alternative accounts of knowledge, or even alternative solutions to skeptical problems. This actually happens in contemporary epistemology – it has happened,

---

6 For an extended argument that our intuitions are not better explained by Fogelin-type warranted assertability maneuvers, see Keith DeRose, "Contextualism: An Explanation and Defense," in John Greco and Ernest Sosa, eds., *The Blackwell Guide to Epistemology* (Oxford: Blackwell, 1999).

for example, in recent arguments against coherentism.[7] Coherentism was originally proposed as a non-skeptical response to the argument from an infinite regress of reasons. The idea is that reasons can be mutually supportive, and so no infinite regress of reasons is necessary to ground knowledge in adequate evidence. But a major problem with coherentism is that it fails to give a psychologically plausible account of the role of experience in forming perceptual beliefs. Take, for example, my current perceptual belief that it is raining. The coherentist contends that all beliefs are supported by other beliefs that serve as its evidence. But against this position, it is not psychologically plausible that I infer my belief that it is raining from other beliefs that I have and that act as its evidence. Surely I know that it is raining because I can *see* that it is.

The coherentist will have a story about perceptual knowledge, but it will not be a psychologically plausible one. For example, the coherentist might say that we unconsciously infer beliefs about objects from beliefs about sensory appearances. But it is psychologically implausible that we typically *have* beliefs about sensory appearances, much less infer beliefs about objects from them. And even if we did typically have such beliefs, what evidence do we have for the supposed unconscious inferences? I certainly do not *seem* to make the relevant inferences in perception. On the contrary, the empirical evidence suggests that such inferences are a philosophical invention.

Where does the empirical evidence regarding our cognitive capacities come from, and who gets to decide what that evidence makes psychologically plausible? On the view defended here, there are two principal sources of empirical evidence: our own reflection and empirical psychology.

In many instances a philosophical position can be recognized as psychologically implausible as soon as the question is raised. For example, it seems obvious upon reflection that we do not typically form beliefs about sensory appearances; in the typical case, we form beliefs about tables and trees, not about how tables and trees appear to us. Sometimes a little experimentation can confirm what seems obvious upon reflection. As Thomas Reid points out, objects not in focus present a double image. This is confirmed by placing your finger in front of your face and then focusing on an object in the distance. Attention to appearances will reveal that your finger presents a double image. Alternatively, if you

---

7 For several examples of this kind of critique of coherentism, see John Bender, ed., *The Current State of the Coherence Theory* (Dordrecht: Kluwer, 1989).

focus on your finger, the object in the distance will present a double image. Reid argues that we must be presented with double images almost all of the time, since almost always some objects are out of focus for us. And yet we do not notice this, confirming the point that we do not typically form beliefs about sensory appearances.[8] This fact constitutes a devastating objection to coherentism, or to any other epistemology on which empirical knowledge requires beliefs about appearances. For since we do not typically have such beliefs, any such theory has the consequence that we typically lack empirical knowledge.

Finally, we can learn about our cognitive abilities from more rigorous empirical research. For example, some coherence theories have a "total evidence" requirement for knowledge and justified belief, laying down a requirement that rational belief acquisition must be sensitive to the total evidence that the person has at the time. But empirical research shows that people are sensitive only to a small number of their total beliefs at any one time. Here again we see a devastating empirical objection to an epistemological theory; if a theory requires sensitivity to all of the beliefs we have, and if our cognition is not capable of that kind of sensitivity, then the theory has unacceptable skeptical results. In this case the theory results in total skepticism, since the psychologically implausible requirement is a completely general one.[9]

The methodology that I am defending here is an extension of what Roderick Chisholm calls "particularism."[10] Chisholm argues that we should follow philosophers like Reid and Moore in testing philosophical

---

8 "Thus you may find a man that can say, with a good conscience, that he never saw things double all his life; yet this very man, put in the situation above mentioned, with his finger between him and the candle, and desired to attend to the appearance of the object which he does not look at, will, upon the first trial, see the candle double, when he looks at his finger; and his finger double, when he looks at the candle. Does he now see otherwise than he saw before? No, surely; but he now attends to what he never attended to before. The same double appearance of an object hath been a thousand times presented to his eye before now, but he did not attend to it; and so it is as little an object of his reflection and memory, as if it had never happened." Thomas Reid, *Philosophical Works*, ed. H. M. Bracken, 2 vols. (Hildesheim: Georg Olms, 1983), vol. 1, p. 164b.

9 The point about total evidence requirements is made by Alvin Goldman in *Epistemology and Cognition* (Cambridge, MA: Harvard University Press, 1986), pp. 204–207. There Goldman cites John Anderson, *The Architecture of Cognition* (Cambridge, MA: Harvard University Press, 1983), and Christopher Cherniak, "Rationality and the Structure of Human Memory," *Synthese* 57 (1985): 163–186. Goldman makes the point specifically against coherentism in his essay "BonJour's *The Structure of Empirical Knowledge*," his contribution to Bender, *The Current State of the Coherence Theory*, p. 112.

10 Roderick Chisholm, "The Problem of the Criterion," in *The Foundations of Knowing* (Minneapolis: University of Minnesota Press, 1982).

theories against pre-philosophical intuitions about particular cases. If a theory has terribly counterintuitive results, then so much for the theory. I am following this basic formula but extending it in four ways. First, I am following Chisholm in holding that a theory should account for intuitions we find clear and obvious, but I am suggesting that a good theory should account for disagreement and vagueness among our intuitions as well. Second, I am suggesting that we use skeptical arguments – both historical ones and ones we make up – to bring out the counterintuitive results of philosophical theories and to focus our unblinking attention on those results. Third, I am suggesting that facts about human cognition as well as intuitions about particular cases can serve to counter philosophical theories. If a theory runs up against our intuition that we know that objects in the world exist, then that counts strongly against the theory in question. But if a theory runs up against our best empirical knowledge, either from science or from our own experience, then here too we have a reason for giving up the theory. I have already pointed out that these two extensions of the methodology are not unrelated; if a theory of knowledge is psychologically implausible, it will generate a skeptical argument with counterintuitive results.

Fourth, I am proposing that implicit assumptions about the nature of knowledge and evidence, as well as explicitly defended theories, should be tested in these ways. Such assumptions in fact amount to philosophical theories, even though they are not defended as such and even though they are the common property of theoreticians and non-theoreticians alike.

Because the methodology that I propose here is a natural extension of what Chisholm calls "particularism," I will call it "strong particularism." This methodology will seem obviously right to some and obviously wrong to others. On the one hand, it is the methodology that many contemporary analytic epistemologists take for granted. On the other, this is one reason why analytic epistemology seems so strange to many outside of it. Many philosophers will think that the methodology is hopelessly question begging, both in its invocation of our non-skeptical intuitions and in its use of results from the empirical sciences. Others will think that it is too conservative, guaranteeing, in effect, that our theories do not challenge our pre-philosophical judgments. But one burden of this book is to defend strong particularism. This will be done in two ways.

First, as with any methodology, this one must be judged by its fruits. In the following chapters I will try to show that real progress can be (and has been) made in philosophy by employing it. Second, the adequacy and appropriateness of strong particularism largely depend on how we conceive of skeptical arguments and how we conceive of the project of engaging them.

If we think of skeptical arguments as coming from real people whom we are to engage as opponents in a debate, then the use of our own intuitions will be contested and the use of empirical psychology will seem question begging. So will the use of these seem pointless if we think that our project is to persuade someone out of her skepticism by mounting a convincing argument. In such a case we would have to start from premises already accepted, and a skeptic would accept neither our non-skeptical intuitions nor the results of empirical sciences. But I will argue in Chapter 3 that these conceptions of the epistemological project are misconceived and misguided. There are no real skeptics, either to be debated or to be persuaded out of their skepticism. In other words, there is no one who actually lives out the skeptical position, or who even believes it outside the study or the classroom. And even if there were, debate and persuasion would be hopeless. A debate with a consistent skeptic cannot be won, especially if we adopt the ground rules that philosophers are wont to concede. Moreover, if we are to persuade someone out of her skepticism, then argument and philosophy are the last thing she needs. Here Reid had it right when he considered the appropriate response to a friend who was found really to be a skeptic: "[Would we] not hope for his cure from physic and good regimen, rather than from metaphysic and logic?"[11]

In any case, that is not what skeptical arguments or their analysis are about. There is no practical or "existential" problem of skepticism, since the position is not one that any person can live. Rather, skeptical arguments constitute *theoretical* problems; they start from assumptions about knowledge and evidence that we ourselves find plausible or even accept, and they show that such assumptions lead to consequences that we cannot accept. As a result we see that some implicit or explicit theory of knowledge is wrong, and we are pushed to develop new and unexpected positions to replace the mistaken assumptions that skeptical arguments expose. If this is the point of engaging skeptical arguments, then it is perfectly reasonable to use our best intuitions and our best science to construct and test alternative positions. We are trying to put together the most plausible account of knowledge and evidence by our

---

11 Reid, *Philosophical Works*, p. 100b.

own lights. If that is our project, then we should use all of the resources that are available to us.

If this is our understanding of skeptical arguments then begging the question does not come into it – there is no one to beg the question against. However, our considered intuitions and science do come into it, for they are the best that we have to go on. As Chisholm puts it, "This may seem the wrong place to start. But where else *could* we start?"[12] Here is another way to gloss Chisholm's point: If a theory of knowledge does not explain our considered intuitions about knowledge, what else could it have going for it? What kind of evidence could we bring to bear to show that the theory is correct?

I have been arguing that we must start with our intuitions. Is that where we must end? In other words, does strong particularism guarantee that skepticism is false? Or worse, does it guarantee that we can never reach *any* conclusion but a conservative one – that is, one that confirms our pre-theoretical intuitions? Well, yes and no. First, there is no guarantee that we will reach any conclusion at all. In other words, strong particularism does not guarantee that we can account for our pre-theoretical intuitions with an adequate theory; it merely lays down criteria for theoretical adequacy. On the other hand, if we *do* reach a theoretical conclusion by using the method, then that theory must preserve at least a great many of our pretheoretical intuitions. But that does not mean that an adequate theory must preserve *all* of our intuitions, since some of these might best be revised along the way. What is more, they might be revised in very important ways.

This consideration can be used to address another kind of objection to strong particularism – namely, that if a theory merely preserves our intuitions about knowledge and evidence, then it cannot be used to criticize them. I would reply by insisting that just the opposite is the case: that a theory can be used to criticize our intuitions only if it *does* preserve a great many of them. The point is that a theory can have a critical function only if we think it is correct. And again, the only reason we could have for thinking that a theory of knowledge *is* correct is that it does a good job of explaining how we know the things that we seem to know. Granting that a theory of knowledge should have a critical function, it can successfully critique some of our intuitions only if it does a good job of explaining others. In the last chapter of the book this

---

12 Roderick Chisholm, *The Theory of Knowledge*, 2nd ed. (Englewood Cliffs, NJ: Prentice Hall, 1977), p. 16. Chisholm is commenting on the adequacy of particularism here.

point is illustrated with respect to our intuitions about moral and religious knowledge. Against the moral and religious skepticism of our times, I argue that an adequate theory of empirical perception opens up the possibility of moral and religious perception. It becomes possible to explain how we might "see" that an action is wrong, or "feel" God's love and presence. This might seem absurd at first, but it follows straightforwardly from an adequate – that is, non-skeptical – empirical epistemology. Strong particularism, then, does not merely preserve our pre-theoretical intuitions.

2

Skepticism about the World: Part One – Reconstructions

In this chapter, I consider two historically prominent skeptical arguments: one from Section XII of Hume's *Enquiry concerning Human Understanding*, and the other from Meditation I of Descartes' *Meditations on First Philosophy*. My purpose is to reconstruct the arguments so as to put them in their most powerful form. But we should remember that by "powerful" I do not mean psychologically convincing. I do not think that either skeptical argument, even in its most powerful form, has the power to convince or persuade. Rather, the arguments can be reconstructed so that they are powerful in another sense: it is not at all easy to see where they go wrong, and rejecting them requires us to give up something that otherwise would seem plausible or perhaps even obvious. Such arguments are powerful heuristic devices in that they drive us to give up plausible but mistaken assumptions about knowledge and evidence, and inspire us to put something substantive in their place.

In the next chapter we will consider how several dismissive responses to skepticism fare against the reconstructed arguments. Remember that dismissive responses are ones that either (a) do not engage skeptical arguments at all or (b) engage them only superficially. Such responses are dismissive because they reject the skeptical conclusion without paying serious attention to the reasoning that leads up to it. Accordingly, dismissive responses miss the lessons that skeptical arguments can teach.

1. AN ARGUMENT FROM HUME

Descartes' argument from Meditation I has probably received more attention than any other skeptical argument and surely has been the target of the most abuse. However, I want to start with the argument from Hume, which I think is in some respects the stronger of the two. More exactly, I argue that the most powerful interpretation of Descartes' argument makes it run on considerations brought out more straightforwardly by Hume's. In this sense the most powerful form of the argument from Descartes reduces to the argument from Hume.

Consider the following passage from Section XII of Hume's *Enquiry*, where he is considering our evidence for the existence of "external objects" and "an external universe."[1]

> By what argument can it be proved, that the perceptions of the mind must be caused by external objects, entirely different from them, though resembling them (if that be possible) and could not arise either from the energy of the mind itself, or from the suggestion of some invisible and unknown spirit, or from some other cause still more unknown to us? It is acknowledged, that, in fact, many of these perceptions arise not from anything external, as in dreams, madness, and other diseases. . . .
>
> It is a question of fact, whether the perceptions of the sense be produced by external objects, resembling them: how shall this question be determined? By experience surely; as all other questions of a like nature. But here experience is, and must be entirely silent. The mind has never anything present to it but the perceptions, and cannot possibly reach any experience of their connexion with objects. The supposition of such a connexion is, therefore, without any foundation in reasoning. (*Enquiry*, pp. 152–153)

In the first paragraph it looks like we are getting the familiar "alternative possibilities" reasoning: How can we know through perceptions that external objects exist if those same perceptions could be caused by a dream, or a spirit, or something else still more unknown? The last sentence of the first paragraph suggests the old "sometimes we make mistakes" argument: Sometimes people *are* deceived by dreams or madness or other diseases, and so how do I know I am not deceived now? But I do not think that Hume has either of these arguments primarily in mind. Rather, his reasoning is suggested by the cryptic second paragraph. The argument contained there is obscure, and we would probably not guess Hume's meaning if we were not already familiar with his reasoning in Section IV of the *Enquiry* regarding unobserved matters of fact. But with that reasoning in mind we can pick out a forceful argument here, for the arguments in Section IV and Section XII have closely analogous structures.

---

1 All references to Hume are from *Enquiries concerning Human Understanding and concerning the Principles of Morals*, 3 ed. L. A. Selby-Bigge, 3rd ed. (Oxford: Clarendon Press, 1975).

The argument of Section IV goes roughly like this: All beliefs about future matters of fact depend for their evidence on both (a) observations of past cases and (b) the assumption that observed cases will be a good indication of future cases, that is, on the assumption that the future will resemble the past. Let us call this the "regularity principle," because it is equivalent to saying that there is a regularity in nature. But now the regularity principle is itself a belief about future matters of fact; it is an assumption that *in the future* observed cases will continue to be a reliable indication of future cases. As such, the only way that the principle could be justified is by inference from (a) past observations and (b) the assumption that the future will resemble the past. In other words, we think that observed cases will be a reliable indication of future cases because we have observed in the past that nature has been regular in that way. But this means that the only evidence we could have for the regularity principle must include the principle itself. Such reasoning is blatantly circular, however, and therefore cannot give rise to knowledge.

More formally, we have the following argument.

(H1)   1. All of our beliefs about future matters of fact depend for their justification on past observations, together with the assumption (A1) that the future will resemble the past.
2. But (A1) is itself a belief about a future matter of fact.
3. Therefore, assumption (A1) depends for its evidence on (A1). (1,2)
4. Circular reasoning cannot give rise to knowledge.
5. Therefore, (A1) is not known. (3,4)[2]

This conclusion is bad enough, but of course Hume's reasoning does not stop there. Because the regularity principle is involved in all of our reasoning concerning future matters of fact, the real conclusion is that there is no knowledge of the future.[3]

6. All of our beliefs about future matters of fact depend on an assumption that is not known. (1,5)

---

2   My custom will be to set out various skeptical arguments with numbered premises. Numbers in parentheses after a conclusion or subconclusion indicate the premises from which the conclusion or subconclusion is supposed to be immediately entailed. Such entailments might depend on the laws of logic, or might depend on the necessary relations of the concepts involved in the premises and conclusions. In presenting the arguments in this manner I am trying to capture the way that the skeptical reasoning is *supposed* to go. It is not my claim, in other words, that conclusions and subconclusions are in fact entailed by the indicated premises. I mean that to remain an open question.

3   Actually, the real conclusion is about all unobserved matters of fact, not just those in the future. This point is made more carefully in Chapter 6, but for present purposes I treat Hume's argument as if it were about our knowledge of future matters of fact specifically.

7. Beliefs that depend on an unknown assumption are themselves not known.
8. Therefore, no one knows anything about the future. (6,7)

We will look at this argument more closely in Chapter 6. At present my purpose is to use it to bring out the structure of Hume's reasoning in Section XII. There Hume is concerned with our evidence for external objects rather than unobserved matters of fact, but, as I have noted, the two skeptical arguments have closely analogous structures.

Let us now look back at the passage that I quoted earlier from Section XII. On the reading I am proposing Hume's first paragraph merely points out that sensory appearances by themselves do not adequately support our beliefs about objects in the world; the fact that objects appear to be a certain way is consistent with their not being that way at all. What is needed together with sensory appearances is the assumption that such appearances are a reliable guide to external reality. In other words, our evidence for our beliefs about objects in the world involves both (a) the way things appear to us through the senses and (b) the assumption that these sensory appearances are a reliable indication of how objects in the world really are. We might not voice such an assumption to ourselves explicitly, but this must be how we are thinking; we are thinking not only that things appear a certain way, but that their appearing that way is an indication that they *are* that way.

But now Hume notes, "It is a question of fact, whether the perceptions of the sense be produced by external objects." In other words, the assumption on which all of our beliefs about external reality depend is *itself* a belief about external reality. It is a belief that our sensory experience is caused by objects in the world that have the properties that our experience presents them as having. But how could we know that this assumption is true? "How shall this question be determined?" The answer is clear: "By experience surely; as all other questions of a like nature." But of course now we have another circularity problem. All of our beliefs about the world depend on two things for their evidence: sensory appearances and the assumption that sensory appearances are a reliable guide to external reality. But that assumption is itself about external reality, and so its evidence depends on itself.

Hume has identified another circle in our reasoning. Or perhaps his point is just slightly different and goes like this: Either our beliefs about the world are based on the assumption that sensory appearances are a reliable guide to reality, or they are not. If they are not, then such beliefs are unsupported, because appearances alone cannot do the job. If they are, then such beliefs are based on circular reasoning. In either case, we have no knowledge of the world.

Immediately following the second passage that I quoted, Hume considers an escape from the argument. It might be supposed, as Descartes argued, that the reliability assumption is not in need of evidence from sensory appearances but can rather be established *a priori* via an argument about God's veracity. Hume responds to this line of reasoning as follows:

> To have recourse to the veracity of the supreme Being, in order to prove the veracity of our senses, is surely making a very unexpected circuit. If his veracity were at all concerned in this matter, our senses would be entirely infallible; because it is not possible that he can ever deceive. Not to mention, that, if the external world be called in question, we shall be at a loss to find arguments, by which we may prove the existence of that Being or any of his attributes. (*Enquiry*, p. 153)

One point Hume is making here is that Descartes' strategy proves too much; if God's veracity guaranteed the trustworthiness of our senses, this would establish infallibility rather than a plausible reliability. But two other points being made are more important for Hume's skeptical reasoning. First, it is not in fact the case that we believe our senses are reliable because we have knowledge of God's veracity. That would be to make an "unexpected circuit." Second, even if we tried to mount such an argument, we would fall back into circles; our knowledge of God must presuppose our knowledge of the world and therefore cannot be used to support it.

Let me take the opportunity to state Hume's argument more formally, in both of the versions I have suggested.

(H2)   1. All of our beliefs about the external world depend for their evidence on sensory appearances, together with the assumption (A2) that sensory appearances are a reliable guide to external reality.
2. But (A2) is itself a belief about the external world.
3. Therefore, assumption (A2) depends for its evidence on (A2). (1,2)
4. Circular reasoning cannot give rise to knowledge.
5. Therefore, (A2) is not known. (3,4)
6. All of our beliefs about the world depend on an assumption that is not known. (1,5)
7. Beliefs that depend on an unknown assumption are themselves not known.
8. Therefore, no one knows anything about external reality. (6,7)

(H3) 1. Any belief about external reality either depends on (A2) for its evidence or depends on sensory appearances alone.
2. If it depends on sensory appearances alone, then it is not adequately supported.
3. If it depends on (A2), then it is supported by circular reasoning.
4. Evidence that is not adequately supporting cannot give rise to knowledge.
5. Circular reasoning cannot give rise to knowledge.
6. Therefore, no belief about external reality amounts to knowledge. No one knows anything about external reality. (1,2,3,4,5)

Before leaving Hume's argument I want to address one possible objection to it. It might be suggested that the argument trades on a particular understanding of sensory appearances. Namely, the argument assumes that sensory appearances are merely causal antecedents to belief, themselves devoid of any conceptual content. On this assumption, when an object appears to a person through the senses, the person's sensory experience does not represent the object as being of a particular kind or as having particular properties. Rather, the experience is only a causal antecedent to a belief that first represents the object that way. It is only on this characterization of sensory appearances, the objection goes, that premise (1) of (H2) seems plausible. If all seeing is "seeing as," however, then it is plausible that sensory appearances alone make probable beliefs about objects in the world. For example, a sensory appearance with the conceptual content that some object is an apple tree makes probable the perceptual belief that the object is an apple tree, and without needing the additional assumption that sensory appearances are a reliable guide to reality. Let us call sensory appearances conceived as having only phenomenal content "thin experience," and appearances conceived as having conceptual content "thick experience." The present objection is that Hume's argument depends on characterizing sensory evidence as thin experience.

This much should be granted to the objection: if we are thinking of sensory appearances as devoid of conceptual content, then Hume's skeptical reasoning goes through straightforwardly. There is no good inference from something's appearing phenomenally a certain way, to a belief that the thing is that way, if only because inferential support is a function of conceptual content.[4] What would be needed is a *belief* to the effect

---

4 This is not the only problem with this characterization of sensory evidence. There are also well-known problems concerning the relationship between the phenomenal properties of

that something is appearing a certain way phenomenally, together with the assumption that the way things appear phenomenally is a reliable indication of the way things are. It is important to see, however, that (H2) and (H3) run just as well on the assumption that sensory appearances do have conceptual content. Either way that we think of sensory appearances, the argument goes through if we grant its other assumptions.

To see that this is so, assume that sensory appearances are thick. When a person sees an apple tree *as* an apple tree, this is understood to involve both a phenomenal aspect and a conceptual aspect, the latter with the content that the object is an apple tree. On this assumption, sensory appearances are always sensory "takings" or "seemings"; to have a sensory experience of an apple tree is not only to be appeared to phenomenally in a particular way, but to take the object appearing to be an apple tree. Of course, not only apple trees can be seen as apple trees. A cherry tree might seem to be an apple tree in this sense, especially if one is not good at discriminating cherry trees from apple trees. Similarly, an apple tree might seem to be something else – for example, seem to be a man at the far end of a darkened field. But in any case, on this view, sensory appearances always come interpreted – they must be understood as having a phenomenal content, but always a conceptual content as well.

Even so, there appearing to be an apple tree (understanding sensory appearances now as having both phenomenal and conceptual content) does not make probable the belief that there is an apple tree, without the assumption that, at least in general, the way things appear is a reliable indication of the way things are. Alternatively, there "seeming visually" to be an apple tree does not make probable the belief that there is an apple tree, without the assumption that the way things seem visually is generally a reliable indication of the way things are. Are such assumptions true? Every indication we have about our perceptual powers is that the answer is yes. But Hume's point in (H2) and (H3) is not to challenge the truth of these assumptions. Rather, his point is that if the assumptions are truths, then they are contingent truths. If it is true that the way things seem to be via the senses is a reliable indication of the way things are, then this is a contingent truth about our cognition and the world

---

appearances and the external properties of objects. I am not concerned with this latter kind of problem, since it does not arise for what I think is the more plausible account of sensory evidence, i.e., the one in which sensory appearances are thick.

rather than a necessary truth about the concepts of sensory seemings and reality. But if this kind of assumption is a contingent matter regarding the way the world is, then our evidence for it must involve empirical observation. In other words, our justification for this sort of assumption must itself be grounded in sensory seemings, and therefore in the assumption that sensory seemings are a reliable indication of the way things are.[5]

This suggests that Hume's arguments can be taken two ways. We *can* interpret the arguments as being about sensory appearances understood as having only phenomenal content. In this case the problem is that my beliefs about the world depend for their justification on the way things appear phenomenally, but appearances so conceived cannot support those beliefs. But we can also interpret Hume's arguments as being about sensory seemings or takings. Now the problem is that my beliefs about the world depend for their justification on the way things seem to be via the senses, but appearances so conceived still do not make my beliefs probable by themselves. In both cases we need to add an assumption in order to make the relevant appearances function as evidence for beliefs about the world. And in both cases there seems to be no noncircular justification for that assumption.

Here is Hume's reasoning reconstructed both ways.

(H2a) 1. All of our beliefs about the external world depend for their evidence on the way things appear phenomenally, together with the assumption (A3) that something's appearing phenomenally a certain way is a reliable indication that it is that way.
2. But (A3) is itself a belief about the external world.
3. Therefore, assumption (A3) depends for its evidence on (A3). (1,2)
4. Circular reasoning cannot give rise to knowledge.
5. Therefore, (A3) is not known. (3,4)
6. All of our beliefs about the world depend on an assumption that is not known. (1,5)

---

5 It might be objected here that I am assuming an internalist theory of content. On externalist theories, the objection goes, it is a necessary truth that the content of one's thick sensory experience refers to an external reality. In reply, even on the strongest versions of externalist theories of content, the necessary connection between content and world is only indirect and tenuous. In other words, the connection does not guarantee the kind of reliability between appearance and reality that is claimed in assumption (A2) of arguments (H2) and (H3). Externalists about content do not dispute this. E.g., see Hilary Putnam, *Reason, Truth and History* (Cambridge: Cambridge University Press, 1981).

7. Beliefs that depend on unknown assumption are themselves not known.
  8. Therefore, no one knows anything about external reality. (6,7)

(H2b) 1. All of our beliefs about the external world depend for their evidence on the way things seem to be via the senses, together with the assumption (A4) that the way things seem to be is a reliable indication of the way things are.
  2. But (A4) is itself a belief about the external world.
  3. Therefore, assumption (A4) depends for its evidence on (A4). (1,2)
  4. Circular reasoning cannot give rise to knowledge.
  5. Therefore, (A4) is not known. (3,4)
  6. All of our beliefs about the world depend on an assumption that is not known. (1,5)
  7. Beliefs that depend on unknown assumption are themselves not known.
  8. Therefore, no one knows anything about external reality. (6,7)

I end this section with a final remark regarding Hume's reasoning. A number of philosophers have denied the plausibility of premise (1) of (H2a). As we have just seen, their reasoning is that appearances conceived as having merely phenomenal content cannot be in the "logical space of reasons" and therefore cannot function as evidence for beliefs, although such appearances still might function as causal antecedents for beliefs.[6] But it seems to me that premise (1) of (H2a) is not wholly implausible. For example, consider my perceptual belief that the cat is sitting on the couch. Isn't my reason for believing this at least partly the fact that things appear phenomenally a particular way? Clearly this is part of the cause of my believing that the cat is on the couch, but isn't it at least plausibly a *reason* in the epistemological sense? For example, isn't it part of what allows me to *know* that the cat is on the couch? Of course one might stipulate that "reasons" or "evidence" by definition involve logical relations, but this would not affect the substantive point at issue. We could still specify a broader sense of epistemic grounds, and it would remain plausible that the way things appear phenomenally makes up at least part of our epistemic grounds for perceptual beliefs.

Perhaps what these philosophers mean to claim is that appearances

---

6 This view is most famously defended by Wilfred Sellars – for example, in "Empiricism and the Philosophy of Mind," in *Science, Perception and Reality* (London: Routledge, 1963). A somewhat similar view is defended in John McDowell, *Mind and World* (Cambridge, MA: Harvard University Press, 1996).

conceived as having merely phenomenal content cannot be *all* of our evidence for perceptual beliefs; that there must be some other aspect of that evidence as well in order to generate knowledge or justified belief. But that claim is consistent with Hume's reasoning in (H2a). In any case, even if we reject (H2a) on the grounds that it involves an inadequate account of sensory appearances, which ultimately I think we should, this still teaches an important lesson about the nature of sensory evidence. Moreover, this line of objection does not offer an adequate diagnosis of (H2b).

I turn next to Descartes' skeptical considerations in the Meditation I. The argument presented there has been interpreted in many different ways. I will argue that its most powerful version reduces to the reasoning we have just seen from Hume.

2. AN ARGUMENT FROM DESCARTES

Although Descartes was no skeptic, he does present some powerful skeptical considerations. Notoriously, he puts forward those considerations because he wants to discard all of his former opinions – everything that he has previously believed and even taken for granted. This is the first step of a wider project in which Descartes tries to rebuild his knowledge according to the "method for rightly conducting reason and seeking truth in the sciences." Roughly, that method involves establishing a solid foundation of clear and distinct first truths and proceeding from those only by demonstrations that are themselves clearly and distinctly valid. Many have thought that Descartes did a better job of undermining his former opinions than he did of rebuilding his knowledge, and I concur with that judgment. But let us take a closer look at how Descartes' skeptical reasoning is supposed to go. It is this first step of his project that is of interest to our own investigation.

As I have just mentioned, Descartes raises doubts in Meditation I because he wants to discard everything that he has formerly believed. But he quickly notes that it would be impossible for him to find reasons for doubting his beliefs one at a time. The more effective alternative would be to find reasons for doubting the sources of his beliefs, thereby implicating all of his beliefs at once, or at least large groups of them at once:[7]

---

7   All quotations from Descartes are from *The Philosophical Works of Descartes, vol. 2*, trans. Elizabeth S. Haldane and G. R. T. Ross (Cambridge: Cambridge University Press, 1979).

And for that end it will not be requisite that I should examine each in particular, which would be an endless undertaking; for owing to the fact that the destruction of the foundations of necessity brings with it the downfall of the rest of the edifice, I shall only in the first place attack those principles upon which all my former opinions rested. (*Meditations*, p. 145)

The "principle" he hits upon, of course, is sensory experience. "All that up to the present time I have accepted as most true and certain I have learned either from the senses or through the senses; but it is sometimes proved to me that these senses are deceptive" (p. 145).

This is the old "sometimes I make mistakes" reasoning again. But a more important point is made next. Namely, it is possible to have the same experience one does now even when one is only dreaming, and when things are not the way they appear at all.

How often has it happened to me that in the night I dreamt that I found myself in this particular place, that I was dressed and seated near the fire, whilst in reality I was lying undressed in bed! At this moment it does indeed seem to me that it is with eyes awake that I am looking at this paper; that this head which I move is not asleep, that it is deliberately and of set purpose that I extend my hand and perceive it; what happens in sleep does not appear so clear nor so distinct as does all this. But in thinking this over I remind myself that on many occasions I have in sleep been deceived by similar illusions, and in dwelling carefully on this reflection I see so manifestly that there are no certain indications by which we may clearly distinguish wakefulness from sleep that I am lost in astonishment. (pp. 145–6)

At first Descartes considers the kind of dream that occurs in sleep, but toward the end of the meditation he raises the possibility of something much more extreme:

Nevertheless I have long had fixed in my mind the belief that an all-powerful God existed by whom I have been created such as I am. But how do I know that He has not brought it to pass that there is no earth, no heaven, no extended body, no magnitude, no place, and that nevertheless [I possess the perceptions of all these things, and that] they seem to me to exist just exactly as I now see them? (p. 147)

It is possible for things to appear to me exactly as they do now even if things are drastically different from what I believe them to be. It is possible, for example, that things appear as they do, but that I am the victim of a powerful and elaborate deception. Perhaps God deceives me, or perhaps I am fooled by an "evil genius" – a being "not less powerful than deceitful," and who "has employed his whole energies in deceiving me" (p. 148).

It is not obvious how the skeptical reasoning is supposed to go here, but one point can be made right away: namely, Descartes never actually believes that there might be an evil genius deceiving him at every turn. Rather, he introduces the possibility of such a demon as a kind of psychological tool; he wants to discard all of his former opinions but finds this psychologically impossible. His solution is to *pretend* that there is a powerful demon bent on deceiving him, so that he may keep in mind his resolution to doubt his former beliefs and to use nothing that is less than certain in his further deliberations.

> But it is not sufficient to have made these remarks, we must also be careful to keep them in mind. For these ancient and commonly held opinions still revert frequently to my mind, long and familiar custom having given them the right to occupy my mind against my inclination and rendered them almost masters of my belief; nor will I ever lose the habit of deferring to them or of placing my confidence in them, so long as I consider them as they really are, i.e. opinions in some measure doubtful, as I have just shown, and at the same time highly probable, so that there is much more reason to believe in than to deny them. That is why I consider that I shall not be acting amiss, if, taking of set purpose a contrary belief, I allow myself to be deceived, and for a certain time pretend that all these opinions are entirely false and imaginary, until at last, having thus balanced my former prejudices with my latter [so that they cannot divert my opinions more to one side than to the other], my judgment will no longer be dominated by bad usage or turned away from the right knowledge of the truth.
>
> I shall then suppose, not that God who is supremely good and the fountain of truth, but some evil genius not less powerful than deceitful, has employed his whole energies in deceiving me. (p. 148)

For this reason alone, much of the abuse that has been heaped on Descartes' argument simply misses the mark. However misguided Descartes' project in the *Meditations*, he never seriously thought that his life might be a dream orchestrated by an evil genius.

If Descartes never takes seriously the possibility that he is deceived, then what is his line of reasoning in the passages we have been reviewing? I think it is essentially this: Descartes sets out to evaluate his evidence for the various beliefs he has long held, and he concludes that his evidence is not very good. And the reason it is not very good is that it fails to rule out other possibilities that are inconsistent with what he believes. Let us take a closer look at this line of thought.[8]

Consider Descartes' belief that he is sitting by the fire in a dressing gown. Presumably he has this belief because this is how things are presented to him by his senses. However, Descartes reasons, things could appear to him just as they do even if he were in fact not sitting by the fire but was instead sleeping, or mad, or the victim of an evil deceiver. The point is not that these other things might well be true, or that they ought to be taken seriously as real possibilities. Rather, it is that Descartes' evidence does not rule these possibilities out. And if it does not rule them out, then it cannot be very good evidence for his belief that he is sitting by the fire.

It should be emphasized that Descartes' reasoning follows from a seemingly obvious principle about adequate evidence. Namely, a body of evidence does not adequately support a conclusion unless that evidence effectively rules out other possibilities which are inconsistent with that conclusion. For example, in murder cases the prosecutor must present evidence that rules out suicide or another murderer. In scientific investigations a hypothesis is confirmed only when the evidence effectively rules out competitors. What Descartes notices is that this general principle has skeptical consequences when applied consistently to our perceptual beliefs about objects in the world. Our evidence in such cases is sensory experience, but that experience fails to rule out a host of alternative possibilities.

Two points need to be emphasized here. First, alternative possibilities to what I believe undermine my knowledge even if they are *false*. For example, if I cannot rule out the possibility of suicide in a suspicious death, then I cannot know that someone committed a murder. And that is true even if there was no suicide – even if the alternative possibility I cannot rule out is in reality false. This is what gives the skeptical reasoning its force. For although there is no reason whatsoever to think that I am in bed dreaming, or that I am the victim of a deceiving demon, it is hard to deny that these are possibilities in some broad sense. That is to say, there is nothing incoherent or logically impossible about them. But

---

8 Here and in the next two paragraphs I follow Barry Stroud, although I depart from him in some respects. See Stroud, *The Significance of Philosophical Skepticism*. For a different reading of Descartes' argument, see Frederick Schmitt, *Knowledge and Belief* (London: Routledge, 1992).

then, that is all that the skeptic needs. For knowledge demands that our evidence rule out alternative possibilities, and these possibilities cannot be ruled out. Second, Descartes' reasoning runs just as well whether we are thinking of sensory appearances as thin or thick. The fact that things appear phenomenally a certain way does not rule out the possibility that I am dreaming, or that I am deceived by an evil demon. But neither does the fact that things present themselves a certain way in thick sensory seemings.

Here is Descartes' reasoning put more formally.

(D1)   1. A person can know something on the basis of her evidence only if that evidence rules out possibilities that are inconsistent with what the person claims to know.
2. A person's evidence for her beliefs about the world is her sensory experience.
3. It is a possibility that one is dreaming, and the possibility that one is dreaming is inconsistent with one's beliefs about the world.
4. Therefore, a person can know things about the world only if her sensory experience rules out the possibility that she is dreaming. (1,2,3)
5. But a person's experience does not rule out the possibility that she is dreaming.
6. Therefore, no one knows anything about the world. (4,5)

We now have a rough characterization of Descartes' skeptical argument. But this characterization is still consistent with a number of interpretations, some of which do not have much force at all. What I want to do now is to get the argument into its most powerful form. I will conclude that there are two versions which are quite powerful in the sense defined earlier: That is, there are two versions of the argument that make no obvious mistake, and that therefore require us to say something philosophically substantive in refuting them. But the most powerful of these two reduces to the argument we have already seen from Hume.

The most significant way in which we get different versions of (D1) is according to how we understand the idea of evidence "ruling out" an alternative possibility. On some interpretations of this idea the argument has little or no force. On others it is hard to see where the argument goes wrong. Before we look at these different interpretations, however, I want to address an objection to the argument that is widely endorsed but seems to me to be off the mark.

3. NEED THE SKEPTIC CHALLENGE ALL OF OUR KNOWLEDGE AT ONCE?

A common objection to Descartes' argument is that it challenges all of our knowledge at once. Sometimes the charge is put somewhat differently: What is wrong with the argument is that it assumes (incorrectly) that we *can* challenge all of our knowledge at once. It incorrectly assumes that such general doubts make sense, or are intelligible. Sophisticated versions of this objection occur in Wittgenstein, J. L. Austin, and Stanley Cavell, and more recently in Barry Stroud and Michael Williams.[9] Now to be fair, all of these philosophers say much more in their critiques of skepticism than this, and none of them can be said to be dismissive in the sense that they do not engage skeptical arguments seriously. But then the frequency of the charge and the quality of its sources is all the more puzzling. For although Descartes in fact presents himself as examining all of his knowledge at once, it seems clear that there is nothing in his skeptical argument that requires him to do so. In other words, there is nothing in his *reasoning* that requires him either to (a) challenge all of his knowledge at once or (b) assume that such general doubts are intelligible. Even if Descartes wants to end that way, there is no reason why he has to begin that way. Therefore his reasoning cannot be criticized along those lines.

It will be interesting to look more closely at how the charge arises. I want to argue that the objection becomes plausible only on misguided conceptions of our engagement with skeptical arguments. For example, one way to think of that engagement is in the context of a debate. In that context we can imagine the skeptic making a particular rhetorical move in response to criticisms. Specifically, the skeptic argues that we cannot pursue any line of objection which assumes that we have knowledge of the world, since that is the very thing in question. The skeptical argument means to challenge all of our knowledge at once, or, more exactly, all of our knowledge of the world at once, and so any line of objection that assumes such knowledge begs the question against the skeptical position. It begs the question, for example, to invoke empirical science as showing that our cognitive faculties are reliable in some important respect.

---

9 See Ludwig Wittgenstein, *On Certainty* (Oxford: Blackwell, 1969); J. L. Austin, *Sense and Sensibilia* (Oxford: Oxford University Press, 1962); Stanley Cavell, *The Claims of Reason* (Oxford: Oxford University Press, 1979); Stroud, *The Significance of Philosophical Scepticism*; and Williams, *Unnatural Doubts*.

Now it seems clear that this charge of question begging is relevant if we think of skeptical arguments as moments in a debate. If the debate is over whether empirical knowledge is possible, we cannot invoke empirical science to show that it is. The question-begging charge is not relevant, however, if we think of skeptical arguments as objects of analysis. I have been suggesting that we should use skeptical arguments as heuristic devices that can drive us to better theories of knowledge and evidence. Skeptical arguments are philosophically interesting because they start from premises that seem plausible *to us*, and yet lead to conclusions that we find implausible. The philosophical task becomes to find something that we can reject, and to replace it with something better. In this context it is irrelevant that an imaginary skeptic could invoke ground rules in an imaginary debate. So far as *we* find a line of critique to be plausible, it does not matter that it begs a question against an imaginary someone else.

Let us make a distinction between (a) assumptions that play the role of premises in an argument and (b) ground rules that play the role of rhetorical restrictions on a conversation. If we are thinking of skeptical arguments as objects of analysis rather than as moments in a debate, then rhetorical ground rules cannot be used to block a critique of an argument's premises. And for exactly the same reasons, a critique of rhetorical ground rules cannot replace a critique of an argument's premises. We need to look at the premises of a skeptical argument, and at the logic that takes us from those premises to its conclusion, and to find something that we can reject there.

We can now return to Descartes' argument with these issues in mind. Does anything in Descartes' skeptical reasoning require that he challenge all of our knowledge at once? Does any premise in his reasoning involve the assumption that we can do this? Put another way, does Descartes assume anywhere in his argument's premises that a general or total assessment of our knowledge is possible, or that completely general doubts are possible? It is true that Descartes *wants* to challenge all of our knowledge at once. But the reason he does is to be found in the wider project he is undertaking rather than in anything essential to the skeptical argument he puts forward. Remember that Descartes wants to clear away all of his former opinions so that he can build back his knowledge according to the right method for conducting his reason. Only after he has cleared away all of his old beliefs can he proceed to establish a certain foundation on which to build back his knowledge. But nothing in the skeptical argument he raises assumes that he can challenge all of his beliefs at once. Neither does his argument assume, in any essential respect, that Descartes can raise completely general doubts. That is where Descartes wants to get to, but it is not where he has to start.

We can see this by looking at Stroud's own reconstruction of Descartes' reasoning. On Stroud's account Descartes considers his belief that he is sitting by the fire as a "best-possible case" from which he can *infer* a more general conclusion.

> The fire and the piece of paper are not too small or too far away to be seen properly, they are right there before his eyes; it seems to be the best kind of position someone could be in for getting reliable beliefs or knowledge by means of the senses about what is going on around him. That is just how Descartes regards it. Its being a best-possible case of that kind is precisely what he thinks enables him to investigate or assess at one fell swoop all our sensory knowledge of the world around us.[10]

On this conception of Descartes' reasoning, the skeptic does not begin by questioning all of our knowledge at once; rather, he begins by looking at our evidence for a best-possible case and concludes that our evidence even in that case is not very good. The skeptic then infers from this that in general our evidence for beliefs about the world is not very good. Stroud implies that the inference is made in something like the following way: I do not know that I am sitting by the fire because my sensory experience does not adequately support that belief over alternative possibilities. But if I do not know that, then I do not know anything about the world on the basis of my sensory experience – this, after all, was a best-possible case. Another way to make the inference is to notice that there is nothing special about the best-possible case that would block the same conclusion in other cases; the reasoning would go pretty much the same way for any belief about the world grounded in sensory appearances. But that includes all of my beliefs about the world, because all of them are grounded, directly or indirectly, on the way things appear to me through my senses.

Here is a reconstruction of the skeptical reasoning beginning from a single case rather than from all of our knowledge at once, with both ways of making the generalization included:

(D2)   1. A person can know something on the basis of her evidence only if that evidence rules out every possibility that is inconsistent with what the person claims to know.

---

10   Stroud, p. 9.

2. My evidence for my belief that I am sitting by the fire is my sensory experience.
3. It is a possibility that I am in bed dreaming, and this is inconsistent with my belief that I am sitting by the fire.
4. Therefore, I can know that I am sitting by the fire only if my sensory experience rules out the possibility that I am dreaming. (1,2,3)
5. But my sensory experience does not rule out that possibility.
6. Therefore, I do not know that I am sitting by the fire. (4,5)
7a. If I do not know that, then I don't know anything about the world.

Or,

7b. The belief that I am sitting by the fire is arbitrary; if I plug in any belief about the world, the argument goes through with respect to that belief as well.
8. Therefore, I have no knowledge of the world. (6,7)

Two comments are in order. First, (D2) presents a formidable problem even if we stop at subconclusion (6). In other words, the argument reaches an unbelievable and unacceptable conclusion even *before* it makes any general skeptical claim, because it is unbelievable that Descartes does not know that he is sitting by the fire. Of course he knows this, and so there must be some mistake in the argument that has nothing to do with its rejection of knowledge of the world in general.

Second, suppose we do follow the argument to its general conclusion in (8). Is there anything about the reasoning presented this way that questions our knowledge of the world "all at once"? Of course the argument's *conclusion* does, but that is the result of the skeptical reasoning, not a presupposition of it. We cannot say that the reasoning presupposes that our knowledge can be questioned all at once, or that what is wrong with the argument is that it *assumes* that it can be. This kind of critique of Descartes' argument, therefore, misses the mark. Even if it presents a problem for the argument as it is presented in (D1), Descartes' reasoning is easily revised along the lines of (D2).[11]

So why does Stroud think that the skeptical argument must challenge all of our knowledge at once, or must assume that we can raise com-

---

11 It is not obvious to me that challenging all of our knowledge at once, or assuming that we can, does create a problem for the skeptical reasoning in (D1). For example, what premise or step in (D1) is thereby made objectionable? But since these aspects of the reasoning are inessential, there is no need to pursue the question.

pletely general doubts, even when Stroud's own reconstruction shows that the argument need not proceed in either of these ways? As I said, the claim becomes plausible if we think of ourselves as debating a skeptic. In that case we can imagine the skeptic making certain rhetorical moves in an effort to head off certain kinds of responses to his skeptical reasoning. The skeptic insists that he is challenging all of our knowledge at once, and that that is why we cannot invoke some aspect of our knowledge to critique the skeptical argument. This rhetorical move amounts to challenging all of our knowledge at once and, in effect, involves the assumption that to do so is intelligible.

Another way that Stroud's claim becomes plausible is if we think of ourselves as engaged in a special kind of philosophical question or project. As Stroud describes it, the special project of traditional epistemology is to answer the skeptic's question about knowledge of the world, but within the context of certain severe restrictions. The traditional epistemologist's task is to show that knowledge of the world is possible, but without assuming any information about the world in doing so. We cannot assume, for example, as Moore did, that we know that here is a hand, and then use this knowledge to show that we have knowledge in general. In the following passage, Stroud makes exactly this point on behalf of the skeptic:

If we have the feeling that Moore nevertheless fails to answer the philosophical question about our knowledge of external things, as we do, it is because we understand that question as requiring a certain withdrawal or detachment from the whole body of our knowledge of the world. We recognize that when I ask in that detached philosophical way whether I know that there are external things, I am not supposed to be allowed to appeal to other things I think I know about external things in order to help me settle the question. *All* of my knowledge of the external world is supposed to have been brought into question at one fell swoop; no particular piece of it is to be available as unquestioned knowledge to help me decide whether or not another particular candidate is true.[12]

Stroud does not stop at ruling out Moore-type refutations of skepticism. He uses the same reasoning to block responses to skepticism by naturalized epistemology and, by extension, responses by any epistemology that invokes empirical knowledge. In the next passage Stroud is considering whether W. V. O. Quine's epistemology could answer the

---

12   Stroud, p. 118.

traditional question about knowledge of the world in general. He concludes that it could not, because Quine assumes the very knowledge that the traditional epistemologist calls into question.

Another apparent difference is that Quine's question about our knowledge is to be answered by making use of any scientific information we happen to possess or can discover, whereas the traditional epistemologist's question was meant to put all that alleged information into jeopardy and hence to render it unavailable for such explanatory purposes. Any question empirical science can answer could not be the traditional philosopher's question.[13]

It is not obvious that Stroud has accurately described the traditional epistemologist's question. Stroud's description of this question does not seem to fit the questions of Plato, Aristotle, or Aquinas, for example. But putting that aside, the essential point for our purposes is that it is rhetorical considerations that have once again imported the issue of total assessment. In other words, even on Stroud's account there is nothing in the skeptical *argument* that challenges all of our knowledge at once, or that raises completely general doubts, or that assumes that it is possible to do these things. By Stroud's own lights, it is only the purpose of the skeptical argument, not the argument itself, that involves such assumptions. And this means that rejecting such assumptions does not touch the argument. Even if we reject the traditional epistemologist's question as Stroud describes it, as surely we should, the skeptical argument remains standing and in need of further analysis.

Michael Williams is another philosopher who recognizes that Descartes' argument can be reconstructed along the lines of (D2) but who nevertheless insists that it assumes, at least implicitly, that all of our knowledge of the world can be challenged at once. Williams endorses Stroud's claim that the assumption can be traced back to traditional epistemology's special project:

In trying to explain how what might otherwise seem to be truisms take on a surprising significance, it is natural to look first to the traditional epistemologist's aim of assessing the *totality* of our knowledge of the world. Because he wants to explain how we are able to know anything at all about the external world, his plan is to assess all such knowledge, all at once. But surely, the argument now goes, if we are to understand how it is possible for us to know *anything at all*

13 Ibid., p. 221.

about external reality, we must trace that knowledge to knowledge we should still have even if we knew nothing about the world.[14]

Williams claims that assumptions about total assessment also show up in skeptical arguments. This is because epistemology's project and skeptical arguments share a deeper assumption: what Williams calls "epistemological realism." According to Williams, it is this concealed theoretical commitment that both (a) makes the project of total assessment plausible and (b) allows the skeptic to draw general conclusions from specific cases along the lines of (D2).

In Williams' sense, epistemological realism is not a metaphysical thesis about the mind independence of reality. Rather, it is a constellation of related epistemological theses about the nature of knowledge. First, epistemological realism treats knowledge of the world like a natural kind.

> The epistemological realist thinks of knowledge in very much the way the scientific realist thinks of heat: beneath the surface diversity there is structural unity. Not everything we call knowledge need be knowledge properly so called. But there is a way of bringing together the genuine cases into a coherent theoretical kind. By doing so – and only by so doing – we make such things as "knowledge of the external world" the objects of a distinctive form of theoretical investigation. We make it possible to investigate knowledge, or knowledge of the world, *as such*. (pp. 108–109)

Second, and seemingly following from this, the epistemic status of a belief is fully objective and radically non-contextual. For this reason the epistemological realist can evaluate abstract propositions as well as particular judgments: the contextual aspects of a particular judgment can be ignored because they are irrelevant to the judgment's epistemic status, which is determined by its propositional content alone. For the realist, "a judgment derives its epistemological status from some highly abstract feature of the content of the proposition it contains" (p. 67; see also pp. 199–200). More specifically, relations of epistemic priority are objective and non-contextual; for an epistemological realist, "there are relations of epistemological priority that hold between propositions independently of the circumstances in which those propositions are advanced, the interests that govern their assessment, or any other such 'contextual' features" (p. 67).

Williams argues that it is exactly these presuppositions of epistemo-

---

14 Williams, *Unnatural Doubts*, p. 89; cited hereafter by page number in the text.

logical realism that allow the skeptic to derive general conclusions from specific examples of knowledge.

When we have a natural kind, we can learn general things about the kind by investigating the properties of appropriate samples. The procedure is legitimate because of the supposed underlying hidden structure. Where there is such a structure, what goes for one sample will go for all; where there isn't, no general lessons can be drawn. . . .

We see, then, that the strategy of arguing from a representative case, far from sidestepping the traditional epistemologist's realist presuppositions with respect to epistemic kinds and relations, brings us right back to them. His procedure is legitimate only if it is reasonable to treat terms like "empirical knowledge" as natural kind terms. There must be something in the epistemic realm analogous to the hidden structure or essential characteristics of naturally occurring substances such as gold. There has to be a microstructure, a hidden essence, of empirical knowledge. We have already seen what this is: context invariant, fully objective and autonomous epistemological constraints: in particular, natural relations of epistemic priority. (pp. 164–165)

In these passages Williams has given up the idea that skeptical arguments must begin by questioning all of our knowledge at once, or that they must involve the assumption that total assessment is possible. His considered position is that skeptical arguments presuppose epistemological realism, and that it is this presupposition which allows the skeptic to *arrive* at total assessment by examining specific cases of knowledge. In later chapters, however, Williams returns to his earlier diagnosis: "When we see that the sceptic's truth talk is really a way of asking his characteristically *general* questions about knowledge and justification, we see that the totality condition on a philosophical understanding of knowledge, and the controversial and implausible ideas it embodies, is the proper target for the theoretical diagnostician"(pp. 246–247). Presumably what Williams should say here is that skepticism depends on epistemological realism, and that epistemological realism makes sense of the skeptical project of total assessment. But as Williams has already agreed, skeptical arguments need not begin by challenging all of our knowledge at once and need not start with the assumption that total assessment is possible.

Is Williams correct that skeptical arguments depend on the assumption of epistemological realism? If they do, and if epistemological realism entails that total assessment is possible, then there is a sense in which skeptical arguments do depend on the possibility of total assessment. Namely, if total assessment is not possible, then, by *modus tollens*, something assumed in the skeptical argument is false – namely, epistemological realism. Perhaps this is all that Williams ever meant by claiming that skeptical arguments assume that total assessment is possible; they do not assume it as a premise, but they are committed to it in the sense that they assume something else (epistemological realism) that entails it.

But putting all of that aside, Williams' claim that skeptical arguments do depend on epistemological realism seems incorrect. We may see this by distinguishing a weak and a strong version of epistemological realism. In the strong sense, epistemological realism claims that the epistemic status of a belief in entirely non-contextual. This seems to be the thesis that Williams intends in his own characterizations of epistemological realism. Let us define a weaker version of the thesis, however. Weak epistemological realism claims that the epistemic status of a belief is not entirely a function of context. In other words, weak epistemological realism claims that some conditions relevant to epistemic status are non-contextual. And now the point is this: Williams claims that skeptical arguments can draw general conclusions from specific cases only by assuming strong epistemological realism. But in fact, all that is needed is weak epistemological realism. So long as *some* conditions relevant to epistemic status are not context dependent, and so long as the skeptical argument exploits only those conditions, the argument need not assume that no other conditions relevant to epistemic status are context dependent.

Put differently, to make the inference to a general conclusion the skeptic need only deny that he has *wrongly exploited* any contextual feature of knowledge; he must deny that the skeptical argument invokes in the specific case some contextual feature that does not carry over to cases of knowledge in general. But denying this does not commit the skeptic to epistemological realism in the strong sense. Strong epistemological realism is the thesis that *no* conditions on knowledge are sensitive to context, whereas the skeptic need only deny that *all* conditions on knowledge are. In particular, the skeptical arguments from Hume and Descartes assume that all beliefs about the world depend, directly or indirectly, on the way things appear to us through the senses. But to affirm that this aspect of empirical knowledge is context invariant does not commit one to holding that all features of empirical knowledge are context invariant.

Suppose that Williams grants this but continues to charge that skeptical arguments assume weak epistemological realism. Now Williams' objection must be characterized as follows: "In order to draw general skeptical conclusions from specific cases, the skeptical argument must assume that some feature of epistemic status is context invariant. But no features of epistemic status are invariant – even weak epistemological realism is false." The problem with this objection is that weak epistemological realism seems *true*. In other words, it seems that *some* conditions relevant to knowledge are context invariant. Specifically, the assumption made by Hume and Descartes that all knowledge of the world depends on sensory appearances seems correct, even platitudinous.

Here Williams would disagree. According to him, not all knowledge of the world depends on the evidence of sensory appearances, since often enough knowledge of the world depends on other knowledge of the world, and sometimes on no evidence at all. In effect, Williams would reject the move from (6) to (8) in (D2) and would reject premise (1) of (H2). Even if some well-chosen belief depends for its evidence on how things appear through the senses, it does not follow that all knowledge of the world depends on that kind of evidence.

As I have said, my own assessment is that it is true that all beliefs about the world depend for their evidence on the way things appear, and that this claim is a truism rather than something we must derive from epistemic realism. A number of points can be made to bring this out. First, we should not build into the claim any particular theory of sensory appearances, or any particular theory about *how* sensory appearances act as evidence for knowledge about the world. The principle of charity requires that we do *not* load philosophical theories into the claim, especially not implausible or false ones. Second, the claim is not that all beliefs about the world depend *directly* on the evidence of sensory appearances. It might be that our most immediate reasons for believing one thing about the world is that we believe other things about the world. But if these other things eventually rest on the evidence of sensory appearances (on how things look, feel, sound, etc.), then this dependence transfers to the belief about the world in question. It is consistent with Williams' point that some knowledge of the world is directly supported by other knowledge of the world, to also claim that all knowledge of the world is indirectly supported by evidence involving the way things appear. Third, the claim need not be interpreted as stating that *all* of our evidence for all of our beliefs about the world must ultimately rest on evidence involving sensory appearances. It is enough to make the case that *some* of our evidence for *each* belief does. The skeptical argument need not assume, therefore, a foundationalism in which all empirical claims are entirely grounded in a foundation of sensory appearances.

But now isn't it plausible that all of our beliefs about the world depend on evidence involving how things appear, at least partly and indirectly? Can we think of any beliefs that do not? Williams' preferred example is Moore's belief that here is a hand. In some contexts, he admits, one might need evidence for such a belief. In others, however, one knows it on no evidence at all. But this seems implausible to me. In some cases where I know that here is a hand, I know it because I can see it or feel it. In other cases I know it because I can reason from other things, including other things that I can see or feel. For example, I can reason that I would have a hand here unless something drastic had happened, and if something drastic had happened I would have seen it or felt it, but I did not. In the first case my knowledge is directly based on the way things look or feel, and in the second case it is indirectly based on the way things look or feel. So even in Williams' preferred example, knowledge about the world is either directly or indirectly grounded in how things appear.

We therefore have no good reason for denying what otherwise seems obviously true: that all beliefs about the world depend for their evidence, in one way or another, on how things look or feel (or taste, or smell, or sound). Moreover, this is the only claim about epistemic priority that the arguments from Hume and Descartes need. At least partly, and at least indirectly, all beliefs about the world depend for their evidence on sensory appearances. If we read that claim charitably and in a common sense manner, then there is no reason for thinking that it is anything less than a truism.

My own diagnosis of (H2) and (D2) concedes that this claim is a truism. However, the skeptical arguments from Descartes and Hume make a different mistake. Those arguments also assume that beliefs about the world must be *inferred* from the way things appear. In other words, they assume a specific account of *how* sensory appearances act as evidence for beliefs about the world. Put differently, the arguments assume that all evidential relations are inferential relations. This is in fact a natural and widely shared assumption. Williams himself seems to accept it, and this is why he must look for a mistake in the skeptical argument elsewhere.

If our knowledge of the external world really does need to be derived, in some general way, from prior experiential data, we ought to be able to explain how. But it is difficult to see how we could give an account of a warrant-conferring form of inference connecting how things appear with claims about how they are in the external world which would be adequate to meeting the sceptic's challenge while doing justice to our sense of the objectivity of the world. The doctrine of the epistemic priority of experiential knowledge over knowledge of the world seems to disconnect our beliefs about the external world from the only evidence available to support them. (p. 56)

In this passage Williams concedes that an adequate inference from appearance to reality is impossible, and for this reason goes on to deny that our evidence for beliefs about the world is how things appear. He is assuming that if sensory appearances are to function as evidence, this must be via good inferences from them. Or consider Williams' endorsement of Ayers' classic analysis of the pattern of skeptical arguments: First it is argued that some kind of knowledge-claim is in need of inferential support from some kind of evidence, and then it is argued that there is no deductive inference and no inductive inference forthcoming. Again, Williams' diagnosis accepts the assumption that good evidence must ground deductive or inductive inferences. What he rejects is the assumption that there are epistemic kinds, carrying with them relationships of epistemic priority.

In later chapters I argue that it is the assumption that evidence is always inferential that is mistaken. To be sure, *some* good evidence is inferential, to be understood in terms of deductive and inductive relations among propositions. But not all evidential relations are inferential relations. Moreover, I argue that an adequate theory of knowledge and evidence can explain why this is so and, specifically, how knowledge grounded directly in sensory appearances can be non-inferential.

It should be noted, however, that Williams' diagnosis is fully consistent with two of my major theses in this book – namely, that traditional skeptical arguments cannot be easily dismissed as making some obvious mistake, and that the close analysis of skeptical arguments reveals substantive but mistaken epistemological assumptions, the rejection of which drives progress in epistemology. Williams himself has defended these theses as persuasively as anyone. In fact, my agreement with Williams goes even deeper than this. Both of us endorse accounts of knowledge which, in broad outline, are contextualist, externalist, and foundationalist, and which require both objective reliability and subjective justification for knowledge. At this level of generality the difference between us is this: Williams identifies epistemological realism as the mistaken assumption of skeptical arguments and thus replaces it with contextualism. I deny that traditional skeptical arguments presuppose epistemological realism, at least in the strong sense that Williams seems to intend. In addition, I argue that agent reliabilism provides a theoretical explanation for the various diagnoses of skeptical arguments that I do think are correct. Put a different way, agent reliabilism provides a deeper theoretical explanation for the contextualist, externalist foundationalism that Williams and I share.[15]

4. TWO MORE WAYS NOT TO UNDERSTAND DESCARTES' ARGUMENT

In the preceding section I have been arguing against a particular interpretation of Descartes' skeptical argument – namely, I have been arguing against the claim that Descartes' reasoning must (a) challenge all of our knowledge at once or (b) assume that completely general doubts are intelligible. I now look at two more ways not to understand Descartes' argument. Remember that we are trying to reconstruct the argument in its most powerful form. In other words, we are trying to reconstruct it employing only assumptions that seem natural and plausible to us. This is in the context of a methodology which uses skeptical arguments as heuristic devices for driving positive epistemology. Reconstructed in their most powerful form, skeptical arguments highlight mistaken assumptions about the nature of knowledge and evidence, the rejection of which must drive us to substantive epistemological positions. The more powerful the argument in terms of its plausibility, the more substantive the position that is required to reject it.

I said earlier that various reconstructions of Descartes' argument are generated by different ways of understanding the idea of evidence "ruling out" alternative possibilities. One way that idea is commonly understood is in terms of entailment. On this reading, premise (1) of (D2) says that one's evidence can give rise to knowledge only if it entails that all alternatives to one's belief are false. That amounts to saying that evidence gives rise to knowledge only if it entails the belief that is based on it.

This interpretation makes premise (1) of (D2) implausible, however. To understand the skeptical argument that way robs it of any force that it might have. It is perhaps a fair reading of Descartes, in that he sometimes seems to accept only demonstration as an acceptable way of building one's knowledge from indubitable first truths. But if this is what he intended, then, as before, it has more to do with his wider project than it does with the skeptical reasoning he puts forward in the first step of that project. Therefore, even if this is a fair reading of the

---

15 See Williams, *Unnatural Doubts*, and "Skepticism," in Greco and Sosa (1999).

argument as it appears in Descartes' text, there is no reason that we have to understand the skeptical argument that way.

Perhaps the most common way to understand the idea of ruling out alternative possibilities is epistemically, so that to rule out a possibility is, for example, to know that it is false, or to have good reason for believing that it is false, or to be certain that it is false. But this way of understanding the phrase also robs (D2) of its force, for on this understanding it seems wrong that I cannot rule out alternative possibilities. Don't I know, for example, that I am not dreaming? Most of us have the strong intuition that we do know that we are not dreaming in the typical case, and so no skeptical argument will have force if it begins from the assumption that we do not know this. What we are looking for, we should remember, is a version of the argument that employs assumptions that seem plausible to us. But on epistemic interpretations of "ruling out," premise (5) of (D2) will seem false to anyone who is not already a skeptic, and so will seem false to us.

Someone wishing to defend the skeptic might concede that these are our intuitions regarding dreams in the normal sense – that is, regarding the kind of dreams we experience when we are asleep in bed, and yet challenge the claim that we have similar intuitions regarding philosophical dreams. Do I know that my whole life is not a dream, as it would be if I were the victim of an evil deceiver? Or consider the possibility that I am the victim of a psychology experiment in the year 3000. How do I know that I am in fact sitting at a table writing on a computer? Perhaps I am a disembodied brain, hooked up to a computer that is thousands of times more powerful and programmed to stimulate my severed nerve endings so as to create exactly the experiences I am having now. If we think of the dream possibility in either of these more radical ways, the argument goes, then it no longer seems obvious to us that we know that we are not dreaming.

But doesn't it? Don't I know that both of these radical dream scenarios are false, because I know that I am sitting at my desk writing on my computer? I must confess, I think it *is* obvious that I do know these things. But even if some would disagree, it surely is not obvious that I do *not* know that these dream scenarios are false. And so interpreted this way, the skeptical argument still depends on a premise that does not seem obvious or compelling.[16]

16 A number of philosophers have thought that premise (5) is intuitively plausible on the

Of course, premise (5) does not have to be intuitively plausible if the skeptic can give independent grounds for it. Stroud puts forward an argument that is supposed to do just this, so we should take a look at that argument. According to Stroud, Descartes thinks that he can know that he is sitting by the fire only if he knows that he is not dreaming. But Descartes cannot know that he is not dreaming, for the following reason. If it really is a condition of knowing anything about the world that one know that one is not dreaming, then one can have knowledge of the world only if some state of affairs or some test establishes that one is not dreaming. But whether such a test exists or is employed successfully is itself a fact about the way things are in the world, and so one must already have knowledge of the world for the test to do its work.

Let us suppose that there is in fact some test which a person can perform successfully only if he is not dreaming, or some set of circumstances or state of affairs which obtains only if that person is not dreaming. Of course for that test or state of affairs to be of any use to him Descartes would have to know about it. He would have to know that there is such a test or that there is such a state of affairs that shows that he is not dreaming. . . . Now strictly speaking if it is a condition of knowing *anything* about the world beyond one's sensory experience that one know that one is not dreaming, there is an obvious obstacle to Descartes's ever having got the information he needs about that test or state of affairs. He would have to have known he is not dreaming to get the information he needs to tell at *any* time that he is not dreaming – and that cannot be done.[17]

This argument is supposed to provide independent grounds for premise (5) of (D2), where that premise is understood to be the claim that I cannot know that I am not dreaming. But if we look closely, we can see that the argument is not a very good one. The argument can be reconstructed as follows:

1. I can know that I am not dreaming only if I can know something about the world – for example, that some test guarantees that I am not dreaming.

---

present reading, but it seems to me that their intuitions have been tutored here. Most non-philosophers, I would think, find it implausible that they do not know they are brains in vats or victims of evil demons. For the contrary view see Keith DeRose, "Solving the Skeptical Problem," *Philosophical Review* 104, (1995):1–52. See also Stewart Cohen, "How To Be a Fallibilist," *Philosophical Perspectives* 2 (1988): 91–123; and Robert Nozick, *Philosophical Explanations* (Cambridge, MA: Harvard University Press, 1981).

17   Stroud, p. 21.

2. But I can know something about the world only if I can know I am not dreaming.
3. Therefore, I cannot know that I am not dreaming.

Here premises (1) and (2) look plausible, but (3) does not follow from them. All that follows from (1) and (2) is that I can know that I am not dreaming only if I can know that I am not dreaming. That is true enough, but of little skeptical force.

Perhaps Stroud means his premises to be temporalized. In that case we get the following reconstruction.

1. I can know that I am not dreaming only if I already know *at some earlier time* something about the world.
2. I can know something about the world only if I already know at some earlier time that I am not dreaming.
3. Therefore, I can know that I am not dreaming only if I already know at some earlier time that I am not dreaming. (1,2)
4. Therefore, I cannot know that I am not dreaming. (4)

Here (3) follows from premises (1) and (2), and (4) follows from (3). But the problem with this version of the argument is that premise (2) no longer seems plausible. Most of us think that we know things about the world *at the same time* that we know we are not dreaming. No one thinks that we must first find out that we are not dreaming and then infer beliefs about the world, or vice versa, for that matter. So on either understanding of Stroud's argument for the claim that we cannot know we are not dreaming, we do not have good independent grounds for that claim. The lesson we should draw from this is that we should not understand the concept of "ruling out" in (D2) in an epistemic sense.

5. DISCRIMINATING EVIDENCE

There are at least two other interpretations of "ruling out" available, and both generate powerful skeptical arguments. The first is that we think of evidence ruling out alternatives in terms of discriminating those alternatives from the state of affairs that is believed to hold.[18] For example, often my evidence for the belief that my wife has come home from work is that I hear her voice announcing her arrival. This auditory

---

18 For a similar understanding of the concept, see Alvin Goldman, "Discrimination and Perceptual Knowledge," *Journal of Philosophy* 73 (1976): 771–791, reprinted in Goldman, *Liaisons: Philosophy Meets the Cognitive and Social Sciences*.

experience discriminates her being home from my neighbor's yelling for his children and from my cat's whining for her dinner. It also discriminates that state of affairs from the television set's being on, but not from my wife having set up a tape recorder so as to fool me into thinking she has come home. If I were to go into the other room and add my visual experience to the evidence that I already have, then my evidence would discriminate my belief from this last possibility as well.

The current idea is that this is how we should understand the skeptical argument in (D2). A set of evidence gives me knowledge only if it discriminates the state of affairs I believe to hold from others that are inconsistent with it. If I believe that my wife is home but on the basis of evidence that does not discriminate her being home from her not being home, then I cannot know that she is home on the basis of that evidence.

More exactly, the current proposal is this:

(Df.1) A set of evidence E rules out alternatives to a belief p for a person S if and only if E discriminates p's being true from possibilities that are inconsistent with p's being true.

And,

(Df.2) E discriminates p's being true from possibilities $q_1 \ldots q_n$ for S if and only if E would cause S to believe that p is true when p is true, and E would not cause S to believe that p is true when any of $q_1 \ldots q_n$ is true.

We then have the following interpretation of key premises in argument (D2):

(D3) 1. S can know that p is true on the basis of evidence E only if E discriminates p's being true from possibilities that are inconsistent with p's being true.
2. My evidence for my belief that I am sitting by the fire is my sensory experience.
3. It is a possibility that I am not sitting by the fire but only dreaming that I am.
4. Therefore, I can know that I am sitting by the fire only if my sensory experience discriminates my sitting by the fire from my only dreaming that I am. (1,2,3)
5. But my sensory experience does not discriminate these possibilities for me.
6. Therefore, I do not know that I am sitting by the fire. (4,5)

At this point the argument is starting to look good. What premise, for example, is it plausible to deny? One might deny premise (1), and I think that ultimately this is the right move to make. But no one should think that (1) jumps out as obviously false, or that denying (1) should be considered uncontroversial. Consider that (1) is equivalent to the following claim: One's evidence can give rise to knowledge only if it discriminates situations where one's belief is true from situations where it is not. That claim is not implausible, and many would consider it to be obviously true. Especially when considered outside the context of the skeptical argument, the proposition might pass as a platitude.

But in fact premise (1) of (D3) is false, or so I argue. This diagnosis of the argument presents itself when we consider that (1) treats all alternative possibilities the same way. In other words, (1) requires that our evidence discriminate the truth of our belief from every alternative possibility whatsoever. But it is questionable whether our ordinary concept of knowledge in fact requires that our evidence do this. Knowing that my wife is home from work requires that I have evidence that discriminates this situation from the one in which only my cat is home and is whining loudly for her dinner. But it does not require, or so I would think, that I can discriminate my wife's being home from her having been abducted by aliens and replaced with a convincing look-alike. It had better not require that, for by hypothesis the imposter is convincing, and so my evidence could not discriminate this possibility from the one in which my wife is home. This possibility, like the evil genius and brain-in-a-vat possibilities, is designed so that my evidence cannot discriminate between it and the usual things that I believe on the basis of that evidence.

These last considerations suggest that not all alternative possibilities to a knowledge-claim carry the same epistemic weight. To know that someone has committed murder we need to rule out suicide. And to know that my wife is home I must rule out the possibility that it is only my cat or a neighbor that is making some noise. I do not need to rule out other things that are nevertheless clearly possibilities in some broad sense. Some possibilities seem to be *relevant*, in the sense that they do need to be ruled out in order to have knowledge, whereas other possibilities seem not to be relevant in that sense.

This suggests that we revise premise (1) of (D3) as follows, requiring an analogous revision in premise (3) to keep the argument valid.

(D4) 1. S can know that p is true on the basis of evidence E only if E discriminates p's being true from all *relevant* possibilities that are inconsistent with p's being true.
2. My evidence for my belief that I am sitting by the fire is my sensory experience.
3. It is a relevant possibility that I am not sitting by the fire but only dreaming that I am.
4. Therefore, I can know that I am sitting by the fire only if my sensory experience discriminates my sitting by the fire from my only dreaming that I am. (1,2,3)
5. But my sensory experience does not discriminate these possibilities for me.
6. Therefore, I do not know that I am sitting by the fire. (4,5)

On this interpretation, premise (1) now seems true. In fact, if what we mean by "relevant possibility" is a possibility that one's evidence must rule out in order to generate knowledge, then (1) becomes a tautology. But now a different diagnosis of the argument suggests itself. First, we can make a distinction between normal dreams that occur in sleep and "philosophical" dreams such as those caused by evil demons and supercomputers in futuristic psychology experiments. We can then say that the possibility that I am fooled by a normal dream is relevant in some cases, but my sensory experience can usually rule it out. In other words, my sensory experience can usually discriminate waking life from a normal dream. Philosophical dreams cannot be so discriminated, but they are not relevant possibilities. So if by dreams we mean normal dreams, then premise (5) of (D4) is false. But if by dreams we mean philosophical dreams, then premise (3) of (D4) is false. Either way, the skeptical argument is unsound.

This approach to (D4) is promising, but we should admit that it is only the beginning of an answer. It *is* a beginning, because it is already a substantive position to hold that one's evidence need not discriminate the truth of a knowledge-claim from all possibilities that are inconsistent with it. But it is only a beginning, because we would like an account of what makes some possibilities irrelevant in this sense and others not. Furthermore, we would like an account of knowledge and evidence that explains why all of this is so.

In Chapter 8, I offer an account of "relevant possibility" that captures our pre-theoretical intuitions about which possibilities are relevant ones and which are not, and I argue that a virtue theory of knowledge and evidence explains why the account has the content that it does. In other words, I argue that a virtue theory explains why our evidence must discriminate the truth of knowledge-claims from some possibilities and not others.

6. SUPPORTING EVIDENCE

Another way we can interpret the idea of evidence ruling out alternatives is in terms of deductive and inductive support. Specifically,

> A body of evidence E rules out a possibility q if and only if E supports (deductively or inductively) not-q.

On this interpretation it is not clear that premise (1) of (D2) needs to be revised so as to be restricted to relevant possibilities. Or, put differently, it is not clear that a distinction between relevant and irrelevant possibilities needs to be made. For on the present interpretation premise (1) of (D2) says that one's evidence ought to support the negation of all possibilities that are inconsistent with what is believed on the basis of that evidence. But that is equivalent to saying that one's evidence ought to support the beliefs that are based on that evidence.

More formally, we have the following argument.

(D5)   1. S can know that p is true on the basis of her evidence E only if, for all q such that q is inconsistent with p, E supports not-q.

Or equivalently,

   S can know that p is true on the basis of E only if E supports p.
   2. My evidence for my belief that I am sitting by the fire is my sensory experience.
   3. It is a possibility that I am not sitting by the fire but only dreaming that I am.
   4. Therefore, I can know that I am sitting by the fire only if my sensory experience supports the proposition, deductively or inductively, that I am not merely dreaming this. (1,2,3)
   5. But my sensory experience does not support the proposition that I am not dreaming.
   6. Therefore, I do not know that I am sitting by the fire. (4,5)

Again, premise (1) of (D5) looks plausible and might even be considered obvious. Moreover, premises (3) and (5) also look good on this interpretation. Since we are no longer required to restrict (1) to relevant possibilities, there is no need to restrict (3) or (5) that way either. Accordingly, premise (3) of (D5) need only claim that my dreaming is possible in some broad sense of possibility, and that claim is hard to deny.

Premise (5) might seem to be the weak point of the argument, but here considerations from Hume can be brought forward to give the premise a strong defense. That my sensory experience does not deductively support the proposition that I am not dreaming is obvious, since it is possible that I have exactly that experience even when I am dreaming. This should be conceded even in the case of normal dreams, but certainly it is true in the case of philosophical dreams. By hypothesis, such dreams replicate the way things appear in waking life.

But more importantly, my sensory experience alone does not *inductively* support the proposition that I am not dreaming. The point here is the same that we saw in the discussion of (H2) and (H3): my sensory appearances do not even make likely the proposition that I am not dreaming, unless I am also assuming, at least implicitly, that sensory appearances are a reliable guide to reality. Without this assumption, or something very much like it, sensory appearances do not make likely anything about the way the world is. But that includes the proposition that I am not dreaming, since that proposition is itself about the way the world is.

And, of course, merely assuming that my experience is a reliable guide to reality is not enough. If my evidence for the proposition that I am not dreaming is to be any good to me, I must *know*, or at least be justified in believing, that the assumption in question is true. But what is my evidence for the proposition that my experience is a reliable guide to reality? As Hume has pointed out, this is itself a matter of fact and therefore could be established only by empirical evidence. But since such evidence must already include the assumption in question, any attempt at justification here would be circular.

I believe that this is the most powerful version of the argument from Descartes' Meditation I. It does not seem susceptible to the relevant possibilities approach that makes a distinction between normal dreams and philosophical dreams, since premise (1) of (D5) is plausible just as it is stated. Who would deny, outside the context of threatening skeptical conclusions, that one's evidence must support the conclusions that are based on it?

But neither do any of the other premises of the argument seem implausible. Consider premise (2) of (D5). When I am sitting by the fire, the reason I believe this is that this is how the world is presented to me in my sensory experience. And isn't this just obvious? Some philosophers have denied it, but usually what they are objecting to is some particular *account* of sensory experience, or some account of how sensory appearance acts as a reason for my belief. Reading the premise in a common sense way, however, who could deny that, in the typical case, the reason that I believe I am sitting in some location is that this is how things appear to me, either visually or by some other sensory modality? Perhaps someone will deny it if they are in the grip of a philosophical theory, or if they think they are pushed to deny it in order to stave off unacceptable skeptical consequences. But no one would deny it pre-theoretically, and we probably should not deny it even post-theoretically.

Next consider premise (3), which claims only that it is a possibility that I am dreaming. Premise (3) need not claim that I have some good reason to think that I am dreaming, or even that I should take the possibility seriously as something that might turn out to be true. Rather, the premise claims only that my dreaming is a possibility in a much broader sense – that is, it is not incoherent, or inconceivable, or logically impossible. And again, this seems hard to deny.

The remaining independent premise is (5), and we have already seen an argument from Hume to support the claim that is being made there. Accordingly, this version of Descartes' argument ultimately depends on the argument from Hume. Both arguments essentially make the claim that beliefs about the world are inadequately supported by their evidence. Descartes' version makes the claim in terms of ruling out alternative possibilities, whereas Hume makes the point more straightforwardly by considering what evidence we have for beliefs about the world. But both arguments ultimately make the point that there is no good inference from sensory appearances to beliefs about the world.

Put another way, both arguments claim that there is no good inference from the way things appear to the way things are. Furthermore, both claim that this is so because even an inductive inference would require the assumption that sensory experience is a reliable guide to the way things are, and there is no non-circular justification for that assumption. But since knowledge requires good inferences from one's evidence, there is no knowledge of the way things are.

3

Skepticism about the World: Part Two – Dismissive Responses

We are finally in a position to consider dismissive responses to skepticism about the world. In Chapter 1 I defined "dismissive responses" as responses that either (a) do not engage skeptical arguments at all, or (b) engage them only superficially. Rather, such responses dismiss skeptical conclusions without paying serious attention to the reasoning that leads up to them. Because such responses fail to engage skeptical arguments seriously, they fail to locate the mistakes that the arguments actually make. This insures, in turn, that they miss the lessons that skeptical arguments can teach.

By definition, dismissive responses fail to engage skeptical arguments seriously. *Type-a* dismissive responses do not engage skeptical arguments at all but instead focus on some aspect, or alleged aspect, of the skeptical conclusion. Type-a responses fall into three categories: charges of self-refutation, pragmatic responses, and rhetorical responses. After considering these I turn to *type-b* dismissive responses, or responses that engage skeptical arguments only superficially. Here the focus is on two versions: (i) the charge that skeptical arguments assume that knowledge requires absolute certainty and (ii) the charge that skeptical arguments assume that knowledge requires deductive evidence. Finally, I consider transcendental arguments as dismissive responses to skepticism. Transcendental arguments can be type-a or type-b responses, depending on how they are understood.

1. CHARGES OF SELF-REFUTATION

Some philosophers have claimed that the skeptical conclusion is inconsistent, and that therefore skepticism is self-refuting. The idea is that in claiming that no one knows, the skeptic is himself making a knowledge-claim, and an inconsistent one at that. The skeptic falls into contradiction, claiming that he knows that no one knows.

A question naturally arises concerning the status of skepticism itself as a claim about the human condition. Can it be known to be true? Is it itself a truth? One can easily see that no coherent answer is possible. If one answers "yes," the original claim is denied. If one answers "no," the original claim is again denied. In effect, the only consistent thing an absolute skeptic can do is to keep silent altogether. As soon as he opens his mouth in speech, he has refuted himself. . . .

The problem, of course, lies in the fact that absolute skepticism refers to itself. As an assertion of a position, it affirms its own truth and hence denies the absolute universality of the skeptical position.[1]

A second version of this objection claims that the skeptic's conclusion is inconsistent with his *premises*. The idea is that the skeptic puts forward knowledge-claims in his premises that contradict his denial of knowledge in his conclusion. Accordingly, the skeptic must either fall into contradiction or must admit that he does not know his premises. If the former, then skepticism is self-refuting. If the latter, then the premises have no power to establish their conclusion.

This kind of response is dismissive because it does not engage any particular skeptical argument; it raises objections that are completely general, and that are supposed to implicate the skeptical conclusion independently of any particular reasoning for it. On the other hand, the objections cannot be sustained on even a superficial consideration of actual skeptical arguments. The arguments from Hume and Descartes, for example, are easily seen not to be self-refuting in the ways that the objections charge.

We can see that skeptical reasoning does not have to be self-refuting by considering two aspects of any skeptical argument.[2] First, let us say that the "scope" of a proposition is its subject matter, so that the scope of the conclusion in argument (D5) in Chapter 2 is knowledge of the world. The scope of Hume's conclusion in Section IV of the *Enquiry* is

---

1 Vincent G. Potter, *On Understanding Understanding* (New York: Fordham University Press, 1994), p. 17.
2 Nicholas Rescher makes the same distinctions in *Scepticism: A Critical Reappraisal* (Totowa, NJ: Rowman and Littlefield, 1980), p. 4. Somewhat similar distinctions are treated by George Pappas in "Some Forms of Epistemological Scepticism," in George Pappas and Marshall Swain, eds., *Essays on Knowledge and Justification* (Ithaca: Cornell University Press, 1978), pp. 309–316.

knowledge of the future. But then a skeptical argument avoids self-refutation of the second kind – contradiction between premises and conclusion – so long as the scope of its premises falls outside of the scope of its conclusion. For example, the skeptic putting forward arguments (H2) or (D5) in Chapter 2 can consistently claim to know his premises while at the same time claiming that no one knows anything about the world, for he can claim that his premises are about our concepts of knowledge and evidence rather than about objects. In other words, the skeptic can affirm that we have conceptual knowledge, and so can know that her premises are true, while denying that we have empirical knowledge, thus avoiding any inconsistency between premises and conclusion. The first kind of self-refutation, involving a conclusion that contradicts itself, can be avoided in essentially the same manner. So long as the conclusion of a skeptical argument is not itself an empirical claim, the skeptic avoids inconsistency when he concludes that he knows (non-empirically) that we have no empirical knowledge.

Second, let us say that the "degree" of a skeptical conclusion is the quality of knowledge or justification that the argument denies we have. For example, a skeptical argument might conclude that, within some scope, we fail to have absolute certainty, or knowledge, or moral certainty, or probable belief, or reasonable belief. Again, the skeptic can avoid self-refutation of the second kind simply by being careful about degree, making sure that he claims a lesser degree of justification for his premises than he denies that we have in his conclusion. For example, it is not inconsistent to claim that reasonable premises entail that nothing is certain. In the same way, the skeptic can avoid self-refutation of the first kind as well. So long as a lesser degree of justification is claimed for the conclusion than is denied in that conclusion, the conclusion does not contradict itself. For example, it is not contradictory to say that it is reasonable to believe that no one has knowledge. Therefore not even a skepticism that is universal in scope must be self-refuting.[3]

We have seen that a skeptic can avoid self-refutation by being careful about the degree of justification claimed for his premises and conclusion. A special case of this is when the skeptic makes no claims at all about the epistemic status of his premises. In this case, the skeptic merely points out that *we non-skeptics* hold those premises to be true and so by our own lights should admit that we have no knowledge. This skeptic makes no claims about knowledge at all but merely calls attention to the

---

3 This is *contra* Potter, p. 17, and Rescher, pp. 14–15.

fact that our own assumptions entail that we do not know what we claim to know. On the one hand, we find several seemingly innocent assumptions to be plausible. On the other hand, we think that we know many things about how the world is. But then it is *our* position that is inconsistent, because those seemingly innocent assumptions entail that we do not know what we think we know. That is not a problem for the skeptic, since he does not claim to know anything. But it is a problem for us, because we do claim to know things that our own assumptions entail we do not.

By paying attention to either scope or degree, the skeptic need not make contradictory claims. In the limiting case the skeptic makes no claims about knowledge at all but instead calls our attention to an inconsistency in our own assumptions about the nature and existence of knowledge.

2. PRAGMATIC AND RHETORICAL RESPONSES

Pragmatic responses claim that skepticism can be refuted by calling attention to the skeptic's actions. One version of this response claims that the skeptic's actions outside of the study are inconsistent with her skeptical conclusion. In acting as we all do to avoid an oncoming bus or secure good tickets to a game, the skeptic demonstrates that her skeptical conclusion is false. Another version of this response claims that the skeptic's actions demonstrate that she does not *believe* her own conclusion. By acting like the rest of us, or even by offering the skeptical argument to us for our consideration, the skeptic reveals that not even she believes that there is no knowledge. She believes, for example, that she knows that we exist to consider her arguments.

Rhetorical responses imply that skepticism can be refuted by making rhetorical points about the skeptic's position in the debate about knowledge. Thus Locke writes, "[I]f all be a dream, then he doth but dream, that he makes the question; and so it is not much matter, that a waking man should answer him."[4] In a similar vein, Reid says of Descartes' skeptic that "[a] man who disbelieves his own existence, is surely as unfit to be reasoned with as a man that believes he is made of glass."[5]

---

4 John Locke, *An Essay concerning Human Understanding*, ed. Peter Nidditch (Oxford: Oxford University Press, 1975), p. 634.
5 Reid, *Philosophical Works*, p. 100a. Reid has much more to say in response to skepticism, and taken in its entirety his response is not at all dismissive. For a largely sympathetic treat-

This kind of response can overlap with pragmatic ones, as when Reid says of Hume, "He believed, against his principles, that he should be read, and that he should retain his personal identity, till he reaped the honour and reputation justly due to his metaphysical *acumen*."[6]

Pragmatic and rhetorical responses are dismissive because they fail to engage the arguments for skeptical conclusions. For the same reason they are completely ineffective. Notice that the premises of Descartes' and Hume's arguments do not mention anything about how one ought to act or how one ought to speak. Rather, they amount to claims about what knowledge requires, together with claims that our own beliefs fail to meet those requirements. No rhetorical or pragmatic point will touch those premises, since the premises do not make rhetorical or pragmatic claims.

This assessment is supported by the following consideration. The skeptical arguments that we have been considering would not lose any of their force if we found no one willing to defend their conclusions. What makes them interesting philosophical problems is that we ourselves find their premises plausible, and yet, by seemingly cogent reasoning, they lead to a conclusion that we find unbelievable. If there never existed a skeptic to be debated, the skeptical arguments would lose none of their interest in this respect. But if the existence of skeptics is irrelevant to the force of skeptical arguments, then observations about either the skeptic's actions or her rhetorical position are irrelevant as well.

Pragmatic and rhetorical responses can be relevant when you are trying to win a debate against a contentious opponent. If, in that situation, you can show that not even she can believe the position she is defending, then that is an effective blow to strike. So might such responses be relevant if we were trying to persuade someone out of her skepticism. In that case it might help to show the poor soul that not even she believes what she is saying, or that no one can consistently act on such a belief. But the point of analyzing skeptical arguments is neither to win a debate nor to persuade someone out of their skepticism. It could not be, since there are no skeptics to be debated or persuaded. At least there are none outside of the study or the classroom, as Hume himself pointed out. In other words, there are no skeptics who need to

---

ment of Reid's critique of skepticism, see my "Reid's Critique of Berkeley and Hume: What's the Big Idea?", *Philosophy and Phenomenological Research* 55 (1995): 279–296.
6 Reid, p. 102a.

be persuaded from a life of skepticism, or whom we need to debate to achieve some other useful purpose.

This last point is noteworthy. Although some very few people are skeptics in the sense that they *endorse* skepticism or *say* that they are skeptics, no one is a skeptic in the sense of living out the position. Hume famously insisted on this, and contemporary philosophers who incline toward skepticism consistently endorse the point. Thus Michael Williams writes that recent years "have seen a remarkable revival of this Humean attitude" and cites Barry Stroud, Thomas Nagel, and P. F. Strawson as "New Sceptics" who, in one way or another, rehearse Hume's point that skepticism cannot be maintained in everyday life.[7]

To say that skepticism cannot be lived is not merely to insist that no one *acts* as a skeptic. It is not merely to say, for example, that no one fails to avoid an oncoming bus. The more important point is that, in the context of everyday life, no one even *believes* that skepticism is true. Even people who profess to be skeptics in their books still make judgments about who ought to be believed, discriminate good from bad evidence, and make other epistemic judgments in the course of their everyday lives. Hume insisted on this as well, as do present-day representatives of the skeptical position.[8] But if no one acts out the skeptical position, and if no one even believes it outside of the classroom or study, then no one needs to be saved from it. There is no practical or "existential" problem of skepticism. And therefore strategies that aim at practical or existential solutions are out of place.

These last considerations raise the question of epistemology's project. What is the question that epistemology is supposed to answer or the problem that it is supposed to solve? Historically, and I think to this day, the project of epistemology has been conceived in five principal ways: (a) to beat the skeptic in a debate; (b) to persuade someone out of his or her skepticism; (c) to prove to someone else that we have knowledge; (d) to prove to ourselves that we have knowledge; and (e) to provide an adequate account of what knowledge is. My claim is that all of these conceptions are misguided except for the last, and that this is rather obvious once the question of epistemology's project is raised explicitly.

We have already seen that the first two conceptions are misguided because there are no skeptics to be debated or persuaded. That is, no

---

7   Williams, *Unnatural Doubts*, p. xiii.
8   See Stroud, *The Significance of Philosophical Scepticism.*, esp. Ch. 2, and Fogelin, *Pyrrhonian Reflections on Knowledge and Justification*, e.g., pp. 9–10.

one exists who lives his life as a skeptic and who therefore needs our help to be brought out of his skepticism. And even if there were such a person, Reid is correct that "physic and good regimen" would be a more likely cure than "metaphysic and logic." Moreover, there is no one whom we need to defeat in a debate over the issue. If we come across a pretend skeptic who wants to play that game, as we sometimes do in a bar or an undergraduate classroom, the better policy is to redirect attention to some more worthwhile activity. But if one likes to play strange games, consider that the pretend skeptic cannot lose, provided that she has the least bit of wit about her. All she need do is refuse to allow any premise against her, and her skepticism will be completely unassailable. Real skeptics are not to be found, and if they are found they are not to be engaged with philosophy. Pretend skeptics should be avoided altogether.

The third and fourth conceptions of epistemology's project either reduce to the first two or are too easy. If the purpose of proving that we have knowledge is to persuade or to win a debate, then we are back in the misguided projects we have already considered. On the other hand, if the point is to prove to *ourselves* or to some other *non-skeptic* that we have knowledge, then the project is pointless, because it is too easy. To prove something is to show that it follows from premises that are already known. But if we are non-skeptics, then it is easy to prove that we have knowledge from such premises. Being non-skeptics, we already know that we know lots of things, and these particular cases vacuously establish that we have knowledge of the kind in question – for example, knowledge of the world. Someone might complain that this kind of proof begs the question. But against whom does it beg the question? Remember that we are not debating with a skeptic in the case being considered.

So the project of epistemology is not to persuade lost souls, or to win debates with contentious opponents, or to prove that we know what we think we know. Rather, it is to construct accurate accounts of knowledge and evidence. In other words, the project of epistemology is to answer Plato's age-old question in the *Theaetetus*, "What is knowledge?" And the point of analyzing skeptical arguments is that they help us to do this. Skeptical arguments highlight mistaken assumptions about knowledge that might otherwise go unnoticed, and they drive us to replace those assumptions with something more adequate. Moreover, to arrive at adequate accounts of knowledge and evidence we must consider our best judgments about which particular cases count as knowledge and which count as good evidence. Here again the analysis of skeptical arguments helps us, because those arguments bring home the counterintuitive results of proposals that inadequately capture those judgments. Of course, skeptical arguments cannot help us if they are dismissed with irrelevant considerations about how imaginary people speak and act. Skeptical arguments can serve as powerful heuristic devices for driving positive epistemology, but only in the context of a project properly conceived.

I have been arguing that epistemology's project is to give an adequate account of knowledge — that is, to answer Plato's question, "What is knowledge?" Some might think that this conception of epistemology is an outdated one, insulated from recent appreciation in philosophy of the social, political, and other contextual factors involved in knowledge and knowledge relations. But this is to misunderstand the project of giving an account of knowledge. Nothing about that project disallows that knowledge has social or political dimensions, or that gender has epistemological significance, or that attention to particulars is necessary, or that knowledge depends on context in some other way. In fact, all of these claims constitute competing epistemologies. They claim that an adequate account of knowledge reveals that it has the contextual dimensions in question.

To drive home the point that recent contextualisms are not antithetical to epistemology, consider that all of them are consistent with what is perhaps the most common position in epistemology today. According to generic reliabilism, knowledge is true belief that arises from reliable cognitive processes, or cognitive processes that reliably produce true rather than false beliefs. Different versions of reliabilism give different accounts of the processes involved, but all agree that knowledge has more to do with the abilities of cognizers to "hook up" with the world than it does with the properties of individual beliefs — for example, properties such as indubitability, incorrigibility, or irrevisability. But note that reliabilism in this broad sense is perfectly consistent with the claims that knowledge is social, political, gendered, or otherwise contextual. All of these questions are in fact wide open within the context of generic reliabilism, since it is an empirical matter how cognitive processes are made reliable or unreliable by social, political or other factors. Moreover, once the question is raised this way, it would be amazing if at least some of these factors were not importantly involved in the production of knowledge.

For this reason, recent self-proclaimed opponents of epistemology are better seen as doing epistemology than as rejecting it. They are offering accounts that emphasize aspects of knowledge and evidence that have been neglected historically, but that are perfectly consistent with more recent epistemological theorizing. Accordingly, what these thinkers reject is not the general project of giving an account of knowledge, but particular outdated accounts that do not recognize aspects of knowledge that contextualists deem to be central. And when I say they are rejecting accounts that are outdated, I mean outdated for the better part of a century. Accordingly, these thinkers need to catch up to epistemology rather than reject it.

3. MORE DISMISSIVE RESPONSES

We are now in a position to consider type-b dismissive responses to skepticism. Such responses also traffic in outdated theories of knowledge, accusing skeptical arguments of presupposing some version of seventeenth- or eighteenth-century rationalism. For example, some philosophers have diagnosed skepticism as requiring absolute certainty for knowledge. Absolute certainty has been conceived variously – as requiring infallibility or incorrigibility, for example. But the general theme is that skeptical arguments set the standards for knowledge outrageously high, and so rejecting the skeptical conclusion requires no more than rejecting implausible skeptical standards.[9]

Another look at our reconstructions of Descartes and Hume shows that this charge is without any force. The point of Hume's argument is that our beliefs about the world are either wholly unsupported by their evidence or else are supported only by reasoning that is logically circular. Such defects in one's evidence do not undermine only absolute certainty. If Hume is right, then our beliefs about the world lack even the lowest degree of positive epistemic status. Of course, that is not to say that Hume is right. The point here is that Hume's argument does not run on a requirement of absolute certainty.

It might be claimed, however, that Hume is requiring that our *evidence* for our beliefs be absolutely certain, and that this is why he conceives of our evidence for objects in the world as incorrigible beliefs about our sensory experience. But although Hume in fact conceived our evidence for objects in this manner, there is nothing about his skeptical reasoning that requires him to do so. The arguments from Hume as

---

9   This kind of diagnosis is quite common. Rescher is one example (see esp. p. 56); see also John Dewey, *The Quest for Certainty* (New York: Minton, Balch, 1929).

reconstructed in (H2) and (H3) in Chapter 2 do not make the claim that beliefs about sensory experience are incorrigible, or that they need to be to give rise to knowledge. Rather, premise (1) of each argument can be read as claiming something seemingly obvious: that our evidence for objects is that things appear a particular way, together with the assumption that the way things appear is a reliable indication of how they are. We do not have to say that sensory appearances are an infallible indication of the way things are, and we do not have to say that appearances are incorrigible. The argument runs just as well on more sane characterizations of sensory appearances and their relation to objects in the world.

Similar things can be said about the charge that skeptical arguments require deductive inferences for knowledge. A close look at Hume's reasoning reveals that he thinks our evidence for objects in the world is neither deductive nor inductive. That it is not deductive is widely recognized. But Hume claims that our evidence is not even inductive, if it does not include some assumption to the effect that appearances are a reliable guide to reality, and he argues quite powerfully that no such assumption can be justified in a non-circular fashion. Again, whether Hume is correct in all of this is not the question; I take it for granted that he is not correct, and that skepticism about the world is false. But Hume's mistake is not that he requires that evidence be deductive, or that knowledge of the world be deduced from the way things appear.

The charge of deductivism might seem to hold against Descartes' reasoning in Meditation I, but only if we read the argument there uncharitably. As we saw in Chapter 2, one way to understand the idea of evidence ruling out alternative possibilities is in terms of deduction, so that one's evidence rules out the possibility that one is dreaming only if one's sensory experience deductively entails that one is not dreaming. But there are at least two other ways to understand this idea that do not make the argument assume an implausible deductivism about evidence.

First, it is a plausible claim about evidence that it must discriminate alternative possibilities from what is believed, where discrimination is understood not in terms of deduction but in terms of the causal properties of one's evidence. The way we defined the notion in Chapter 2, evidence discriminates the truth of a belief p from alternatives if it would cause you to believe that p is true when p is true, but would not cause you to believe that p is true when the alternatives are. Consideration of everyday cases brings out the plausibility of Descartes' principle understood in this manner, but whether the principle is true or false, it clearly does not involve the thesis that evidence must be deductive.

Second, we can read Descartes' argument as making essentially the same point as Hume's. On this reading the claim that sensory experience does not rule out alternative possibilities is understood as the claim that such evidence does not support the negation of those possibilities either deductively or inductively. It does not support their negation deductively, because it is possible to have exactly the same experience when the possibilities are true. But it does not support them inductively either, because such support would require the assumption that sensory experience is a reliable guide to reality, which assumption cannot itself be justified in a non-circular fashion.

To see that deductivism is not the real issue here, consider this: even if we did have some adequate justification for the assumption that experience is a reliable guide to reality, that still would not make our evidence deductive. For that assumption claims only that sensory experience is a reliable indication of how things are, not an infallible indication. So even if the assumption could be used as part of our evidence for beliefs about the world it would provide only inductive or probable support. Accordingly, the point of the skeptical argument is not that deductive support is required for knowledge. The real point is that inductive support is required, and we do not have even that for our beliefs about the world.

I said that type-b responses to skepticism are dismissive because they do not consider skeptical arguments seriously; rather, they depend on uncharitable readings of such arguments, failing to consider that more powerful reconstructions are easily available. Accordingly, these responses reject the arguments from Descartes and Hume for the wrong reasons, and so fail to recognize the more interesting lessons that those arguments can teach.

4. TRANSCENDENTAL ARGUMENTS

Before closing this chapter I want to consider one more kind of response to skepticism about the world. Transcendental arguments are a kind of dismissive response, because they fail to consider skeptical arguments or only consider them superficially. As we will see, transcendental arguments are type-a or type-b depending on how we interpret the way they are being employed against the skeptical conclusion.

By "transcendental arguments" I mean arguments of a certain form. Such arguments start by considering the conditions for the possibility of some undisputed phenomenon and argue to the conclusion that some disputed object exists or that some disputed state of affairs is actual. For example, Kant argued that a condition for the possibility of experience is that spatial–temporal objects exist, and Heidegger argued that a condition for the possibility of inquiry is that we already dwell in the world at which inquiry is directed. More recently Hilary Putnam has argued that a condition for inquiring about knowledge of the empirical world is that such a world exists,[10] and Donald Davidson has argued that a condition of our having any beliefs at all is that most of them are true.[11]

These arguments vary in their details, but their general strategy is the same and puts them in a common class. All of them start with some phenomenon that even the skeptic acknowledges, or that he must acknowledge as a presupposition of his own inquiry. And from there each argues that a necessary condition for the possibility of that phenomenon is that some other thing the skeptic disputes is true. By this line of argument the skeptic is refuted by making explicit the conditions of his own skeptical inquiry.

Accordingly, transcendental arguments share the following structure:

(TAS) 1. Some undisputed phenomenon is possible only if some disputed phenomenon is actual.
2. The undisputed phenomenon is actual.
3. Therefore, the disputed phenomenon is actual.

Whether transcendental arguments are sound depends nearly entirely on their first premise. This is because their argument form is clearly valid, and the examples I have given do trade on undisputed phenomena in their second premises. So, for example, it is undisputed that we have sensory experience, or that we are inquirers, or that we have beliefs.

On the other hand, anyone familiar with these arguments knows that establishing their first premise is no walk in the park. The arguments here are long and complex, and depend in several places on claims that

---

10 Putnam, *Reason, Truth and History*.
11 Donald Davidson, "A Coherence Theory of Truth and Knowledge," in Ernest LePore, ed., *Truth and Interpretation: Perspectives on the Philosophy of Donald Davidson* (Oxford: Blackwell, 1992), reprinted from D. Henrich, ed., *Kant oder Hegel* (Stuttgart: Klett-Cotta, 1983). See also, Donald Davidson, "The Method of Truth in Metaphysics," in P. A. French, T. E. Ueling, Jr., and H. K. Wettstein, eds., *Midwest Studies in Philosophy 2: Studies in the Philosophy of Language* (Morris: University of Minnesota Press, 1977) and reprinted in Donald Davidson, *Inquiries into Truth and Interpretation* (Oxford: Clarendon Press, 1985).

are, at the very least, controversial. However, none of my criticisms of transcendental arguments depends on the controversial nature of their major premises. On the contrary, I think such arguments are ineffective responses to skepticism even if they are exactly right from start to finish. Neither do any of my criticisms depend on charges of question begging. Since I am not conceiving the present context as a debate with the skeptic, concerns about begging questions are not really relevant. To beg a question there has to be someone to beg it against, but, as we have seen, there are no skeptics that we ought to be debating.

Perhaps the most natural way to interpret transcendental arguments is to view them as type-a responses to skepticism. On this interpretation they do not engage skeptical arguments at all but instead try to show that the skeptical conclusion must be false and so can be rejected independently of how one gets there. But on this interpretation there are several reasons why transcendental arguments are ineffective responses to skepticism.

The first reason they are ineffective is that the conclusions they try to establish are extremely general. For example, Kant concludes that a condition for the possibility of experience is that spatial–temporal objects exist. But he does not claim which objects must exist, or when, or where. And so even if Kant's argument is correct, it leaves untouched any skepticism about knowledge-claims that are more particular. The same is true of Heidegger's argument as well as Putnam's and Davidson's. As a rule, the more general the conditions that a transcendental argument establishes, the less effective it is against skepticism about particular knowledge-claims. On the other hand, the less general the conditions established by the argument, the less plausible the argument becomes. For example, no one would even think to argue that a condition of the possibility of my current sensory experience is that I am here and now in front of a computer, or even that there are any computers at all.

The second reason that transcendental arguments fail to refute skepticism is that they do not touch even the most general skeptical conclusions. This is because skeptical arguments are about knowledge rather than truth. For example, the arguments reconstructed from Descartes and Hume conclude that we lack knowledge of the world, not that the world does not exist. Therefore no argument that establishes that the world exists, or that we dwell in it, or that most of our beliefs are true touches the conclusion that skeptical arguments put forward.

Even a superficial analysis of skeptical arguments shows that this is the case. In Chapter 1 we saw that all skeptical arguments can be boiled down to two essential premises, one stating that knowledge requires that some condition be fulfilled, and one stating that the condition in question is not fulfilled. Looking at the arguments from Descartes and Hume, we see that they do not claim that the truth-condition on knowledge is not fulfilled. Rather, they claim that we lack appropriate evidence for our beliefs. According to these arguments, even if our beliefs are true, they do not amount to knowledge.

Skeptical arguments do not claim that the world does not exist, or that we do not dwell in the world, or that most of our beliefs are not true. For this reason, arguments with the purpose of establishing such things cannot be effective responses against them – or at least such arguments cannot be effective as direct responses. Is there some other way in which transcendental arguments are supposed to refute the skeptical conclusion? One possibility presents itself, but it can quickly be rejected.

It might be thought that transcendental arguments refute skepticism indirectly, because they can be used to *give* us knowledge that would otherwise be lacking. In other words, even if skeptical arguments are right that we typically lack evidence for our beliefs, transcendental arguments can provide evidence for at least some very general claims about the world. We can prove, for example, that such a world exists. Or we can prove that most of our beliefs are true, even if we do not know which. But this line of thought is highly problematic. If the idea is that only these very general truths about the world can be known, and that only a small group of philosophers have ever known them, then the proposal is highly counterintuitive. On the other hand, if the idea is that this is how Jane and Joe in the street get knowledge in typical cases, then the claim is still highly problematic, because it is psychologically implausible. Any argument, transcendental or otherwise, can give one knowledge only if one understands the argument and uses it. But the suggestion that the relevant transcendental arguments are actually used in non-philosophical contexts is perhaps too implausible ever to have been suggested.

So far I have been interpreting transcendental arguments as type-a responses to skepticism; such arguments do not engage skeptical arguments at all but rather try to show that the skeptical conclusion cannot be true. Another interpretation is to view them as type-b responses. On this understanding, transcendental arguments are not supposed to prove that skepticism is false but instead are used to reject something in the skeptical reasoning. Specifically, they show that the possibilities that skeptical arguments raise as alternatives to knowledge-claims are not real possibilities, and that therefore an essential assumption of skeptical arguments is mistaken. For example, Descartes considers the possibility that he is the bodiless victim of an evil genius, who makes it appear that there are earth and stars and the like when in fact all of these things are false. But this is not in fact a possibility, transcendental arguments show, and so an assumption of Descartes' reasoning is mistaken.

On this interpretation transcendental arguments constitute type-b responses to skepticism – that is, they engage skeptical arguments, but only superficially. Each of several considerations shows that this is the case.

First, not all skeptical arguments invoke alternative possibilities to knowledge-claims. For example, Hume's argument does not. Second, not even Descartes' argument must assume that total illusions or nearly total illusions are possibilities. For example, argument (D5) from Chapter 2 runs as well on the possibility of normal dreams as on the possibility of philosophical ones. Third, even demon scenarios can be constructed so that deception is highly restricted. Consider the possibility that the world is for the most part as it appears to be but a deceiving demon steps in from time to time to make one of our most confident judgments false. The problem in this kind of scenario is not that *all* of our beliefs might be false, but that *any* of our beliefs might be false. For any particular knowledge-claim that one might make, it might be the case that the demon makes that claim false while keeping many other claims true. This last possibility is not ruled out by the argument from Davidson or by any other transcendental argument we have considered.

This point echoes one that was made in Chapter 2: namely, skeptical arguments need not start out by questioning all of our knowledge at once. Another possibility, and one that is reflected in our reconstructions of Descartes' argument, is that the skeptic may begin by raising doubts about an individual knowledge-claim. But if there is nothing special about that claim in particular, then the same doubts can be generalized so as to undermine other knowledge-claims as well.

In conclusion, dismissive responses to skepticism fail to touch the skeptical arguments we have reconstructed from Descartes and Hume. One version of Descartes' argument seems to be open to a relevant possibilities approach, although there remains work to be done there. But argument (D5) does not seem open to that approach, and neither do the arguments from Hume. These latter claim that there is no good inference from appearance to reality, and so far we have seen nothing to challenge that basic claim.

In Chapter 4 we turn to a different kind of response to skepticism about the world. Specifically, we investigate the claim that the arguments from Descartes and Hume depend on a faulty ontology, or perhaps a faulty philosophy of mind. This kind of response is not dismissive, since it engages the skeptical arguments in question seriously. It *is* mistaken, however – or so I argue in the next chapter.

4

Skepticism about the World: Part Three – Dualism, Realism, and Representationalism

At present, Western philosophy is divided among various schools. For reasons that are partly philosophical and partly historical, philosophy as it is practiced in the Anglo-American or "analytic" tradition often looks very different from what goes on in traditional continental philosophy, the tradition of American pragmatism, or the so-called post-modern school. But across these various factions one discovers a point on which there is odd agreement. A great many philosophers, including representatives from each of the schools mentioned, have defended essentially the same diagnosis of skepticism about the world. Namely, they claim that skepticism is not an epistemological problem at all, but is rather the necessary consequence of a misguided modern ontology. Once that ontology is given up, these philosophers agree, the problem of skepticism cannot even get off the ground.

Richard Rorty calls this characterization of the relationship between skepticism and the modern ontology "the usual story," citing Etienne Gilson and J. H. Randall as two of the story's prominent proponents.[1] Here are some characteristic statements of the position, beginning with two from a founding father of Anglo-American philosophy, George Berkeley:

[W]e have been led into very dangerous errors, by supposing a two-fold existence of the objects of sense – the one *intelligible* or in the mind; the other *real* and without the mind, whereby unthinking things are thought to have a natural subsistence of their own, distinct from being perceived by spirits. This, which, if I mistake not, hath been shown to be the most groundless and absurd notion,

---

1 See Richard Rorty, *Philosophy and the Mirror of Nature* (Princeton: Princeton University Press, 1979), p. 49, n. 19, and pp. 51–52, n. 21.

is the very root of Scepticism. (*A Treatise concerning the Principles of Human Knowledge*, pp. 107–108)

[S]o long as men thought that real things subsisted without the mind, and that their knowledge was only so far forth *real* as it was *conformable to real things*, it follows they could not be certain that they had any real knowledge at all. . . . All this sceptical cant follows from our supposing a difference between *things* and *ideas*, and that the former had a subsistence without the mind or unperceived. (Ibid., p. 108.)

In the next passage another great of analytic philosophy, J. L. Austin, takes a swipe at Berkeley but makes essentially the same point in different terms.

But what is generally, and most importantly, wrong with [the anti-skeptic's] argument is simply that he has got into (perhaps has let Berkeley lead him into) the position of swallowing the two-languages doctrine – temporarily, at least, appearing to swallow the two-entities doctrine on the way. And the resulting question about how the evidence-language ('idea'-language) is related to the material-object-language, which he tries to answer, is a question that *has* no answer, it's a quite unreal question. The main thing is not to get bamboozled into asking it at all. (*Sense and Sensibilia*, p. 142)

While this diagnosis of skepticism can be found in analytic philosophy, it is almost ubiquitous in the Continental tradition. In this regard it is helpful to understand that much of Continental philosophy is essentially Kantian, beginning from the premise of Kant's Copernican revolution.[2] Roughly, the line of thinking is that Hume's skepticism presupposes a distinction between mind and mind-independent reality. To avoid skepticism we must give up empirical realism in favor of transcendental idealism. In other words, we must give up the idea of a knowable mind-independent reality. On the basis of roughly this line of thought, many Continental philosophers now take it for granted that the object of knowledge is created (or at least shaped) by the mind that knows it, and Continental philosophy is largely devoted to exploring the implications of this idea.

Martin Heidegger's analysis differs in critical respects from Kant's, but it is clear that Heidegger agrees at least with this much: the problem of skepticism is rooted in inadequate ontology – and more specifically, in a dualism of internal knowing subject and external object of knowledge.

---

2 A notable exception is the realist tradition in phenomenology.

Now the more unequivocally one maintains that knowing is proximally and really 'inside' and indeed has by no means the same kind of Being as entities which are both physical and psychical, the less one presupposes when one believes that one is making headway in the question of the essence of knowledge and in the clarification of the relationship between Subject and Object. For only then can the problem arise of how this knowing subject comes out of its inner 'sphere' into one which is 'other and external,' of how knowing can have any object at all, and of how one must think of the object itself so that eventually the subject knows it without needing to venture a leap into another sphere. (*Being and Time*, p. 87)

In Continental philosophy the Kantian–Heideggerian diagnosis of skepticism is found to be so convincing that it is not an exaggeration to say that it is taken for granted. It is largely for this reason that there is no recognizable subdiscipline of epistemology in Continental philosophy, and it is the reason that so many Continental philosophers accept some form of anti-realism.[3]

Unfortunately, a similar line of thinking has been convincing to some in America as well. In the following passages John Dewey joins Kant and Heidegger in blaming bad ontology for skepticism, and with the same anti-realist results:

For these questions [of epistemology] all spring from the assumption of a merely beholding mind on one side and a foreign and remote object to be viewed and noted on the other. They ask how a mind and world, subject and object, so separate and independent can by any possibility come into such a relationship to each other as to make true knowledge possible. (*Reconstruction in Philosophy*, p. 123)

Those who have followed the previous discussions will not be surprised to hear that, from the standpoint of experimental knowing, all of the rivalries and connected problems [of epistemology] grow from a single root. They spring from the assumption that the true and valid object of knowledge is that which has being prior to and independent of the operations of knowing. (*The Quest for Certainty*, p. 196)

Finally, essentially the same diagnosis of skepticism is embraced by the post-modern school. Influenced by Heidegger and Dewey, post-

---

3   Dreyfus argues that Heidegger is not an anti-realist. See Hubert L. Dreyfus, *Being-in-the-World* (Cambridge, MA: MIT Press, 1991), esp. pp. 252–265. This is controversial, but in any case my purpose here is not to contribute to Heidegger scholarship; rather, I am interested in critiquing a general line of thought that has been influential in Continental philosophy, whether or not it can be correctly attributed to Heidegger.

modernists like Richard Rorty view epistemology as the activity of working out solutions to the problem of skepticism. But that activity and the problem it tries to solve both depend on the modern ontology for their existence. Once that ontology is given up, there is no place left for either epistemology or its central concern:

> The idea of a discipline devoted to "the nature, origin, and limits of human knowledge" – the textbook definition of "epistemology"– required a field of study called "the human mind," and that field of study was what Descartes had created. The Cartesian mind simultaneously made possible veil-of-ideas skepticism and a discipline devoted to circumventing such skepticism.[4]

These passages show that philosophers representing a wide range of traditions can nevertheless share common ground. Let us take a closer look at what that common ground is.

First, all of these philosophers call attention to a recognizably "modern" ontology of the self and the world. By this I mean one that is Cartesian in its inspiration, and that distinguishes between an internal knowing subject and an external object of knowledge. Here "internal" is essentially a designation for mental or spiritual stuff, whereas "external" is used to designate a different ontological kind. We can use the terms "physical" or "material" here, but they do not make explicit what is perhaps the most important point at issue. That is, whereas subjects are by nature a kind of mental substance, objects are *mind independent* in the following sense. According to the modern ontology, objects in the world exist and have many of the properties they do, independently of whether any mind exists or how any mind thinks.

This is opposed to mental things such as minds, sensations, thoughts, and thinkings, which depend for their existence on the existence and activity of minds. There are no thoughts without a thinker and (trivially) no thinkers without a thinker. Mind-independent reality is also opposed to socially constructed things such as marriages and home runs. Marriages and home runs are not mental things, but they depend for their existence on mental things. Unlike rocks and trees, they are mind dependent in the sense that they would not exist, or have many of the properties they do, if minds did not think in one way rather than another.

So understood, the modern ontology combines a dualism of mind and material world with a realism about the latter. Another thesis often

---

4 Rorty, p. 140.

associated with the modern ontology, but only hinted at in the quoted passages, is representationalism. According to this last doctrine, thought about objects requires thought about ideas that represent them. A sub-thesis of this position is that perception is representational, requiring thought about the sensations that material objects cause in perception. As we shall see, representationalism is not really an ontological thesis at all but is rather a position in the philosophy of mind that is sometimes confused with the modern ontology.

A second shared theme in these passages is that the problem of skepticism is created by the modern ontology. More specifically, the problem arises as to how internal subjects can come to know external objects, or to even think such objects in the first place. This second theme can be broken down into two claims. First, it is claimed that the modern ontology is necessary for generating skepticism about the world. Thus Heidegger claims that "only then can the problem arise of how this knowing subject comes out of its inner 'sphere' into one which is 'other and external'." Second, the claim is made that the modern ontology is sufficient for generating skepticism. Thus Berkeley suggests that accepting the modern ontology inevitably results in skepticism about the objects of sense. A corollary of the first claim is that rejecting the modern ontology is sufficient for resolving the problem of skepticism. A corollary of the second claim is that rejecting the modern ontology is necessary for resolving that problem.

A third theme in the quoted passages is that the modern ontology should be given up in favor of some version of anti-realism. With the exception of Austin, all of the authors cited suggest that the objects we know are created or shaped by our thinking. Of course, none of our authors would call himself an anti-realist. All of them would say that to accuse them of anti-realism is to remain in the false ontology that makes the distinction between realism and anti-realism possible. But on the standard meaning of the term, "anti-realism" is the position that the object of knowledge is not independent of our knowing it. Put differently, anti-realism claims that the reality we know is created by, or at least shaped by, the way we know it, or more generally, the way we think about it. This position is in opposition to the view that we know things as they are – that is, as they are independently of our knowing them or thinking them.

Now if this is what is meant by anti-realism, then Berkeley, Heidegger, Dewey, and Rorty are endorsing some form of anti-realism over the modern ontology. They all think that the ontological distinction between mental subject and mind-independent object of knowledge is at the root of skepticism about the world, and they all recommend that we erase the distinction by denying that the object of knowledge is independent of the way we know it or think about it. Another way to understand their common position is to say that for them *all* objects of knowledge are like marriages and home runs, in that they are somehow constructed by our thinking. On Berkeley's idealism all objects are literally mental objects. On less radical forms of anti-realism there is a distinction between the mental and the non-mental, but even non-mental objects depend for their existence and properties on the ways we think about them.

My thesis in this chapter is that all of this is wrong-headed. I argue that the modern ontology is not necessary for generating skepticism, since powerful arguments for skepticism can be constructed without it. Such arguments depend on an innocent appearance–reality distinction rather than any specific way of cashing out that distinction, modern or otherwise. Neither do skeptical arguments depend on representationalism, or the thesis that thinking about objects requires thinking about ideas that represent them. Representationalism has been closely associated with the modern ontology and is sometimes confused with it. But skeptical arguments depend on neither the modern ontology nor a representationalist theory of ideas.

Second, neither the modern ontology nor representationalism is sufficient for generating skepticism, since the best skeptical arguments depend on incorrect assumptions about knowledge and evidence. It is these assumptions that really drive the skeptical arguments, and that should be the focus of our inquiry. On the view that I am defending, different ontologies and theories of ideas amount to so much window dressing, sprucing up the arguments but playing no substantive role in their reasoning.

Finally, because skepticism is an epistemological problem and not an ontological one, the most common motivation for anti-realism is just misguided. On the one hand, it is not necessary to embrace anti-realism to refute skeptical arguments. On the other, embracing anti-realism does not do the job; the best skeptical arguments from Descartes and Hume run just as nicely on anti-realist ontologies. So, for example, even if we adopted Berkeley's radical idealism, the skeptical argument from Hume would still be a powerful one.

In Part I of this chapter, I consider whether the modern ontology or representationalism is necessary for generating powerful skeptical arguments about our knowledge of the world. In Part II, I consider whether either of these doctrines is sufficient. But before proceeding it should be stressed that my purpose is not to defend either the modern ontology or representationalism. Rather, it is to show that the relationship between these theses and skepticism is not what it is commonly and widely claimed to be. Accordingly, skeptical arguments teach epistemological lessons, not lessons in ontology or the philosophy of mind.

I. *What Is Necessary for Skepticism about the World*

It is now time to take a closer look at how the modern ontology and representationalism are supposed to give rise to skepticism. In order to do so we should look at the best skeptical arguments available and ask where they depend on the doctrines in question. Of course, I argue that they do not depend on the modern ontology or on any particular ontology whatsoever. Neither do they depend on a representationalist theory of ideas. To the contrary, such arguments run nicely on any ontology or theory of ideas that is even minimally plausible.

What I mean by this last point is the following: To be even minimally plausible, any ontology and any theory of ideas must recognize certain distinctions and be consistent with certain assumptions that are in themselves platitudinous. So, for example, any minimally plausible ontology must recognize a distinction between appearance and reality, since it is a platitude that things are not always as they appear. Although different theories cash out the distinctions and assumptions in different ways, all must include them as part of the data to be explained. Once these distinctions and assumptions are in place, however, the skeptical arguments we have been considering are off and running.

Skeptical arguments are mistaken somewhere – that much is a working assumption of the present methodology. But they need not make any mistake about ontology, or about how the way things appear represents the way things are. This, in any case, is the thesis of Part I.

1. THE MODERN ONTOLOGY AND SKEPTICISM

I argued in Chapter 2 that the best arguments for skepticism from Descartes and Hume are versions of the "no good inference" argument. Both of those arguments begin with the assumption that, in some broad sense and at least in part, our beliefs about the world depend on the way things appear to us. The second claim they share is that this dependence is broadly evidential. If we give these two claims charitable readings, then they are platitudes – no one who is not in the grip of a philosophical theory would think to deny them. But if we do accept them, then we have most of the materials for a powerful line of skeptical reasoning. Consider the following, which I think captures the common structure of "no good inference" arguments for skepticism about the world:

(NGI)   1. Our beliefs about objects in the world depend, at least in part, on the way things appear to us via the senses.
2. The nature of this dependency is broadly evidential – the fact that objects in the world appear a certain way is often our reason for thinking that they are that way.
3. Therefore, if I am to know how objects in the world are, it must be via some good inference from how things appear to me. (2,3)
4. But there is no good inference from the way things appear to the way things are.
5. Therefore, I cannot know how objects in the world are. (3,4)

Let us consider the initial force of this argument. As I said, premise (1) is properly considered to be a platitude. It states only that our beliefs about objects in the world partly depend on the way those objects appear to us. But then premise (2) is eminently plausible as well. It seems clear that, at least in typical cases, something's appearing to be a certain way constitutes a reason for thinking that it is that way. In Chapter 2 I said that this is plausible even if we are characterizing sensory appearances merely phenomenally. But certainly it seems right if we are thinking of sensory appearances as already having conceptual content. In that case, premise (2) says that something's seeming to be a certain way via the senses is often one's reason for thinking that it is that way.

Moving to premise (4), which is the remaining independent premise of the argument, we have what looks to be another plausible claim. Initial support for (4) is provided by the uncontroversial claim that things are not always as they appear. But we have seen that Hume gives an independent argument for the premise. In a nutshell, any inference from appearance to reality would have to be circular, since it must depend on an empirical premise to the effect that the way things appear is a reliable indication of the way things are. So even if (4) is not as obvious as (1) and (2), there are good reasons to think it is true.

Now to the question of the present section – namely, how is argument (NGI) supposed to involve the modern ontology? I can think of only two ways in which it might be thought to do so. First, the argument talks of appearances being our evidence for objects in the world, and it might be thought that this in itself commits the argument to the modern ontology of internal subjects and external objects. Second, it might be thought that premise (4) implicitly assumes the modern ontology, since only such an ontology would make (4) seem plausible. I now consider each of these suggestions in turn.

a. The Appearance–Reality Distinction

As we have seen, argument (NGI) talks about appearances being our evidence for objects in the world. And certainly one interpretation of this talk is to think of ourselves as internal subjects, and to think of objects in the world as having a fundamentally different and independent ontological status. Appearances are then the mental intermediaries by which internal subjects are allowed to think the external objects of knowledge. On this interpretation, which is perhaps the interpretation that both Descartes and Hume would endorse, the argument claims that our knowledge of internal appearances cannot provide sufficient evidence for knowledge of external objects in the world.

But is there any reason why we *must* understand the skeptical argument in this manner? There seem to be at least two other options. First, we could refrain from further cashing out the language of argument (NGI) in any way. In other words, we could attempt to critique (NGI) without committing ourselves to any deeper ontology of sensory appearances and reality. Certainly we understand the thrust of the argument as it stands, and so we could simply opt to take it at face value and assess it accordingly.

Our second option is to cash out the skeptical argument in terms of a different ontology, one that does not involve the offending distinction between internal knower and external object of knowledge. For example, we could employ Chisholm's adverbial theory of perception, which takes sensory appearances to be modes of the perceiver rather than mental objects.[5] On Chisholm's view, to have a blue sensation is to be appeared to bluely, thus avoiding ontological commitment to intermediate objects between the knower and the thing known. If we are thinking of sensory appearances as having conceptual content, to have a sensory appearance of a tree is to be appeared to in a characteristic way

---

5 Roderick Chisholm, *Perceiving: A Philosophical Study* (Ithaca: Cornell University Press, 1957).

phenomenally (to be appeared to treely), and to take the object appearing to be a tree. Alternatively, we could understand the skeptical argument as materialists, considering appearances to be material (or perhaps functional) states of the knower, and understanding beliefs in a similar manner.

On any of these options we get a skeptical argument that is at least as forceful as any involving a modern ontology. More specifically, what drives the skeptical argument is (a) an innocent distinction between the way things appear and the way things are and (b) some assumptions about the nature of our evidence for objects in the world. But both the distinction and the assumptions about evidence are independent of the modern ontology. I have more to say regarding the assumptions about evidence in Section I.1b. But let us consider the appearance–reality distinction now.

First, the distinction between the way things appear and the way things are is independent of any specific ontology. The modern ontology of external objects and internal ideas represents one way to cash out the distinction, but it is not the only way, or even the most plausible way. Second, it is a mere platitude that things are not always as they appear, and so any minimally plausible ontology will have to cash out the distinction in some fashion or another. Third, it is the distinction itself, not the modern understanding of it, that is driving the skeptical argument. If anything, the argument is stronger without the modern interpretation, since it is thereby relieved of what is only excess baggage.

But perhaps this last point is incorrect. For even if the language of (NGI) can be cashed out independently of the modern ontology, perhaps the argument depends on that ontology in a different way. Specifically, one might think that premise (4) becomes plausible only by adopting the modern version of the appearance–reality distinction. In other words, one might think that only the modern ontology makes it plausible that there is no good inference from how things appear to how things are. In order to decide this point we must look more closely at the considerations that can be given in support of premise (4) and at whether these considerations involve the modern ontology in any essential respect.

b. *Inference from Appearance to Reality*

It seems to me that there are three main considerations that can be brought in favor of premise (4) of (NGI). The first is the Humean argument about the impossibility of a non-circular inference from appearances to reality. As we have seen, the main idea of this argument is that premises about how things appear cannot give support to conclusions about how things are, unless such premises include an assumption about the relationship of appearances to reality. In other words, there will have to be some assumption to the effect that the way things appear via the senses is a good indication of the way things are. But then the problem arises as to how that kind of assumption could be justified. As Hume points out, any such justification would itself require the evidence of appearances, and so would require the very assumption whose justification is in question. Therefore, Hume concludes, a non-circular inference from appearances to reality is impossible.

My own view is that this argument from Hume in favor of premise (4) is correct. Or, to qualify, it is correct on an important understanding of "support" that we will consider more closely in subsequent chapters. What is relevant for present purposes is that the Humean argument, whatever its merit, is completely independent of any particular reading of the appearance–reality distinction. Once again, it is the appearance–reality distinction itself that is driving the argument, not any modern interpretation of the distinction. The problem would not go away, for example, if we were to think of appearances as the adverbialist does or as the materialist does. For on any interpretation of the appearance–reality distinction it will seem that we need an assumption to the effect that appearances are a reliable guide to reality. And on any remotely plausible interpretation of that distinction, such an assumption will not itself be a necessary truth but rather a contingent truth about the way things in fact are. But then the central premises of the Humean argument are in place, and the problem of circularity arises.

Even if these Humean considerations could be avoided, there is another argument in favor of premise (4) that is, in my opinion, unanswerable. Even if a non-circular inference from appearances to reality were in principle possible, no such inference would be psychologically plausible. In other words, it would not be plausible that such an inference is actually used when we form beliefs about objects on the basis of sensory appearances. This is because an inference takes us from belief to belief, but we do not typically have beliefs about appearances. In the typical case, we form our beliefs about objects in the world without forming beliefs about appearances at all, much less inferring beliefs about the world from beliefs about appearances. And notice that this point holds independently of how we are thinking of the ontology of appearances. For example, we do not typically have beliefs about the ways in which we are appeared to, and we certainly do not typically form beliefs about what functional states we are in.

A third argument in favor of premise (4) also involves considerations of psychological plausibility and would hold even if we could remove the difficulty regarding beliefs about appearances. The argument is made by Hume, but it has not been adequately appreciated. Specifically, any inference that is particularly clever or sophisticated is unlikely to play a role in perceptual knowledge, because even brutes and small children learn from experience. And so invoking any complex inference here is, once again, psychologically implausible. It is not plausible, for example, that we actually make some complex inference to the best explanation when we see that there is a cup on the table. Introspection certainly does not reveal any such inference. And a small child knows that there is a cup on the table before she is capable of much simpler reasoning. This is a place where the empirical facts of human cognition trump philosophical theorizing. And once again, these points do not depend on our understanding appearances in any specific way, modern or otherwise.

We may conclude that the skeptical argument represented in (NGI) does not involve the modern ontology in any essential respect. A quick look at arguments (H2), (H3), and (D5) from Chapter 2, all versions of the "no good inference" argument, confirms the points that have been made with regard to (NGI). All of these arguments are driven by an appearance–reality distinction and some assumptions about the nature of our evidence for objects in the world, but neither that distinction nor those assumptions require a modern ontology for their interpretation or their support. Therefore, the modern ontology of internal subjects and external objects is not necessary for generating powerful arguments for skepticism about the world. For the same reasons, rejecting the modern ontology is not sufficient for refuting these arguments. Philosophers who have thought that it is have taken false refuge in that position.

2. REALISM AND SKEPTICISM

I have been arguing that skepticism about the world does not depend on a dualistic modern ontology. The strategy I have used to make the argument is rather simple: I have shown that the best skeptical arguments run just as well on other ontologies. More specifically, I have shown that the arguments can run on a monistic materialist ontology, and that they can run on an adverbialist ontology that is consistent with both dualism and monism. But here someone might object that I have been missing the point. What is wrong with the modern ontology, the objection goes, is not its dualism but its realism. So long as we think that objects in the world are mind independent we will have the skeptical problem, and that is why skeptical arguments run on materialism and adverbialism as well as on Descartes' dualism.

It is fairly easy to see, however, that this objection to the reasoning of Section I.1 is incorrect. It is incorrect because adverbialism is not committed to realism; although an adverbialist understanding of appearances is consistent with realism about objects in the world, it is also consistent with anti-realism about objects in the world. Therefore, the reasoning in Section I.1 shows that the best skeptical arguments do not depend on realism. They can run on adverbialism combined with anti-realism.

To drive home the point, consider that even a radical idealist like Berkeley should be worried by "no good inference" arguments. That is, even on Berkeley's extreme anti-realism those arguments run just as well. The reason this is so is that even Berkeley must maintain a distinction between appearance and reality – any minimally plausible ontology must do so. But this is enough to get "no good inference" arguments going, and nothing about Berkeley's ontology blocks the reasoning to their skeptical conclusion.

Let us take a closer look. In Berkeley's idealism all that exists are minds and ideas. Leaving aside the niceties, objects such as tigers and trees are essentially well-ordered bundles of ideas. But even here we have a distinction between "real" objects and mere appearances. For example, Berkeley's ontology makes a distinction between actual tigers and hallucinations of tigers. The latter, of course, are not well ordered – they lack the coherence and stability that bundles of ideas constituting "real" tigers possess. But then what is our evidence, on Berkeley's view, that there is a real tiger before us? In cases of perception, it has to be the sensory appearances that we have *at the moment*. And of course momentary appearances, even if they are over several moments, can be deceiving. What appears to be a real tiger need not be, since initial stability and coherence might later give way to the incoherence of an illusion.

All of this is as it would have to be. For of course our evidence for objects in the world is the way that things appear to us, and of course appearances can be deceiving. Berkeley accepts these as the platitudes that they are and tries to account for them within the framework of his idealism. But since he accepts these platitudes, the skeptical argument is off and running. Certainly premises (1) and (2) of (NGI) remain true on Berkeley's anti-realism. And the reasoning for premise (4) will be the same as well.

Therefore, "no good inference" arguments run as well on radical idealism as they do on realism. This is an important result. The most common motivation for anti-realism is the attempt to avoid skepticism, but anti-realism does not do the job.

3. REPRESENTATIONALISM AND SKEPTICISM

Some philosophers, however, will charge that I am still missing the point. It is not the mind–body dualism of the modern ontology that leads to skepticism, or even its realism about objects in the world. Rather, the problem with the modern ontology is its representationalist theory of ideas. A necessary assumption of the skeptical arguments, the objection goes, is that we think about objects by first thinking about ideas. This in turn sets up the requirement that our ideas "agree" with their objects, or that our ideas accurately "represent" them. But once we conceive things this way, it becomes impossible to know that our representations do in fact agree with their objects. That is the real point of the Heideggerian and post-modern critiques.

The following passages from Heidegger and Rorty suggest that this is indeed what these philosophers have in mind:

What is thus perceived and made determinate can be expressed in propositions, and can be retained and preserved as what has thus been asserted. This perceptive retention of an assertion about something is itself a way of Being-in-the-world; it is not to be Interpreted as a 'procedure' by which a subject provides itself with representations of something which remain stored up 'inside' as having been thus appropriated, and with regard to which the question of how they 'agree' with actuality can occasionally arise. [Heidegger, *Being and Time*, p. 89]

In Descartes's conception – the one which became the basis for "modern" epistemology – it is *representations* which are in the "mind." The Inner Eye surveys these representations hoping to find some mark which will testify to their fidelity. Whereas skepticism in the ancient world had been a matter of a moral attitude, a style of life, a reaction to the pretensions of the intellectual fashions of the day, skepticism in the manner of Descartes's *First Meditations* [sic] was a perfectly definite, precise, "professional" question: How do we know that anything which is mental represents anything which is not mental? (Rorty, *Mirror of Nature*, pp. 45–46)

If this is the point of Heidegger's and Rorty's critiques, then it is badly put when in other places they blame ontology for skepticism.[6] For representationalism is not an ontological thesis at all but a thesis about how objects are thought. In other words, it is a position in the philosophy of mind. To see that this is so, consider that the modern ontology does not entail representationalism, and representationalism does not entail the modern ontology.

First, representationalism does not entail the modern ontology. Remember that representationalism is the thesis that one can think about objects in the world only by thinking about ideas that represent those objects. But nothing about this thesis suggests that either objects or ideas must have any particular ontology. So, for example, an adverbialist about ideas can be a representationalist, holding that one can think about objects in the world only by thinking about the modes of thought that represent them. Appearances or ideas considered as modes of thought can serve just as nicely to represent objects as appearances or ideas considered as mental objects. Neither does representationalism entail anything about the ontology of objects in the world. Even an idealist can be a representationalist, and Berkeley's theory of perception bears this out.

Second, the modern ontology does not entail representationalism. As we saw, that ontology is best characterized as a dualism between mind and body, combined with a realism about the latter. Minds are mental or spiritual substances while bodies are material substances, and the two are considered to be of independent ontological kinds, meaning that neither depends for its existence on the other. But nothing in that position entails that thinking about material objects takes place by thinking about mental objects that represent them. An alternative position is that minds can think about material objects directly. In other words, a modernist can hold that although we think about objects *with* ideas, we do not do this by thinking *about* the ideas. As the medievals put it, ideas are the *medium quo* rather than the *medium quod* of thought about material objects.

To make the point a different way, consider that there are two senses of the term "object." In an ontological sense an object is a relatively

---

6   Dreyfus (p. 50) claims that it is not Heidegger's point.

stable and independent entity. In this sense of "object," the modern ontology posits two kinds: mental and material. The second sense of object is intentional. In this sense, to be an object of thought is to be thought about. And of course something does not have to be an object in the ontological sense to be an object in the intentional sense. Thus one can think about acts, modes, and events as well as material objects and persons. And now the point is this: the modern ontologist can hold that ideas and appearances are objects in the ontological sense without holding that they must always be objects in the intentional sense. Ideas *qua* ontological objects might function in our thinking without being intentional objects.

So the modern ontology is logically independent of a representationalist theory of ideas. One can be a representationalist without being a modern ontologist, and one can be a modern ontologist without being a representationalist. But that question aside, is representationalism necessary for generating skepticism? The answer is no, since nothing in the skeptical arguments presupposes representationalism. Let us focus again on argument (NGI).

Premise (1) of (NGI) says that our beliefs about objects in the world depend on the way things appear to us. But it does not say *how* our beliefs depend on appearances – it does not say, for example, that appearances must be objects of our thought before we can think about objects in the world. On the contrary, (1) is consistent with the thesis that appearances are the *medium quo* of thought about objects.

Premise (2) does say something about the way beliefs depend on appearances; it says that the dependence is in some sense evidential. But once again, this is consistent with the thesis that appearances are the *medium quo* of thought. One might hold that the way things appear serves as our evidence for the way things are but hold that one need not actually think about that evidence for it to play its epistemic role. This might sound odd, since it seems odd that something could serve as evidence without our thinking about it. But we can see that the position is not odd if we are careful about an important distinction. Namely, there is a distinction between thinking about something and being conscious of it. Put differently, there is a difference between thinking about a thing and its being within one's consciousness.

To illustrate the difference, consider that you might drive on a highway for miles while absorbed in conversation. During this time you might not think about the road at all – a kind of automatic pilot kicks in until either your interest in the conversation wanes or something on the highway requires your attention. But although you do not think about the highway, presumably you are conscious of it all the time. Otherwise you would crash. Another example that illustrates the distinction is proprioception. At nearly every waking moment we are conscious of the position of our bodies, owing to receptors in our muscles. This is why we do not bump into things, fall down, or knock things over more often than we do. But we hardly ever think about the position of our bodies. Our body position, in other words, is not constantly the object of our thought. Again, we can be conscious of things without thinking about them.

It is plausible that this is the case with sensory appearances as well: we are at every moment conscious of appearances, but we hardly ever think about them. What we think about are the objects doing the appearing, and that is why we are often ignorant of, or even wrong about, their phenomenal properties. Of course, there are exceptions to this. While an artist is painting, she might think hard about how a thing appears, and any of us can turn our attention to the many shades of color presented by a single facing wall. But these exceptions prove the rule; we do not typically think about appearances, although we are conscious of them at nearly every waking moment.

If this is right, then we can make good sense out of the claim that sensory appearances serve as evidence without our thinking about them. For although we do not typically think about appearances, we are at every waking moment conscious of them. And our being conscious of them is what allows them to serve as our evidence for beliefs about the world. This position not only makes sense – it is almost certainly correct. On the one hand, we do not typically think about appearances. On the other hand, it seems obvious that our evidence for beliefs about the world involves the way things appear to us through the senses. Consider again my perceptual belief that the cat is on the couch. As I have already said, it seems obvious to me that the reason I believe this is that this is how things visually appear. And I mean that this is my reason in the epistemic sense of "reason" – this is how I know that my cat is on the couch. How else would I know?

Finally, premise (4) of (NGI) does not presuppose representationalism. In fact, one of the reasons I gave in favor of premise (4) was that we do not typically have beliefs about how things appear to us, and so an inference from appearance to reality would be lacking in premises. Even if such an inference were possible in principle, I argued, the claim that we actually employ it in forming beliefs about the world is psychologically implausible. Far from requiring representationalism, premise (4) is well supported by a denial of representationalism.

In conclusion, "no good inference" arguments run on an innocent appearance–reality distinction together with some assumptions about the nature of our evidence for beliefs about the world. Such arguments do not depend on mind–body dualism, realism about objects in the world, or a representationalist theory of ideas.

II. What Is Sufficient for Skepticism about the World

We have seen that the modern ontology is not necessary for generating arguments for skepticism about the world. But many philosophers have thought that it is sufficient. Their reasoning is that once we posit an ontological gap between mind and world, there is no way that the gap can be bridged. They accept the skeptical reasoning that appearances cannot be good evidence for a mind-independent world, and attempt to block the conclusion by denying that there is any mind-independent reality that we could want to know. Unfortunately, these philosophers fail to notice that the skeptical reasoning works as well for mind-dependent objects as it does for mind-independent ones. As we have seen, "no good inference" arguments work as well on Berkeley's idealism as they do on Descartes' realism.

What this shows is that skeptical arguments make some other mistake. Specifically, "no good inference" arguments make some mistake in their assumptions about our evidence for beliefs about the world, and this mistake is preserved throughout different interpretations of their ontology. This means that the modern ontology is not sufficient for generating skepticism about the world – you need the bad epistemology to get the skeptical result. Or to put things more carefully, this shows that the modern ontology is not sufficient for generating skepticism within the context of "no good inference" arguments.[7]

To establish these claims it will be necessary to identify some mistaken

---

[7] In Chapter 8, I will argue that the modern ontology is not sufficient to generate skepticism via any argument at all. In this regard I apply the relevant possibilities approach to argument (D4) from Chapter 2, and argue that an adequate theory of evidence reveals that the skeptical scenarios are not relevant possibilities. This, in turn, shows that (D4) makes a mistake about the nature of evidence. But if the modern ontology is not sufficient here either, then all of the best arguments for skepticism about the world will have been considered and I will be warranted in drawing this conclusion without qualification.

epistemological assumption in the skeptical arguments we have been considering. This is the purpose of Section II.1. Second, we will need to show that a rejection of the argument along such lines is consistent with the modern ontology. This is done in Section II.2.

1. THE BIG MISTAKE

What part of the skeptical argument can be plausibly rejected? As I have said, premises (1) and (2) of (NGI) are mere platitudes. Part of what I mean by this is that anyone should accept (1) and (2), no matter what her ontology, her philosophy of mind, or her theory of evidence.

Many attempts to answer the skeptic have focused on premise (4), but I think that this approach is misguided. I have already said that I find Hume's argument about circularity convincing when it is understood appropriately. But more importantly, it seems to me that it is empirically false that human cognition employs anything like an inference from appearance to reality. The very notion of an inference involves a movement from belief to belief on the basis of deductive or inductive relationships of their contents. But it is psychologically implausible that we typically have beliefs about sensory appearances, and, even if we do, it is implausible that we infer anything from them on the basis of anything approaching adequate reasoning.

The point I am making here is not just about conscious beliefs and conscious inferences. I think that the attribution of even subconscious beliefs or inferences is empirically implausible. First, if we typically have beliefs about appearances, then we should be able to remember them. But on the contrary, I cannot reconstruct the way things appeared to me even moments ago. I take this as evidence that I never had beliefs about appearances in the first place. Second, it is well documented that people are often wrong about the way things appear to them. For example, people will say that a facing wall appears to be uniform in color, but a more careful introspection reveals that it presents a myriad of different shades. In a similar fashion, people will report that shadows on a field of snow appear gray, while in fact such shadows appear blue, as is also revealed by a closer introspection. A good explanation for this kind of mistake is that people are not used to thinking about appearances at all, and so when our attention is called to the way things appear we are not very good at forming accurate beliefs about this.

Someone might nevertheless think that such beliefs are subconscious, even if they are difficult to recall or articulate. For even if I am not very good at remembering or describing appearances, surely I can say something about them when asked. But here we have to make a distinction between a subconscious belief and a disposition to believe.[8] That is, the fact that I am disposed to form some beliefs about my sensory experience when asked does not show that I had those beliefs all along. It is more likely, I think, that such beliefs are originally formed upon consideration of the question. In this case beliefs about appearances would be like beliefs about previously unconsidered sums; if I ask you the sum of 122 and 345, you will form an accurate belief about this, but that is no indication that you believed the answer all along. When we have this distinction in mind, it is hard to maintain that we typically have even subconscious beliefs about how things appear. And if we do not have the beliefs, then we do not make inferences from them. Premise (4) of the argument looks good.

What options for rejecting something in (NGI) are left? I suggest that we focus on the move from premises (1) and (2) to (3). That move seems initially plausible, but a closer look will reveal that it is not as obvious at it might first appear. More specifically, the move implicitly assumes that all evidential relations are inferential relations – or at least it assumes that the evidential relation between sensory appearances and reality is inferential. Although these assumptions seem plausible and are even widely accepted, I believe that this is the mistake that "no good inference" arguments make.[9]

In the remainder of this section I try to make an initial case that this is indeed the mistake made by the skeptical arguments we have been considering. In Chapter 7, I defend a theory of knowledge that is consistent with this diagnosis, and that provides a theoretical basis for it. In other words, agent reliabilism not only shows that not all evidential relations are inferential but explains why this is so. Very roughly, the idea is as follows: According to agent reliabilism, knowledge is true belief that arises out of reliable cognitive faculties and habits, or what we may call "cognitive virtues." Such faculties and habits reliably put us in touch with the world, providing a good cognitive fit between ourselves

---

8 A similar distinction is treated in Robert Audi, "Dispositional Beliefs and Dispositions to Believe," *NOÛS* 28 (1994): 419–434.
9 Many discussions of skepticism seem to endorse the assumption, at least implicitly. I have already mentioned Ayers' classic account of skeptical arguments in *The Problem of Knowledge* (Harmondsworth: Pelican, 1956), and Williams' endorsement of this. See also Baysean and traditional coherentist accounts of evidence, both of which attempt to define evidential relations in terms of various kinds of inference relations.

and our environment. But not all cognitive faculties are inferential faculties. Our perceptual faculties, for example, put us in touch with the world by reliably producing true beliefs directly on the basis of sensory inputs. Here "directly" does not mean without prior training, concepts, or presuppositions. Rather, it means non-inferentially – that is, not on the basis of inferences from prior premises serving as reasons. If this very general picture is correct, then sensory appearances can be good evidence without the benefit of any inference from appearances to reality. Inference from prior beliefs to further beliefs is one way to reliably form true beliefs about one's environment, but there are non-inferential ways as well.

I say this is only the "rough idea" because knowledge requires more than reliability. For one thing, beliefs must be subjectively justified as well as objectively reliable to count as knowledge. But we will see that agent reliabilism can accommodate this condition on knowledge as well. What we need is an account of subjective justification on which the forming of beliefs about the world directly on the basis of sensory appearances turns out to be so justified. Again, I begin the initial case in the remainder of this section and continue it in Chapter 7.

a. The Elements of Perception

I am presently challenging the implicit assumption of argument (NGI) that all evidential relations involve inferential relations. Put another way, I am challenging the assumption that all evidential relations involve a deductive or inductive inference from one set of beliefs to some further set of beliefs. What one would like is a theory of evidence that allows this diagnosis of the skeptical argument.

The most general characterization of evidence is as follows: A cognitive state is evidence for another cognitive state if and only if being in the first state tends to confer some positive epistemic status on the second state. For example, hearing the doorbell ring is evidence for my belief that there is someone at the door, insofar as hearing the doorbell ring tends to make the belief in question rational, or justified, or warranted. What we are looking for is a theory of evidence that allows cognitive states to be in such an evidential relationship to our beliefs about the world, but that does not characterize that relationship in terms of deductive or inductive inferences from belief to belief. Later in this chapter I argue that there are at least two broad approaches to evidence that would do the job, and I throw my hat in with one of them. But at this point a short detour is necessary. Before we can take a closer look at these approaches it will be necessary to consider the elements of perception in a very general way.

I am interested here in quickly making some distinctions that we can all agree upon, even if we would not agree about how to cash them out. On a very general level, then, we may distinguish three elements in the perception of an object: the phenomenal content involved in the perception, the conceptual or representational content involved in the perception, and the perceptual judgment arising out of such contents. These elements need not be thought of as being temporally or even ontologically distinct, and the distinctions are not meant to be exhaustive. My point is only that one can make these distinctions in a rough-and-ready manner, and I make them here because they will help us to understand the theories of evidence to be discussed shortly. Accordingly, we can talk about the following elements of perception, my stipulated name for each appearing in italics.

i. The uninterpreted *qualia* of sensations. (Sensory appearances characterized as lacking conceptual content.)
ii. Interpreted *experience*. (Sensory appearances characterized as involving conceptual content.)
iii. *Beliefs* about objects in the world.

The elements of perception distinguished here are commonly considered to be in relations which are in a broad sense causal, but they are also considered to be in broadly evidential relations. As we have seen, which elements are the essential ones for the evidential relation is a matter of dispute, but in general philosophers agree that one or both of the elements in i and ii act as evidence for the beliefs in iii, in the sense (explained earlier) that being in such states tends to confer positive epistemic status on beliefs about the world. Some philosophers argue that we should collapse i and ii into a thick concept of experience, thinking that further distinctions are irrelevant to the evidential story. The important relation, according to this way of thinking, is between thick experience and belief. Others collapse the distinction between ii and iii, thinking that the important relation is between uninterpreted *qualia* and interpreted experience/belief. A third possibility is that we must keep the distinctions among *qualia*, experience, and belief, thinking that there is not one important evidential relation but two: one between *qualia* and interpreted experience, the other between interpreted experience and belief.

In Chapters 7 and 9, I defend a substantive account of perception that endorses the first position. On this view of perception, sensory appearances *qua* perceptual evidence have both phenomenal and conceptual content. My purpose in the present chapter, however, is to avoid all such controversies. This is the appropriate way to proceed at this point in the discussion, since I am arguing that the problem with (NGI) is *not* that it assumes one account of sensory appearances or another. The argument does not depend on a characterization of sensory appearances as thin or thick, and it does not depend on any particular ontology of sensory appearances.

There are now two points that need to be emphasized in this context. First, it is relatively uncontroversial that the elements we have distinguished really are elements of perception. No matter how we understand the perception of objects, it must be acknowledged to somehow involve phenomenal *qualia*, conceptual content, and belief. Second, no matter how we understand these elements of perception, epistemological problems arise. For on any plausible theory of evidence, *either qualia* are evidence for interpreted experience/belief, or interpreted experience is evidence for belief, or both. But how are such evidential relations to be understood? I have claimed that these relations are not to be understood in terms of deductive or inductive inferences from belief to belief. Once again, we are looking for a theory of evidence that allows either *qualia* or thick experience to be evidence for beliefs about the world, but that does not characterize this relationship in terms of inferences.

We are now in a position to look at two approaches to evidence that can do this. As I have said, I will not argue here that my favorite approach is correct. For the purposes of this section I will only attempt to motivate the intuition that one of these approaches is correct, and to show that either of them would provide the materials for rejecting the skeptical reasoning in (NGI). It will then be relatively easy to show that both of these approaches to evidence are consistent with a modern ontology. That will be done in Section II.2.

b. *Two Approaches to Evidence*

In order to understand the two approaches to evidence I have in mind it will be useful to make an analogy to ethics. In ethics, theories of right action may be distinguished into two general camps. The first understands right action in terms of an objective relationship to morally valuable consequences, so that an action is right if and only if, as a matter of fact, it produces (or has a tendency to produce) such consequences. The second general approach understands right action in terms of correct norms or rules. Here what makes an action right is not whether some relation to consequences in fact obtains, but whether the action is allowed by some relevant set of action-guiding norms. The first approach is broadly consequentialist, whereas the second approach is broadly deontological.

We can characterize approaches to evidence in an analogous fashion. Broadly speaking, a consequentialist approach in epistemology understands positive epistemic status in terms of epistemically valuable consequences. On this approach, a cognitive state is evidence for a belief p if and only if believing p on the basis of the cognitive state tends to result in the agent believing truly with respect to p. Sometimes the basing relation here is understood to be inferential, so that a belief q is good evidence for a belief p if inferring p from q (when q is true) tends to lead to believing p truly. But that is only one way to satisfy the basing relation. Alternatively, on this approach we may say that an experience e is good evidence for a perceptual belief p if believing p on the *causal* basis of e tends to result in believing p truly. In this latter case there is no question of a deductive or inductive inference from beliefs about experience to beliefs about objects in the world. Rather, the point is that the experience itself is evidence for the belief, insofar as having that experience tends to result in believing the truth.

I have talked here in terms of the relationship between experience and belief. But a similar account could be given regarding the relationship between *qualia* and belief, or between *qualia* and interpreted experience.[10]

Not surprisingly, a deontological approach in epistemology understands epistemic status in terms of correct epistemic norms. On this approach a cognitive state is evidence for a belief if and only if correct epistemic norms permit forming that belief on the basis of that cognitive state. Here again the basing relation is sometimes understood as inferential, the idea being that correct epistemic norms permit some inferences and not others. But again the basing relation can be satisfied in other ways as well. Thus it is possible that correct epistemic norms permit a certain belief whenever one has a certain kind of experience.

---

10 Alvin Goldman has developed a series of this broad kind of position. See, e.g., his "What Is Justified Belief?", in George Pappas, ed., *Justification and Knowledge* (Dordrecht: Reidel, 1979).

Alternatively, there could be norms governing the interpretation of *qualia*, thus taking a cognitive agent from uninterpreted *qualia* to interpreted experience or even to full-blown belief. The idea here is that there are epistemic norms that govern the formation of beliefs directly on the basis of either *qualia* or experience, as opposed to norms which govern inferences from beliefs about *qualia* and experience.[11]

Consequentialist theories of positive epistemic status stress "objective" or *de facto* reliability, whereas deontological theories stress "subjective" factors such as conformance to countenanced norms. A third approach to evidence would be a mixed theory, requiring both an objective and a subjective element for positive epistemic status. This is a plausible approach in epistemology, since knowledge would seem to require both an objective relation to the truth and appropriate cognitive conduct. In somewhat different terms, knowledge would seem to require both objective reliability and subjective justification. Accordingly, a mixed approach might hold that a cognitive state is evidence for a belief p if and only if *both* (a) believing p on the basis of the cognitive state tends to result in the agent believing truly with respect to p, and (b) believing p on that basis is permitted by some relevant set of belief guiding norms. But there are other ways to capture the idea of appropriate cognitive conduct, or subjective justification, without reference to norms or rules. Such an alternative is preferable, I will argue, insofar as the thesis that our cognition is governed by norms or rules is a controversial one. This second kind of approach is defended in Chapter 7, under the guise of agent reliabilism.

We are now in a position to draw the conclusion of this section: namely, either of the two broad approaches to evidence just considered would ground the objection to (NGI) that I have proposed. If you will remember, that objection questioned the move from premises (1) and (2) to (3) in the skeptical argument. My thinking was that this move in the argument implicitly assumes that all evidential relations involve inferential relations, and I objected to that assumption. Clearly, either of the two approaches to evidence just considered would ground the present objection. If either approach is correct about the nature of perceptual evidence, then argument (NGI) is invalid.

---

11 For a developed version of this kind of position, see John Pollock, *Contemporary Theories of Knowledge* (Totowa, NJ: Rowman and Littlefield, 1986), esp. Ch. 5.

2. THE MODERN ONTOLOGY AGAIN

In the preceding section, I argued that the skeptical argument depends on a controversial assumption about the nature of evidence, and that either of two broad approaches to evidence would vindicate an objection to that assumption. My final task is to show that those theories of evidence are consistent with the modern ontology. Doing so establishes that the modern ontology is not sufficient for generating the skeptical argument in (NGI), and that rejecting the modern ontology is not necessary to defeat that argument.

It is fairly easy to see that the two theories of evidence are consistent with the modern ontology. For both theories were explicated in terms of various relations among *qualia,* thick experience, and belief, with no commitment being made regarding the ontological statuses of these entities; rather, I purposely characterized such entities in the most general and neutral terms. That being the case, it is now easy to show how the modernist can accommodate the various moments of perception, taking such moments themselves to be uncontroversial data that any ontology would have to allow. For good measure we will note how the adverbialist and materialist can do this as well.

How would a proponent of the modern ontology understand our categories of perceptual elements? Presumably she would understand *qualia* as some sort of mental objects and would understand experience in that way too. Beliefs about the world would then be intentional attitudes which somehow go through these mental intermediaries. A strong version of this story weds representationalism to modernism, so that beliefs about the world are directly *about* the mental intermediaries, and only indirectly about mind-independent objects insofar as the mental entities represent, or copy, or picture those objects.

On the other hand, we need not understand our categories in that way. Thus the adverbial theorist considers both *qualia* and thick experience to be modes of the knower, thereby avoiding ontological commitment to separately existing mental objects of any kind. On this view beliefs are intentional attitudes that can be directly about objects in the world, there being no intermediary objects for intentionality to go through. Alternatively, the materialist thinks of *qualia,* experiences, and beliefs as various material or functional states of the knower, invoking no kind of non-material object or state or attitude.

But then each of the two theories of evidence considered above is consistent with a modern interpretation. On the consequentialist theory this amounts to saying that a *quale* or experience e (now understood as mental objects serving as intermediaries between subject and object) is evidence for an external object belief p if and only if believing p on the causal basis of e tends to result in believing p truly. The deontological approach can make a similar application. In this case a *quale* or experience e (again, conceived as mental intermediaries) is evidence for an external object belief p if and only if some relevant set of epistemic norms permit believing p on the basis of e. A mixed approach could accommodate the modern ontology by combining the consequentialist and deontological conditions in the obvious manner.

What all of this shows is that the skeptical argument in (NGI) depends on a controversial assumption about evidence that is independent of the modern ontology. Therefore the modern ontology is not sufficient for generating the skeptical argument, and rejecting that ontology is not necessary for defeating the argument.

3. REPRESENTATIONALISM AGAIN

Section II.2 also shows that representationalism is not sufficient for generating skepticism, or at least not within the context of "no good inference" arguments. This is because both consequentialist and deontological theories of evidence are consistent with representationalism, and so the denial that all evidential relations are inferential is also consistent with that position.

It is interesting to ask whether representationalism is sufficient to generate skepticism by a different route. After all, one would think that there must be something to the critique of skepticism that has been taken for granted in so many circles, and this would seem to be the last possibility that the modern ontology, or at least a representationalist version of it, is closely related to skepticism.

It might seem obvious that representationalism does lead to skepticism. For if thought about objects in the world requires thought about ideas, then thought about objects is indirect. And if thought about objects is indirect, then it must proceed by inferences from thought about ideas. But then the materials for a "no good inference" argument are in place, and the skeptical conclusion would seem to follow in this way from representationalism. Let us take a closer look at this reasoning, which in effect suggests the following skeptical argument:

(R) 1. The immediate or direct object of thought is always some idea in the mind.
2. All thought about other things must be indirect, mediated by thought about ideas of those things.
3. Objects in the world are not ideas.
4. Therefore, all thought about objects in the world is indirect, mediated by thought about ideas of those objects. (1,2,3)
5. Therefore, thought about objects in the world requires an inference from thought about our ideas of them. (4)
6. But there is no good inference from ideas to objects in the world.
7. Knowledge requires good inferences.
8. Therefore, there is no knowledge of objects in the world. (5,6,7)

Premises (1) and (2) of the argument amount to representationalism, and (1) and (3) suggest a modern version. The remaining independent premises, (6) and (7), are common property of "no good inference" arguments. So it looks as though a combination of the modern ontology and representationalism is sufficient to generate skepticism about the world.

That analysis is mistaken, however, because (5) does not follow from (4). The subconclusion stated in (4) is that thought about objects in the world must be mediated by thought about ideas. This indeed follows from the representationalist assumptions stated in (1) through (3). Let us call this kind of mediation "conceptual," since it involves conceiving (or thinking about) one thing in order to conceive (or think about) another thing. The subconclusion stated in (5), however, is that thought about objects must be mediated by *inferences*. It only remains to note that conceptual mediation does not imply inferential mediation, or mediation by inferences from prior premises. One might hold that thinking about Xs requires thinking about Ys, without holding that beliefs about Xs require inferences from beliefs about Ys.

To see that this is so, consider the process of interpreting a piece of art. To interpret a painting, for example, presumably one must think about it: for example, one must form beliefs about certain physical aspects of the painting. But the way in which interpretation takes place is not that we *infer* an interpretation from premises about the physical features of the painting; beliefs about the painting's physical features do not figure in an argument from which we deductively or inductively draw a conclusion about the painting's meaning. If you think that this is how interpretation works, then try to reconstruct the argument. At best the result will be awkward and unconvincing.

These considerations show that interpretation can take place in some other manner. And this might be the case for the interpretation of sensory appearances as well as for the interpretation of art. But then, even if representationalism were correct – even if we did form beliefs about the world on the basis of thought about sensory appearances – it would not follow from this that we infer beliefs about the world from beliefs about sensory appearances.

Is there another way in which representationalism entails skepticism? Reid sometimes speaks as if he thinks that there is. Reid thinks that a representationalist theory of ideas was shared by ancient and modern philosophers alike, and that it was sufficient to generate skepticism:

Modern philosophers, as well as the Peripatetics and Epicureans of old, have conceived that external objects cannot be the immediate objects of our thought; that there must be some image of them in the mind itself, in which, as in a mirror, they are seen. And the name *idea*, in the philosophical sense of it, is given to those internal and immediate objects of our thoughts. The external thing is the remote or mediate object; but the idea, or image of that object in the mind, is the immediate object, without which we could have no perception, no remembrance, no conception of the mediate object. (*Essays*, p. 226a–b)

We ought, however, to do this justice to the Bishop of Cloyne and to the author of the "Treatise of Human Nature," to acknowledge, that their conclusions are justly drawn from the doctrine of ideas, which has been so universally received. . . . The theory of ideas, like the Trojan horse, had a specious appearance both of innocence and beauty . . . but carried in its belly death and destruction to all science and common sense. (Ibid., p. 132a–b)

In these passages Reid calls our attention to a representationalist theory of ideas that he thinks is common property throughout the history of philosophy, and he credits Berkeley and Hume with recognizing that theory's skeptical consequences. But is it the representationalism of the theory of ideas that is the culprit? Reid attributes the following skeptical argument to Berkeley. Notice that it is not a "no good inference argument," but instead trades on the inability of ideas to represent a material world.

Bishop Berkeley gave new light to this subject, by shewing, that the qualities of an inanimate thing, such as matter is conceived to be, cannot resemble any sensation; that it is impossible to conceive anything like the sensations of our minds, but the sensations of other minds. . . . But let us observe the use the Bishop makes of this important discovery. Why, he concludes, that we can have no conception of an inanimate substance, such as matter is conceived to be, or of any of its qualities; and that there is the strongest ground to believe that there is no existence in nature but minds, sensations, and ideas.... But how does this follow? Why, thus; We can have no conception of anything but what resembles some sensation or idea in our minds; but the sensations and ideas in our minds can resemble nothing but the sensations and ideas in other minds; therefore, the conclusion is evident. (*Inquiry*, pp. 131b–132a)

The argument that Reid here attributes to Berkeley may be reconstructed as follows:

(B) 1. The only immediate objects of thought are ideas and sensations.
2. All thought of other things must be by means of ideas or sensations that represent them.
3. In the case of material objects, the ideas or sensations that mediate our thought must be images or resemblances of those objects.
4. No idea or sensation resembles any material object.
5. Therefore, there is no thought or perception of material objects. (1,2,3,4)

Premises (1) and (2) of Berkeley's argument amount to representationalism, and so that theory is playing a role here. Moreover, Reid is convinced by other arguments from Berkeley that (4) is true. But premise (3) is a thesis of Berkeley's empiricism rather than an essential aspect of representationalism. That is, representationalism *per se* is not committed to the thesis that representation must be by resemblance. But then representationalism is not sufficient to generate skepticism via Berkeley's inconceivability argument. For that you need a bad theory of representation; that is, you need the assumption that representation must be by resemblance.

Here we might have a case where the analysis of a skeptical argument drives positive philosophy of mind rather than epistemology. For premise (3) is not an epistemological thesis, but a thesis in the philosophy of mind, or perhaps in semiotics. On the other hand, the thesis that representation requires resemblance is so implausible that it is hard to say that we have learned any lesson at all. This is perhaps one of those cases where an assumption can be rejected as soon as it is made explicit.

4. CONCLUSIONS

I close by drawing some conclusions from the discussion so far. First, neither the modern ontology nor representationalism is necessary for constructing powerful arguments for skepticism about the world. Specifically, "no good inference" arguments require neither a mind–body dualism, a realism about objects in the world, nor a representationalist philosophy of mind. Such arguments are consistent with these but by no means need them.

Second, neither the modern ontology nor representationalism is sufficient for generating skepticism about the world, since the best skeptical arguments make an epistemological mistake. "No good inference" arguments assume that all evidential relations are inferential, or at least that the evidence of sensory appearances must be inferential. But although these assumptions are pretheoretically plausible and even widely accepted, this is not how perceptual knowledge works. An adequate theory of knowledge and evidence should show why this is so, explaining how sensory appearances can act as evidential grounds for beliefs about the world, even if there is no good inference from appearance to reality.

Third, all refutations of skepticism that are pragmatic or rhetorical are also misguided. Since the problem of skepticism is not an existential one, pragmatic and rhetorical considerations regarding the skeptic's way of life, or her sanity, or her position in a debate are all out of place. What makes skepticism a philosophical problem is not that there are skeptical people, but that there are skeptical *arguments*. So long as those arguments proceed on assumptions and reasoning that seem plausible to us, they present a problem about how we are to rethink our previous opinions about knowledge and evidence. As such, skeptical arguments are not merely problems, but are also valuable methodological tools for driving us toward better epistemologies.

Finally, all of this means that Heidegger, Dewey, Rorty, and others are wrong about the legitimacy of epistemology's project. If skepticism is conceived as a philosophical problem – that is, as an argument that begins from plausible assumptions and ends in an unacceptable conclusion – then the only way to refute it is to challenge something essential to the argument and to replace it with something better. This is a legitimate philosophical enterprise, and it is exactly what epistemology tries to do. If, on the other hand, skepticism is conceived as an existential problem, then there is no problem. No one lives in the grip of skepticism – not even philosophers who proclaim themselves to be skeptics. For this reason there is no need for philosophical "therapy" in addressing skepticism. There is no existential sickness for therapy to cure.

5

The Argument from an Infinite Regress of Reasons

In the first four chapters I have been claiming that skeptical arguments play an important role in philosophical inquiry. Such arguments act as heuristic devices for driving positive epistemology in particular, as opposed to ontology or philosophy of mind. I mean this thesis to be both prescriptive and descriptive. On the one hand, I am claiming that skeptical arguments *ought* to play this methodological role. On the other, the claim is that such arguments *do in fact* play it. Nothing supports the descriptive thesis more than the literature on the skeptical argument from an infinite regress of reasons. That argument is beautifully simple, but it has inspired debate over the nature of knowledge and evidence for over two millennia.

1. THE REGRESS ARGUMENT AND STRONG PARTICULARISM

The problem arises because it seems that one must have good reasons for whatever one claims to know. But not any reason is a good reason; one must have reasons for thinking that one's reasons are true. Accordingly, it seems that knowledge requires (*per impossibile*) an infinite regress of reasons. An early version of the argument is attributed to the ancient skeptic, Pyrrho. The passage quoted next is taken from Sextus Empiricus's discussion of Agrippa's five skeptical modes leading to the suspension of judgment. Agrippa, in turn, was systemizing the skeptical teachings of Pyrrho.[1]

---

[1] For an excellent discussion of Agrippa's "Five Modes" and their relationship to contemporary theories of knowledge, see Fogelin, *Pyrrhonian Reflections on Knowledge and Justification*, esp. Part II.

The Mode based on the extension to infinity is the one in which we say that the proof offered for the verification of a proposed matter requires a further verification, and this one another, and so on to infinity, so that since we lack a point of departure for our reasoning, the consequence is suspension of judgement. (Sextus Empiricus, *Outlines of Pyrrhonism*, 1.15)

A similar problem is found in Plato's *Theaetetus*. Socrates is considering the definition of knowledge as "true opinion, combined with definition or rational explanation" and raises the problem of where an explanation might end. Here Socrates recounts something he heard in a "dream":

But none of the primeval elements can be defined; whereas the things which are compounded of them, as they themselves are complex, are defined by a combination of names, for the combination of names is the essence of a definition. Thus, then, the elements or letters are only objects of sense perception, and cannot be defined or known; but the syllables or combinations of them are known and expressed, and are apprehended by true opinion. When, therefore, any one forms the true opinion of anything without rational explanation, you may say that his mind is truly exercised, but has no knowledge; for he who cannot give and receive a reason for a thing, has no knowledge of that thing; but when he adds a rational explanation, then, he is perfected in knowledge and may be all that I have been denying of him. (202b–c)

In Plato's terms, the problem is that knowledge seems to require a rational explanation, but no explanation is possible with the "primeval elements." Eventually Socrates seems to endorse a kind of foundationalism, insisting that the "simple elements" are known even though they are not susceptible to further explanation:

Then, if we argue from the letters and syllables of which we have experience to other simples and compounds, we shall say that the letters or simple elements as a class are much more distinctly known than the syllables, and much more indispensable to a perfect knowledge of any subject; and if someone says that the syllable is known and the letter unknown, we shall consider that either intentionally or unintentionally he is talking nonsense? (206b)

The problem is more clearly articulated by Aristotle in the *Posterior Analytics*, and he more clearly opts for foundationalism:

Some people think that because you must understand the primitives there is no understanding at all; others that there is, but that there are demonstrations of everything. Neither of these views is either true or necessary.

The one party, supposing that you cannot understand in any other way, claim that we are led back *ad infinitum* on the ground that we shall not understand the posterior items because of the prior items if there are no primitives. And they are right – for it is impossible to survey infinitely many items. And if things come to a stop and there are principles, then these, they say, are unknowable since there is no *demonstration* of them and this is the only kind of understanding there is. . . .

The other party agree about understanding, which, they say, arises only through demonstration, But they argue that nothing prevents there being demonstrations of everything; for it is possible for demonstrations to proceed in a circle or reciprocally.

We assert that not all understanding is demonstrative: rather, in the case of immediate items understanding is indemonstrable. And it is clear that this must be so; for if you must understand the items which are prior and from which the demonstration proceeds, and if things come to a stop at some point, then these immediates must be indemonstrable. (*Posterior Analytics*, Book Alpha, Chapter 3)

In these passages the problem is put in terms of giving "proofs," "rational explanations," and "demonstrations." Accordingly, these historical formulations might be criticized for setting the requirements for knowledge too high. Alternatively, someone might think that the arguments do not threaten knowledge at all, since they are directed at "understanding," or *scientia,* or some other property requiring stronger conditions than knowledge does.[2] But either of these responses would miss the real force of the skeptical reasoning being considered. The central theme that drives the regress argument is that positive epistemic status *in general* requires being based on good evidence. To put the idea another way: anything that counts as knowledge (or understanding, or *scientia)* must be believed on the basis of good reasons for thinking that the thing in question is true. Accordingly, the infinite regress argument can be reconstructed as follows:

(IR)   1. To know that something is true one must believe it on the basis of good reasons, or reasons that indicate that the thing is likely to be true.
            2. But not any reason is a good reason. Good reasons themselves must be backed up by good reasons for thinking that they are true, which reasons will in turn be in need of further good reasons.

---

2   For a position along these lines, see Eleonore Stump, "Aquinas on the Foundations of Knowledge," *Canadian Journal of Philosophy,* supplementary volume 17 (1992): 125–158.

3. Therefore, to know that something is true one must believe it on the basis of an infinite number of good reasons. (1,2)
4. No human is capable of basing her belief on an infinite number of reasons.
5. Therefore, knowledge (for humans) is impossible. (3,4)

When we understand the argument this way it is a powerful one, for it depends only on premises that are initially plausible and reasoning that is seemingly valid. Moreover, the argument is directed at knowledge in the ordinary sense. Premise (1) says that knowledge must be based on good evidence – a platitude in most circles and true by definition in some. Premise (2) makes the plausible claim that not anything counts as a good reason or good evidence. Presumably one must have some good reason for thinking that one's evidence is true. But since the question regarding the value of one's evidence can be raised at each level of supporting reasons, it would seem to follow that an infinite number of reasons is required to ground a knowledge-claim. Premise (4) points out that human cognition is incapable of such a feat, and the skeptical conclusion follows from there straightaway. Something in argument (IR) must be wrong, but it is not obvious what it is. As we will see, refuting (IR) requires taking substantive positions regarding the nature of knowledge and evidence.

It should be clear at this point that (IR) is immune to dismissive responses to skepticism. Pragmatic and rhetorical responses are irrelevant here for the same reasons they were irrelevant regarding skepticism about the world. The skeptical problem represented in (IR) has nothing to do with how we should speak or act, and therefore cannot be solved by making pragmatic or rhetorical points. Rather, (IR) takes assumptions that are initially plausible – in the sense that they would be accepted by nearly anyone pre-theoretically – and shows that those assumptions lead to a total skepticism about human knowledge. The only way to solve that kind of problem is to find something in the argument to reject.

It is also clear that (IR) does not trade on unrealistically high standards for knowledge. Nothing like absolute certainty is being required, for the argument insists only that our evidence makes it likely that our knowledge-claims are true. That is hardly a high standard. For the same reason it is also clear that deduction is not being required. Sextus and Aristotle talk in terms of "proof" and "demonstration," but nothing in the skeptical reasoning requires that the argument be put that way. The requirement that knowledge be based on inductive evidence issues in the regress just as effectively, and so deduction has nothing to do with it.

Finally, it is worth mentioning that (IR) does not depend on a modern ontology. Nothing whatsoever in (IR) makes use of one ontology over another, and therefore the idea that skepticism about the world depends on Cartesianism is refuted by that point alone. The scope of (IR) is total skepticism rather than skepticism about the world, but the narrower kind of skepticism follows from the broader. Accordingly, if a completely general skepticism does not depend on a modern ontology, then skepticism about the world does not either.

With dismissive responses aside, we are now in a position to consider non-dismissive challenges to the regress argument. The three most important positions that have been taken in response to (IR) are foundationalism, coherentism, and contextualism. Foundationalism is the position that some things are known even though they are not believed on the basis of justifying reasons. As such, foundationalism denies premise (1) of (IR). Foundationalism also denies (2), since within a foundationalist framework "basic" or non-inferred knowledge can also serve as good evidence for knowledge that is inferred from the foundations. Coherentism accepts premises (1) and (2) but rejects the reasoning to (3). The idea is that although all knowledge must be based on good reasons, there is no implication of an infinite regress since justifying reasons can be in a relation of mutual support. This relation is called "coherence," with different versions of coherentism spelling out the nature of the relation in different ways.

A third response to (IR) is contextualism. The central thesis of contextualism is that the requirement for further good reasons depends on context. For example, in normal situations a person can know that there are two sleeping cats in the room merely by seeing each cat separately and then inferring that there are at least two. What is not required is that the person have further good reasons for thinking that each individual cat is there – it is enough in a normal context just to see them. On the other hand, we can imagine other contexts where seeing each cat would not be enough. If one were visiting a taxidermist, for example, one would need further reasons for thinking she sees individual living cats rather than individually stuffed cat skins. In different contexts, different beliefs will be contextually basic.

Contextualism therefore heads off an infinite regress of reasons by allowing a stopping point at beliefs that are contextually basic. But a question arises whether contextually basic beliefs are themselves cases of knowledge. Contextualists have come down on both sides of the issue. If the position is that such beliefs are knowledge, then contextualism denies both premises (1) and (2) of the skeptical argument. If the position is that these beliefs are not knowledge, then contextualism denies only premise (2).

Below we will look more closely at each of these various positions. But at this point I want to emphasize that all three are driven by consideration of the regress argument. Foundationalists, coherentists, and contextualists all think that their position is necessary to avoid something like (IR), confirming that the analysis of skeptical arguments can and does drive positive epistemological theory.

We have already seen that Aristotle's foundationalism is a direct response to the problem of an infinite regress. The same is less clear in Plato, although he seems to follow a similar dialectic, embracing foundationalism rather than admitting that "compounds" are known whereas their "simple elements" are unknown. In this respect Plato and Aristotle have been followed by many over the centuries. In the following passage Chisholm endorses foundationalism as the correct response to the regress problem:

In many instances the answers to our questions will take the following form: "What justifies me in thinking that I know a is F is the fact that it is evident to me that b is G." For example, "What justifies me in thinking I know that he has that disorder is the fact that it is evident to me that he has those symptoms." . . .

We might try to continue *ad infinitum*, justifying each new claim that we elicit by still another claim. Or we might be tempted to complete a vicious circle: in such a case, having justified "a is F" by appeal to "b is G," and "b is G" by reference to "c is H," we would then justify "c is H" by reference to "a is F." But if we are rational beings, we will do neither of these things. For we will find that our Socratic question leads us to a proper stopping place.[3]

Not only foundationalists are driven by the regress argument. Consider the following passage from the coherentist Laurence BonJour.

The main watershed which divides the [coherentist theory of knowledge] from opposing epistemological views is a familiar problem which I shall call "the regress problem." This problem arises directly out of the justification condition of the traditional explication of knowledge as adequately justified true belief. The most obvious way in which beliefs are justified is *inferential justification*. In

---

3 Chisholm, *Theory of Knowledge*, 2nd ed., pp. 18–19.

its most explicit form, inferential justification consists in providing an argument from one or more other beliefs as premises to the justificandum belief as a conclusion. But it is obviously a necessary condition for inferential justification that the beliefs appealed to as premises be themselves *already* justified in some fashion; that a belief follows from unjustified premises lends it no justification. Now the premise-beliefs might also be justified inferentially, but such justification would only introduce further premise-beliefs which would have to be justified in some way, thus leading apparently to an infinite, vicious regress of epistemic justification. . . . Any adequate epistemological position must provide a solution to this problem, a way of avoiding the skeptical result – and the character of that solution will determine, more than anything else, the basic structure of the position.[4]

Finally, David Annis contends that his contextualism is an alternative to foundationalist and coherentist responses to the regress argument.

Philosophers who have accepted foundationalism have generally offered a version of the infinite regress argument in support of it. Two key premises in the argument are the denial of a coherence theory of justification and the denial that an infinite sequence of reasons is sufficient to justify a belief. But there is another option to the conclusion of the argument besides foundationalism. A contextualist theory of the sort offered above stops the regress and yet does not require basic statements in the foundationalist's sense.[5]

These passages show that foundationalism, coherentism, and contextualism are offered quite explicitly as solutions to the regress argument. As such the literature on this debate offers a clear confirmation that the analysis of skeptical arguments drives positive epistemology. The dialectic at work here is that theorists assume that there must be some mistake in the argument. A particular theory is then offered as explaining exactly where the argument goes wrong. Moreover, it is not uncommon for philosophers to argue against an alternative solution on the grounds that it does not really avoid skepticism. In the following passage Goldman criticizes BonJour's coherentism for placing unrealistic demands on knowledge and therefore having unacceptable skeptical results:

It should be clear on reflection that this is a severely unrealistic demand. It is most implausible to suppose that garden-variety perceptual beliefs and memory

---

4 BonJour, "The Coherence Theory of Empirical Knowledge," in Paul Moser, ed., *Empirical Knowledge* (Totowa, NJ: Rowman and Littlefield, 1986), p. 117. Reprinted from *Philosophical Studies* 30 (1976): 281–312.
5 David Annis, "A Contextualist Theory of Epistemic Justification," in Moser (1986), p. 208. Reprinted from *American Philosophical Quarterly* 15 (1978): 213–219.

beliefs are based on inferences from premises of the indicated sort. Yet we commonly impute knowledge and justification in these cases. Not only are very few beliefs actually based on such inferences, it seems likely that the only people who possess the relevant premise beliefs (or even possess the constituent concepts) are people with epistemological training and sophistication. It would therefore follow on BonJour's view that only these people are deserving subjects of the terms "knower" and "justified believer." But is it plausible to suggest that philosophical sophisticates are the only people with knowledge or justified belief?[6]

Here the assumption is that skepticism is false, and that therefore any theory of knowledge that has skeptical consequences, intended or otherwise, is also false.

In this regard Fogelin charges the literature on the regress argument with blatant question begging. According to Fogelin, it is not appropriate to assume that skepticism is false and then defend one's own position on that basis. But this, he says, is exactly what so many contemporary analytic philosophers do:

> The third success condition for a theory of epistemic justification is that it not beg the question against Pyrrhonism by making the argument depend on assuming its falsehood. It is remarkable how often epistemologists do this, quite explicitly, without a blush. The following specimen comes from Chisholm:
>
>> There is the Aristotelian argument to the effect that some of the things I am justified in believing are self-justifying. The argument is easier to ridicule than to refute. If my justification for accepting a certain proposition q requires me to go beyond and to appeal to a certain other proposition p, then I'm also justified in accepting q. Therefore these are the three possibilities; either there is an infinite regress; or there is a circle; or some propositions I'm justified in believing are self-justifying. But the first two of these three possibilities are inconsistent with the fact that I do know something. Therefore some propositions are self-justifying.
>
> The underlying assumption of this passage is that beliefs that we take to be justified already are justified. The task is to show how.[7]

He remarks,

---

6 Goldman, "BonJour's *The Structure of Empirical Knowledge*," in Bender (1989), p. 108. Several essays in Bender object to coherentism on the basis of psychological implausibility. See esp. Hilary Kornblith, "The Unattainability of Coherence," and James Bogen, "Coherentist Theories of Knowledge Don't Apply to Enough Outside of Science and Don't Give the Right Results."
7 Fogelin, p. 141. He quotes Chisholm, "Comments and Replies," *Philosophia* 7 (1978): 597–636, at p. 598.

This is a feature, expressed in various ways, of a great many contemporary theories of epistemic justification. *All* such theories beg the question against Pyrrhonism, and do so blatantly.[8]

But if so many epistemologists blatantly beg the question against skepticism, and without even a blush, then maybe Fogelin has missed what they are up to. My claim has been that charges of question begging are irrelevant in the context of analyzing skeptical arguments because there is no skeptic with whom we ought to be engaged in a debate, or against whom we have to be careful not to beg the question. Rather, the philosophers that Fogelin is criticizing are trying to give an adequate account of the nature of knowledge, and a condition of adequacy for such an account is that it explain our pre-theoretical intuitions about what does and does not count as knowledge. Since these intuitions are overwhelmingly non-skeptical, this means that an adequate account must avoid skepticism. That is why it makes perfect sense to look at the regress argument and to argue that one's position offers a solution to it, and why it makes perfect sense to point out that some alternative account does not.

In other words, what Fogelin is missing is contemporary epistemology's particularism. Philosophers like Chisholm quite explicitly adopt the methodological rule that epistemic theories ought to be consistent with what we pre-theoretically take ourselves to know.[9] Philosophers like Goldman quite explicitly add the rule that epistemic theories ought to be consistent with what we know empirically about our own cognitive capacities. As I have argued, these two methodological strategies are related, since any theory of knowledge that is psychologically implausible will generate skeptical results, and will therefore fail to capture our pre-theoretical intuition about what we do and do not know.

As we saw in Chapter 1, Fogelin would not admit that a skeptical position must fail to account for our pre-theoretical intuitions. According to him, our intuitions about what we know and do not know become unstable under the weight of skeptical reasoning, and a sophisticated skepticism is able to explain this very feature of our pre-theoretical judgments. In other words, a sophisticated skepticism carries

---

8 Fogelin, p. 143.
9 See Chisholm, "The Problem of the Criterion." See also *The Theory of Knowledge*, 2nd ed., p. 16: "We presuppose, first, that there *is* something that we know and we adopt the working hypothesis that *what* we know is pretty much that which, on reflection, we think we know. This may seem the wrong place to start. But where else *could* we start?"

with it an explanation of why we think we know in ordinary contexts, and why we tend to change our minds about this in the extraordinary contexts in which we take skeptical arguments seriously. But still, it seems to me that a non-skeptical theory that explains our intuitions remains overwhelmingly preferable, other things being equal. This is because a non-skeptical theory accounts for our common sense intuitions about what we know by showing that they are for the most part *true*. A skeptical theory accounts for those intuitions only by showing that they are false, and by adding an explanation about why we do not normally realize that they are false. Only a non-skeptical theory, therefore, explains the majority of our intuitions in a sense that *preserves* them. But if such a theory is preferable, then the methodological assumption that radical skepticism is false is warranted. For the purposes of theory construction we should assume that radical skepticism is false, and we should work out a position that entails this. This methodology is in fact implicit in the passages that I have quoted. When foundationalists and coherentists argue against other positions, they are not *merely* assuming that skepticism is false; rather, they are implicitly claiming that their own position accounts for our intuitions about knowledge successfully.

So far we have seen how foundationalism, coherentism, and contextualism can be understood as responses to the skeptical regress argument. Each of these positions assumes that a completely general skepticism is false, and that therefore something in the argument is wrong. Accordingly, each tries to identify exactly where the argument is mistaken, and to replace that mistake with a substantive thesis about the nature of knowledge and evidence. In the remainder of the chapter I argue that foundationalism provides the best account of knowledge in light of the regress argument.

More exactly, I argue that foundationalism provides the best account of *human* knowledge, or knowledge for beings with our kind of cognition. First, I argue that plausible versions of contextualism are best understood as a kind of foundationalism and therefore do not represent an alternative means of stopping the regress. Second, I argue that coherentism does represent an alternative to foundationalism, but that it is psychologically implausible as an account of knowledge for beings like us. The conclusion is that a contextualist version of foundationalism gives the only account of human knowledge that both avoids the regress argument and is psychologically plausible.

"Contextualist foundationalism" might sound like an oxymoron, but that is because critical treatments of foundationalism have failed to pay sufficient attention to what that theory is supposed to be about. In other words, foundationalism is supposed to be a response to the skeptical argument from an infinite regress of justifying reasons. As we have seen, the way that foundationalism does this is to posit beliefs that are known even though they are not backed up by further beliefs that act as their evidence. But nothing about stopping the regress of reasons this way requires that foundational beliefs be insensitive to context. Therefore, there is no legitimate reason to burden foundationalism with an absolutist or non-contextualist theory of evidence.

In Section 2, I look at foundationalism more closely and show how attention to (IR) reveals what is and is not required by a foundationalist response to the regress argument. In Section 3, I consider several versions of contextualism and argue that the plausible ones reduce to foundationalism. In Sections 4 through 7, I look at coherentism. The best-known objections raised against that position might be called *a priori*; they charge that, in principle, coherence is insufficient for justification and knowledge. However, I argue that coherentism falls to *a posteriori* objections, or objections to the effect that coherentism is psychologically implausible as an account of knowledge for beings like us. I end by drawing some conclusions.

2. FOUNDATIONALISM

The purpose of this section is to sketch the strategy that foundationalism employs to respond to argument (IR) and to give a preliminary defense of the position in the face of a few objections. However, my defense of foundationalism is only preliminary; there are many interesting objections to the position that I do not even consider. This is because my main concern is to show how attention to skeptical arguments can drive progress in epistemology. Accordingly, I restrict my attention to a certain class of objections: those that are ineffective against foundationalism precisely because they fail to attend to the skeptical reasoning to which foundationalism is supposed to be a response.

The central thesis of foundationalism is that some things are known even though they are not based on further justifying reasons. A second thesis is that foundational knowledge can be used as supporting evidence for other beliefs, thereby giving rise to non-foundational knowledge that *is* based on justifying reasons. As we have seen, this means that foundationalism denies premises (1) and (2) of (IR). What I want to do next is look more closely at the various ways that knowledge might be foundational. Traditionally, foundationalists have embraced four kinds of foundational knowledge.

a. Four Kinds of Foundation

i. First, some foundationalists have claimed that foundational knowledge may be based on states of awareness such as sensory or introspective experience. The idea is that foundational knowledge is based on evidence, but the evidence is experience rather than belief. The regress of justifying reasons is thereby ended, because experience is not a "reason" that in turn needs to be justified or made known by further reasons. This way of understanding foundational knowledge is sometimes called "givenism," presumably because experience is simply "given" to consciousness, without further need for justifying grounds.
ii. Some philosophers have held that knowledge is foundational due to the *way* in which it is believed. For example, Descartes thought that any proposition that is clearly and distinctly conceived amounts to certain knowledge. Such beliefs are sometimes called "self-justifying" or "self-evident," because they are justified or evident, but not on the basis of any further belief or experience.
iii. Some foundationalists have claimed that beliefs may constitute foundational knowledge in virtue of their being of a certain intrinsically specified kind. Thus it has been claimed that beliefs about one's current mental states are foundational.
iv. Finally, some beliefs have been considered foundational by virtue of their external relationship to truth. For example, historically it has been claimed that infallible beliefs qualify as foundational knowledge. More recently it has been claimed that beliefs that are formed in highly reliable ways are thereby justified and can even amount to knowledge. If the way in which such a belief is formed does not involve further beliefs that serve as its evidence, then the belief would qualify as foundational.

Notice that any of these four strategies for understanding foundational knowledge would provide an adequate basis for rejecting (IR). Each is such that, if it is correct, then premises (1) and (2) of (IR) are false. This is because each describes a way in which a belief can amount to knowledge even though that belief is not based on further reasons acting as its evidence. But then not all knowledge must be based on further reasons, and not all reasons are in need of further reasons for their own justification.

b. Objections

There have been many objections to foundationalism, but by far the most common is that foundational beliefs are impossible. More specifically, a great amount of time and energy has been spent showing that no beliefs are absolutely certain, or infallible, or incorrigible, or indubitable, or irrevisable. But this kind of objection is easily dismissed if we understand foundationalism as a response to the regress argument. For nothing in the foundationalist strategy for stopping the regress requires that foundational beliefs be absolutely certain, or infallible, or incorrigible, or indubitable, or irrevisable. What is required is that some knowledge not be based on further beliefs that act as its evidence. It is also required that this foundational knowledge can act as evidence for further knowledge. But that's it. There is nothing associated with stopping the regress that requires the high-powered epistemic properties just mentioned and commonly invoked in critiques of foundationalism.[10]

Why have so many philosophers missed this point? One reason, I suggest, is that they have misconceived the project of epistemology and therefore the motivation for foundationalism as well. If the project of epistemology were to prove to the skeptic that knowledge is possible, then the requirement that foundational knowledge be infallible, or incorrigible, or indubitable might make sense. The idea would be that we need premises that not even a skeptic could intelligibly deny, and that we need to show how the remaining knowledge we have can be based on those unchallengeable premises. But we have seen that it is a misconceived enterprise to offer proofs to skeptics. Similar things can be said about engaging skeptics in debate. If this were epistemology's project, then, again, the quest for absolutely certain foundations might make sense. But we should not be engaging skeptics in debate any more than we should be offering them proofs. It is not a misconceived enterprise, however, to investigate how knowledge must be structured to avoid the problem of an infinite regress of reasons. This is one important aspect of constructing an adequate theory of knowledge, which is the real project of epistemology and the one in which foundationalists, coherentists, and contextualists alike are engaged.

---

10 Similar points are made by William Alston in "Has Foundationalism Been Refuted?", *Philosophical Studies* 29 (1976): 287–305, and by Laurence BonJour in "Can Empirical Knowledge Have a Foundation?", *American Philosophical Quarterly* 15 (1978): 1–13. See also Robert Audi, *The Structure of Justification* (Cambridge: Cambridge University Press, 1993).

A second major objection to foundationalism is that there are not enough foundational beliefs to support all of the knowledge that we have. Even if some beliefs are infallible, or incorrigible, or indubitable, and so forth, there are not enough of these to act as evidence for knowledge that is not in the foundations. The answer to the first objection, however, answers this one as well. Since the foundations of knowledge can be understood much more broadly than both objections assume, there is no reason to think that there will not be enough foundational beliefs to do the job. Beliefs based on sensory appearances, for example, will be plentiful if givenism can be made to work.

Of course, such beliefs would not be plentiful if they had to be *about* sensory appearances. We have already seen that it is psychologically implausible that we typically have beliefs about how things appear to us via the senses. But once we give up requirements like infallibility and incorrigibility there is no reason to think that beliefs based on sensory appearances must be about sensory appearances. It is more plausible that appearances give rise directly to perceptual beliefs about *objects in the world*, making fallible beliefs about material objects rather than infallible beliefs about appearances foundational. This account of perception is consistent with the theories of evidence that we considered in Chapter 4, and if it is correct, then there would be no shortage of foundational perceptual knowledge. An account of perception and perceptual evidence along these lines is further developed in Chapters 7 and 9.

3. CONTEXTUALISM

We have noted that the central thesis of contextualism is that the need for good reasons is context dependent, so that different beliefs are contextually basic in different situations. As such, contextualism denies at least premise (2) of argument (IR). We also noted that there are two major kinds of contextualism, depending on whether contextually basic beliefs are themselves considered to be instances of knowledge. Let us call the position that basic beliefs are not knowledge "type 1" contextualism, and the position that they are knowledge "type 2" contextualism. Type 2 contextualism denies premise (1) of (IR) as well.

The position that contextually basic beliefs are *not* knowledge is suggested by Ludwig Wittgenstein in *On Certainty*. The idea is that knowledge and other epistemic concepts are essentially tied to the practice of giving reasons for one's claims, or at least being able to do so. But then concepts like knowledge and justification are simply out of place where a belief is contextually basic. In such a case there will be nothing to appeal to as a reason. This interpretation of Wittgenstein is endorsed by Marie McGinn:

> The second criticism Wittgenstein makes of the traditional epistemologist's use of the words "I know" concerns the connection between knowing and giving grounds. Our use of the expression "I know" is, he claims, connected 'in grammar' with the possibility of saying *how* we know, and hence with the possibility of stating the *grounds* on the basis of which our claim to know is made.[11]

In support of the position, McGinn quotes Wittgenstein:

> One says "I know" when one is ready to give compelling grounds. "I know" relates to the possibility of demonstrating the truth. (*On Certainty*, # 243)

Wittgenstein holds that knowledge rests on a foundation, but not an epistemic foundation. The reason the foundation is not epistemic is that concepts such as knowledge and justification apply only to beliefs that are based on reasons or grounds. Or, as Wittgenstein writes,

> What we have here is a foundation for all my action. But it seems to me that it is wrongly expressed by the words "I know." (Ibid., # 414)

The Wittgenstein–McGinn position has some plausibility as a thesis about the way certain expressions are used. It is not implausible that when one uses the expression "I know" one implies that one is ready to give good grounds. Moreover, epistemic terms such as "reasonable," "justified," and "evident" are closely connected to having reasons, giving justifications, and offering evidence. But these verbal points should not be allowed to mask a more fundamental issue, which is whether contextually basic beliefs must have some sort of positive epistemic status to play their grounding role. Whatever we call it, it seems that there would have to be some feature of contextually basic beliefs that makes them fit to serve as reasons or evidence or justifications for other beliefs.[12]

Consider that not just anything counts as a contextually basic belief, even for Wittgenstein and McGinn. McGinn argues with Wittgenstein that what makes a belief contextually basic is its special role in the language game rather than its epistemic certainty.

---

11   Marie McGinn, *Sense and Certainty* (Oxford: Blackwell, 1989), p. 109.
12   Sosa makes this point forcefully in *Knowledge in Perspective*, p. 89.

These judgements are absolutely secure, but not in the sense that they are 'intrinsically certain,' as this is understood by the traditional epistemologist. Our conviction in them is not properly conceived as epistemic certainty regarding the truth of empirical propositions, for which the question of justification must inevitably arise, but as the immediate exercise of our practical mastery of our techniques for describing the world, for which the question of justification makes no sense.

Whatever the merits of this account of basicality, the relevant point here is that there must be *something* that distinguishes beliefs that are appropriately basic in a given context from beliefs that are not; there must be something that gives some beliefs but not others their epistemic efficacy, so to speak. But once this point is clearly understood, what is left to the claim that contextually basic beliefs are not known or epistemically justified? If the point is just a verbal one about the terms "known" and "justified," then it does not address the substantive issue at hand. But if the point is that such beliefs have no positive epistemic status whatsoever, then it is implausible. Perceptual beliefs that describe the world around me and that are used as evidence for believing other things are superior in epistemic status to flightful fancies and wild guesses. That is why they *can* be used as evidence for believing other things, while fancies and guesses cannot.

Versions of contextualism that deprive contextually basic beliefs of positive epistemic status are therefore implausible. Once the issue is clearly put, it appears that the contextualist should say that basic beliefs do have positive epistemic status, although their having such depends on the context in which a given belief arises. This is what I called type 2 contextualism.

This second position is explicitly endorsed by Annis. According to his version of contextualism, a central issue of justification is whether a believer is capable of answering relevant objections. Second, justification is relativized to an "issue-context," which determines both the level of understanding required of the believer and the persons whose objections must be answerable. Without going into the details, a belief is contextually basic on this view so long as it evokes no relevant objections. The idea is that after a point all legitimate objections will be met and the regress of reasons appropriately ends at that point. But since this stopping place is partly determined by context, Annis's view is rightly considered a version of contextualism.[13]

---

13 Annis, "A Contextualist Theory."

A different version of type 2 contextualism is implicitly endorsed by Rorty. In a passage where he is arguing against foundationalism Rorty writes the following:

> There is, to be sure, a place for the notion of "direct knowledge." This is simply knowledge which is had without its possessor having gone through any conscious inference. But there is no suggestion that some entities are especially well suited to be known in this way. What we know noninferentially is a matter of what we are familiar with. Some people (those who sit in front of cloud-chambers) are familiar with, and make noninferential reports of, elementary particles. Others are familiar with diseases of trees, and can report "another case of Dutch elm disease" without performing any inferences.[14]

Rorty's contextualism is different from Annis's. It does not centrally involve the ability to answer relevant objections, but instead trades on a notion of familiarity that Rorty does not spell out. But clearly Rorty thinks that some beliefs are contextually basic in the sense in which we have been understanding that notion: some beliefs are known even though they are not inferred from other beliefs, and their status as knowledge depends on contextual features.

Again, I am not interested here in either the details or the merits of these accounts. Rather, the question I want to raise is why type 2 contextualism is not foundationalism. Both Annis and Rorty present their views in opposition to foundationalism, but it seems to me that their views are versions of foundationalism rather than alternatives to it.

To see the point, recall the way that foundationalism was defined. Since foundationalism is a response to the regress argument, we defined it in relation to that argument, saying that the central theses of the position are the denial of premises (1) and (2) of (IR). More explicitly, foundationalism is the position that some things are known not on the basis of inferences from further reasons, and that such foundational knowledge can act as reasons that allow other things to be known. I propose that the present brand of contextualism answers the regress argument in exactly the same way and therefore constitutes a version of foundationalism. Contextualist versions of foundationalism simply add the thesis that whether a belief is foundational depends on contextual features.[15]

Critics of foundationalism might accuse me of abusing terminology; they might insist that foundationalism has never been understood so that

---

14 *Philosophy and the Mirror of Nature*, p. 106.
15 For a similar assessment of Rorty, see Sosa, *Knowledge in Perspective*, p. 93.

foundational beliefs can be determined by context. Thus Michael Williams writes,

> For foundationalism, a judgement derives its epistemological status from some highly abstract feature of the content of the proposition it contains.... Given foundationalism, we might as well talk about basic propositions as about basic judgements (expressed by propositions advanced in particular circumstances). But if Wittgenstein is right, the distinction is crucial: a terminating judgement derives its status from its context, and not just from its content.... Whatever the merits of this response to the regress, it is nothing like traditional foundationalism.
>
> The contrast we have just noted provides the first hint of what I shall claim to be foundationalism's decisive feature, its commitment to a strongly realistic conception of epistemic relations. For the foundationalist, there are relations of epistemic priority that hold between propositions independently of the circumstances in which those propositions are advanced, the interests that govern their assessment, or any other such "contextual" factors.[16]

But as I have already argued, there is no legitimate motivation for burdening foundationalism with theses that are irrelevant to stopping the regress of reasons. In Williams' terminology, there is no good motivation for saddling foundationalism with epistemic realism. There is simply nothing in the logic of the foundationalist strategy for stopping the regress that requires a "realist" position.[17]

Annis seems to recognize this point when he defines foundationalism at the beginning of his essay:

> Foundationalism is the theory that every empirical statement which is justified ultimately must derive at least some of its justification from a special class of basic statements which have at least some degree of justification independent of the support such statements may derive from other statements. Such *minimal* foundationalism does not require certainty or incorrigibility; it does not deny the revisability of *all* statements, and it allows an important role for intrasystematic justification or coherence.[18]

But for some reason Annis fails to recognize that, by his own definition, his contextualism is a version of foundationalism.

---

16 Williams, *Unnatural Doubts*, p. 67.
17 Williams makes a distinction between formal and substantive foundationalism, where only the latter is committed to epistemic realism. However, he does not use the distinction to make the present point; rather, his discussion of the relationship between foundationalism and skepticism focuses on substantive foundationalism. See *Unnatural Doubts*, esp. pp. 114–121.
18 Annis, "A Contextualist Theory," p. 203.

I now want to take the point a step further. Specifically, I want to challenge the notion that there has ever been a foundationalist who was not also a contextualist. I take Descartes as my test case, since he is usually the whipping boy for critics of foundationalism. In the *Meditations* Descartes claims that only what is certain amounts to knowledge. Some things are known for certain immediately, insofar as they are clearly and distinctly conceived by the light of reason, whereas others must be demonstrated from what it known immediately. We therefore have a classic foundationalist structure, with non-inferential knowledge acting as a basis for inferential knowledge. But Descartes says quite explicitly that whether something is conceived clearly and distinctly depends on context, as does whether something is known immediately.

And although amongst the matters which I conceive of in this way, some indeed are manifestly obvious to all, while others only manifest themselves to those who consider them closely and examine them attentively; still, after they have once been discovered, the latter are not esteemed as any less certain than the former. . . . And as regards God, if my mind were not pre-occupied with prejudices, and if my thought did not find itself on all hands diverted by the continual pressure of sensible things, there would be nothing which I could know more immediately and more easily than Him. (Meditation V, *Meditations*, p. 183)

Descartes thinks that whether something is known immediately depends on contextual features such as prior training, degree of attention applied, the influence of prejudices, and the presence of distractions. What this shows is that the real issue is not *whether* there are contextual factors involved in the determination of basic beliefs, but *which* contextual factors are involved. Different versions of contextualism try to give an adequate account of exactly this issue. Moreover, no version of foundationalism ignores context entirely, not even the extreme rationalism of Descartes. We may conclude, therefore, that type 2 contextualism reduces to foundationalism.

4. COHERENTISM

The alternative to foundationalism is not contextualism but coherentism. According to that position, the regress of justifying reasons is not infinite because reasons can stand in a relationship of mutual support or "coherence." Accordingly, coherentism accepts premises (1) and (2) of argument (IR) but it rejects the move to (3); even though all knowledge must be supported by justifying reasons, no infinite regress is entailed.

Coherence theories may be divided into two kinds, according to how a given theory fills in the details regarding the coherence relation. Traditional coherence theories understand that relation in terms of the usual inference relations recognized by logicians and other philosophers, foundationalists included. Thus coherence is defined in terms of deductive and inductive inference relations, including, for example, inferences to the best explanation. A leading advocate of this kind of theory has been BonJour.[19] Nontraditional coherence theories develop some alternative account of coherence. In recent years examples of this kind of theory have been provided by Keith Lehrer.[20]

The two best-known objections to coherentism are (a) that highly coherent belief systems can nevertheless be isolated from reality and (b) that there are a multiplicity of equally coherent systems with no nonarbitrary means of choosing among them. These may be called *a priori* objections to coherentism, since they are objections to the effect that, in principle, coherence relations cannot give rise to knowledge or justified belief. Coherentists have been much occupied with objections of this kind. However, I will not be concerned with them here. Rather, I want to argue that coherentism falls to *a posteriori* objections, or objections that coherentism cannot give an adequate account of knowledge and justified belief for beings with our cognition.

I argue that the coherentist position in general is threatened by the following line of objection: Traditional coherence theories hold that inference always figures into the justification of belief, and so such theories must claim (implausibly) that even perceptual beliefs are inferentially justified. Nontraditional theories hold that traditional inferences never play a role in justification, and so must deny (implausibly) that making a correct inference ever makes a difference. Finally, no kind of coherence theory can give an adequate account of the role of sensory appearances in perceptual knowledge. Because coherence theories allow only other beliefs to serve as evidential grounds, coherence theories must misdescribe the way that appearances ground perceptual knowledge.

---

19 See BonJour, "The Coherence Theory of Empirical Knowledge," and *The Structure of Empirical Knowledge* (Cambridge, MA: Harvard University Press, 1985).
20 See, e.g., Keith Lehrer, "The Coherence Theory of Knowledge," *Philosophical Topics* 14 (1986): 5–25, and Lehrer, "Coherence and the Truth Connection: A Reply to My Critics," in Bender (1989).

According to this line of objection, there may be nothing wrong with coherence theories in principle. Rather, coherence theories fail to provide an empirically adequate account of human knowledge. Some human knowledge is inferential and some is not, and human perceptual knowledge is grounded directly on sensory appearances rather than belief.

5. THE OBJECTION TO TRADITIONAL COHERENCE THEORIES

In the following sections we will be pursuing the argument that coherentism is psychologically implausible. But since different kinds of coherentism are implausible in different ways, it will be necessary to consider traditional and nontraditional theories separately.

The following passage from BonJour indicates that he conceives of the coherence relation in terms of traditionally accepted inference relations.

> What, then, is coherence? Intuitively, coherence is a matter of how well a body of beliefs "hangs together": how well its component beliefs fit together, agree or dovetail with each other, so as to produce an organized, tightly structured system of beliefs, rather than either a helter-skelter collection or a set of conflicting sub-systems. It is reasonably clear that this "hanging together" depends on the various sorts of inferential, evidential, and explanatory relations which obtain among the various members of the system of beliefs, and especially on the more holistic and systematic of these. Thus various detailed investigations by philosophers and logicians of such topics as explanation, confirmation, probability, and so on, may reasonably be taken to provide some of the ingredients for a general account of coherence.[21]

BonJour's view is therefore an example of a traditional coherence theory. The objection I want to raise against this kind of theory is summed up by John Pollock's observation that perception is not inference. The problem for such theories is that at least some of our beliefs are both non-inferential and justified, but according to traditional coherence theories all beliefs having positive epistemic status get it by being inferentially supported by other beliefs. In the following passage Pollock considers the proposal that his perceptual belief that a book on his table is red depends for its justification on an inference from reasons:

---

21 BonJour, *The Structure of Empirical Knowledge*, p. 93.

The trouble with this proposal is that there are no plausible candidates for such a reason. What could such a reason be? One suggestion I have heard is that our reason is the second-order belief that we believe the book to be red, but the claim that we ordinarily have such second-order beliefs is no more plausible than the foundationalist claim that we ordinarily have appearance beliefs. Furthermore, what could our reason be for the second-order belief? . . . The general difficulty is that perception is not inference. When I believe on the basis of perception that the book is red, I do not infer that belief from something else I believe. Perception is a causal process that inputs beliefs into our doxastic system without their being inferred from or justified on the basis of other beliefs we already have.[22]

BonJour's strategy for avoiding this kind of objection is to show just how inferential justification for perceptual beliefs proceeds. BonJour asks what sort of inferential justification might be available for the perceptual belief that there is a red book on the table:

First, the belief in question is a visual belief, i.e. it is produced by my sense of sight; and I am, or at least can be, introspectively aware of this fact. Second, the conditions of observation are of a specifiable sort: the lighting is good, my eyes are functioning normally, and there are no interfering circumstances; and again, I know or can know these facts about the conditions, via other observations and introspections. Finally, it is a true law about me (and indeed about a large class of relevantly similar observers) that my spontaneous visual beliefs in such conditions about that sort of subject matter (viz., medium-sized physical objects) are highly reliable, i.e. very likely to be true; and, once more, I know this law.[23]

These observations suggest to BonJour the following general account of inferential justification for perceptual beliefs:

(i) I have a spontaneous belief that P (about subject-matter S) which is an instance of kind K.
(ii) Spontaneous beliefs about S which are instances of K are very likely to be true, if conditions C are satisfied.
(iii) Conditions C are satisfied.

Therefore, my belief that P is (probably) true.
Therefore, (probably) P.[24]

Several comments are in order. First, it would seem that to be justified in believing P via premises (i) through (iii), one must be justified in

---

22 Pollock, *Contemporary Theories of Knowledge*, p. 75.
23 BonJour *The Structure of Empirical Knowledge*, p. 291.
24 Ibid., p. 295.

believing each of the three premises. It is not enough, as BonJour suggests, that the person "can be" introspectively aware, or that she "can know" that the premises obtain. One reason is that evidence can do me good only if I use it, and I cannot use it unless I am already aware of it. Another reason is that evidence-beliefs cannot give rise to justification unless they enjoy positive epistemic status themselves. For example, if I am just guessing that the postcard in my mailbox is from you, then that hardly allows me to know that you are in Paris. This is so even if I "can know" that it is from you just by looking more closely.

Second, premises cannot give rise to justification unless the person actually makes the relevant inference; the mere availability of a justifying inference is not enough to give a belief positive epistemic status. If I know how many apples and how many oranges are in the refrigerator, but I have not put two and two together, then I do not know how many fruits are in there. Third, it is extremely implausible that we are justified in believing the relevant premises or that we make the relevant inference every time we are justified in some perceptual belief. As we have already noted, typically we believe no such premises and make no such inference.

These considerations are sufficient to illustrate the problem inherent in any theory that conceives coherence in terms of traditional inference relations. Any such theory must give an implausible account of perceptual knowledge, since it is implausible that perceptual beliefs are inferred from premises about sensory appearances, or from premises about the conditions in which perceptual beliefs are formed, or from anything else.

6. THE OBJECTION TO NONTRADITIONAL COHERENCE THEORIES

An example of a nontraditional coherence theory is provided by Lehrer's position in "The Coherence Theory of Knowledge." According to Lehrer, knowledge depends on "complete justification," which in turn involves both an objective and a subjective element. Each of these elements is understood in terms of coherence with a certain system of beliefs. More specifically, S is personally (subjectively) justified in accepting that p if and only if p coheres with the acceptance system of S. S is verifically (objectively) justified in accepting that p if and only if p coheres with the verific system of S.[25] S's acceptance system corresponds

---

25 Lehrer, "The Coherence Theory of Knowledge," p. 6.

roughly to those propositions that S accepts for the purposes of obtaining truth and eschewing error. S's verific system is obtained by deleting falsehoods from S's acceptance system.

Next Lehrer defines the key idea of coherence in terms of the undefined locution "it is more reasonable for S to accept that p on the assumption that c than to accept q on the assumption that d on the basis of system A." The central intuitive idea is that "something coheres with a system of a person if it is more reasonable to accept it than to accept anything with which it conflicts on the basis of the system."[26] This intuitive idea is made explicit by means of the following definitions:

p competes with q for S on the basis of system A if and only if it is more reasonable for S to accept p on the assumption that not q than on the assumption that q on the basis of system A.

p beats q for S on the basis of system A if and only if p competes with q for S on the basis of system A and it is more reasonable for S to accept p than to accept q on the basis of system A.

n neutralizes q as a competitor of p for S on the basis of system A if and only if q competes with p for S on the basis of system A, and n is such that the conjunction of q and n does not compete with p for S on the basis of system A when it is as reasonable for S to accept the conjunction of q and n as to accept q alone on the basis of system A.

Lehrer then defines the coherence relation as follows:

p coheres with the system A of S if and only if, for every q that competes with p for S on the basis of the system A, q is either beaten or neutralized for S on the basis of the system A.[27]

It is clear that on Lehrer's account coherence is not understood in terms of the inference relations commonly recognized by traditional theories of knowledge. In place of the familiar inference relations of deduction and induction Lehrer defines coherence in terms of his technical notions of competition and neutralization. Accordingly, Lehrer's theory is what I have called a nontraditional coherence theory.

The objection I want to raise against nontraditional theories like Lehrer's is that they cannot account for inferential knowledge. More exactly, we know some things *because* we infer them from other things we know. But nontraditional coherence theories do not recognize a justificatory role for traditional inferences.

26 Ibid., p. 9.   27 Ibid., pp. 10–11.

An example from Wayne Davis and John Bender will help to illustrate the problem:

Consider an acceptance system containing the following propositions.

(1) All and only those with at least a 90 on a prelim get an A on it.
(2) All and only those with an A on every prelim are exempt from the final.
(3) I got at least a 93 on every prelim.
(4) I got an A on every prelim.
(5) I am exempt from the final.

On Lehrer's theory, any subject with such an acceptance system is justified in accepting (5), as long as the propositions are all true for that subject. For the probability of (5) relative to the rest of the system is 1. Any such subject has a conclusive reason to accept (5). But compare Alan and Bob, for both of whom all the propositions are true. Alan inferred (4) from (1) and (3), and he inferred (5) from (2) and (4). Bob inferred (5) from (1) and (4), (1) from (2), (2) from (3) and (4), and (4) from (5).[28]

Davis and Bender argue that on Lehrer's theory both Alan and Bob come out justified, even though Bob's reasoning is viciously circular and idiotic. But this is counterintuitive – a person's belief cannot be justified on the basis of circular and idiotic reasoning. How the person arrives at his belief matters for justification and knowledge.

Davis and Bender argue that Lehrer is exposed to the counterexample because he does not distinguish between merely having reasons for a belief and believing for those reasons. But I think that the problem is deeper than that. To see this, notice that we can revise Lehrer's theory to accommodate the distinction between having reasons and believing for reasons. For S to be personally justified in accepting p, we might require not only that p coheres with S's acceptance system in Lehrer's sense, but also that S is aware of this and accepts p for that reason.

If we revise the theory in this way we will now get a correct ruling on Bob. Since Bob does not believe (5) *because* (5) coheres with his other beliefs, Bob's belief will not be ruled justified. However, the revised version now rules incorrectly about Alan. For although Alan clearly *is* justified in accepting (5), he does not accept (5) because he is sensitive to the Lehrerian coherence relation between (5) and the remainder of his beliefs. This consideration presents a problem for any

---

28 Wayne Davis and John Bender, "Fundamental Troubles with the Coherence Theory," in Bender (1989), p. 58.

nontraditional coherence theory. Namely, Alan has justified belief in the example at least partly because he has made certain traditional inferences, but a nontraditional coherence theory does not recognize a justificatory role for *these* inferences, and that by its very nature.

Before accepting this last conclusion we should consider a final strategy by Lehrer to account for the role of traditional inferences in justification. In his latest defense of the coherence theory Lehrer argues that in cases of traditional inferential justification, coherence is impossible unless a person accepts that her belief follows (in a traditional way) from her evidence for her belief. Thus Lehrer establishes a role for traditional inferences by requiring that a person accepts that there is a traditional inference relation between her belief and the evidence she has for her belief.[29]

But in fact this latest move does not avoid the current objection against coherentism. Waving aside the point that people typically accept no such thing about their beliefs, the current objection is that in certain cases what matters for justification is that a traditional inference has been *made*. What matters for justification is not that a person believes or accepts that her belief follows from her evidence, but that she has actually made an inference from her evidence to the belief in question. Thus I take it that the above example from Davis and Bender would not lose its force if we added that Bob accepts that (5) follows from (1) through (4). So long as no good inference was actually made, Bob is not justified in believing that he is exempt from the final, and the fact that Bob thinks that a good inference could be made seems irrelevant.

Consider a second example. Suppose that Mary is a geometry student who accepts certain axioms and accepts a theorem that in fact follows from those axioms. We may stipulate further that Mary accepts that the theorem follows from the axioms and that she accepts that she can tell whether this is so. Finally, let us suppose that all of these beliefs are true. But now suppose that Mary has not in fact made a correct inference from the axioms to the theorem. Atypically, Mary has reasoned fallaciously in this case. It is clear that Mary does not have either justification or knowledge regarding the theorem. Furthermore, the reason she lacks these is that she has failed to make a correct inference. The example shows that in certain cases whether a person is justified in believing something depends at least partly on whether she has made a traditional

---

29   Lehrer, "Coherence and the Truth Connection," p. 272.

inference. It is this fact about human knowledge that non-traditional coherence theories cannot explain.

The considerations of Sections 5 and 6 show that traditional coherence theories cannot account for perceptual knowledge and nontraditional theories cannot account for inferential knowledge. This is because traditional theories must hold that traditional inferences are always involved in knowledge, while nontraditional theories must hold that traditional inferences are never involved. In the next section I want to consider an objection that can be raised against all coherence theories. It is another *a posteriori* objection, claiming that coherence theories cannot account for the role of sensory appearances in perceptual knowledge.

7. THE ROLE OF SENSORY APPEARANCES

The essential point of this objection is that positive epistemic status depends on what sensory experience a person actually has. Just as inferential knowledge depends on what inferences are actually made, perceptual knowledge depends on how things actually appear. But since the way things appear is not itself a belief, coherence theories cannot account for the importance of sensory appearances in perceptual knowledge.

To focus on the objection I have in mind we may consider a counterexample to coherentism formulated by Ernest Sosa. Sosa asks us to consider person A, who has the belief that he has a headache, in a case where A does indeed have a headache. Sosa correctly notes that the belief in question will have few relevant relations with other beliefs that A currently holds. These beliefs might include that he is not free of a headache, that he is in pain, and perhaps some few others. But now consider the case of person B, who also has a splitting headache, but who has exactly the same beliefs as A save the following few changes: change the belief that B has a headache to the belief that he does not have a headache, change the belief that B is not free of a headache to the belief that he is free of a headache, and make the other few changes necessary to bring into coherence all of B's beliefs relevantly related to the existence or nonexistence of a current headache. Sosa's point is that although A is justified in believing that he has a headache, B is *not* justified in believing that he does not have a headache. And this is so despite the fact that B's beliefs enjoy the same coherence as A's. The reason is that B's *having* a splitting headache affects the epistemic status of B's beliefs about his headaches, even though his having a headache is neither a belief nor a relation among beliefs and so does not affect the coherence of B's beliefs.[30]

Sosa's example involves an introspective belief about one's own mental state, but a similar example can be constructed for sensory perception. For example, visual beliefs are typically involved in few relevant relations with other beliefs. In the case where I have a perceptual belief that there is a tree before me, an equally coherent system can easily be constructed for the belief that there is a stump before me. And now Sosa's reasoning can be applied to these perceptual cases. In the first case, part of what justifies me in believing that there is a tree is surely my experience that there seems to be a tree. In the second case, I am not justified in believing that there is a stump, despite the fact that, by hypothesis, this new belief fits into an equally coherent system – for my experience is that there seems to be a tree and not a stump.

Notice that this kind of objection is effective against coherentism whether we are thinking of appearances as thin or thick. On the one hand, it seems that I cannot be justified in my belief that there is a stump before me if things appear phenomenally as if there were a tree rather than a stump. But even more clearly, I cannot be justified in believing that there is a stump before me if the representational content of my sensory experience is that the thing is a tree. Either way we think of appearances, the justification of perceptual beliefs depends on the way things appear, and not merely on our having beliefs about the way things appear.

As I have already noted, the present objection mirrors the main objection brought against nontraditional coherence theories; just as what inferences one *makes* counts in determining whether an inferential belief is justified, what experiences one *has* counts in determining whether a perceptual belief is justified. But then, *contra* coherentism, the justification of perceptual beliefs is not reducible to beliefs or relations among beliefs.

8. CONCLUSIONS

We may conclude that coherence theories cannot give an account of human knowledge that is empirically adequate. Some of our knowledge

---

30 Ernest Sosa, "The Raft and the Pyramid: Coherence versus Foundations in the Theory of Knowledge," in *Knowledge in Perspective*, pp. 184–185. Reprinted from *Midwest Studies in Philosophy* 5 (1980): 3–25.

is non-inferential and some is inferred from what is already known. Moreover, perceptual knowledge is based directly on sensory appearances as its evidential grounds. This suggests that foundationalism gives the correct account of the structure of human knowledge, since it is the only account that both answers the skeptical regress argument and is psychologically plausible. We may also note that these conclusions confirm the lessons of Chapter 4: that not all evidential relations are inferential, and that perceptual knowledge is not inferred from beliefs about the way things appear.

Finally, the kind of foundationalism here affirmed is contextualist. This is because how things are perceived and what inferences are made both depend on context. This is trivially so in that the causal antecedents of perception and inference are dependent on contextual factors. But the details of a correct view will not be trivial. Substantive issues arise regarding *which* contextual factors influence human cognition, and how. For example, substantive issues arise regarding how class, race, gender, and other social factors affect human cognition. Different versions of contextualism decide these questions differently. No epistemology that I am aware of, however, has claimed that context is irrelevant to human knowing.

6

Hume's Skepticism about Unobserved Matters of Fact

In the preceding chapters we have considered arguments for skepticism about the world from Descartes and Hume. We also looked at the Pyrrhonian infinite regress argument, which is universal in its scope. A third kind of skepticism regards our knowledge of unobserved matters of fact. Arguments for this position have their most famous articulation in Hume and charge that we can never make adequate inferences from the observed to the unobserved. Skeptical arguments of this kind have sometimes been called "the problem of induction."

Various objections have been raised against Hume's reasoning here. The three that I will be concerned with are (a) that Hume's arguments depend on his empiricist theory of ideas, (b) that the arguments assume that absolute certainty is required for knowledge, and (c) that Hume's arguments assume deductivism, or the position that inductive reasoning cannot give rise to knowledge.

If any of these objections were effective, then Hume's skeptical arguments would teach no important lesson. No one today thinks that Hume's theory of ideas is adequate, or that knowledge requires either absolute certainty or deduction. But in fact none of these objections is effective against Hume's skeptical reasoning. This is because Hume's reasoning does not essentially depend on the various implausible assumptions that the objections attribute to it. As we have seen in other cases, the skeptical reasoning in question can be reconstructed so as to employ only assumptions that are pre-theoretically plausible, and that would be accepted by nearly anyone outside the context of philosophical inquiry.

My strategy for defending Hume's reasoning against the present objections is to distinguish between two skeptical arguments in the *Enquiry* – one from Section IV and one from Section VII. With the arguments clearly distinguished we can see that objection (a) is effective only against the argument from Section VII. Objections (b) and (c) are effective against neither argument.

In Part I of this of chapter, I reconstruct the two skeptical arguments from Hume and evaluate the force of objections (a) and (b). I consider these objections to be type-b dismissive responses, since they engage Hume's actual reasoning only superficially. In Part II I consider objection (c), which we will see is not a dismissive response. However, I think that this very common objection to Hume ultimately misunderstands his skeptical reasoning about unobserved matters of fact. Hume is not a skeptic about the epistemic efficacy of inductive inferences. Rather, he is skeptical that our beliefs about unobserved matters of fact have even inductive support. Understanding Hume's argument this way makes it far more powerful than it is usually understood to be, for almost everyone thinks that inferences must be at least inductive to give rise to knowledge. I argue that such is not the case, and that this is the real lesson of Hume's argument. This in turn poses a problem for positive epistemology: any adequate account of knowledge must explain how evidence can produce knowledge even if that evidence does not inductively support its conclusions. I end by pointing to a theory of knowledge that would do the job. Chapter 7 develops this theory with an eye on the lessons from the preceding chapters as well. In the next chapter, therefore, we make the transition to positive epistemology.

I. Hume's Arguments and Dismissive Responses

We may distinguish two Humean arguments for skepticism about unobserved matters of fact. Hume runs the two arguments together in *A Treatise of Human Nature*, and as a result commentators often fail to distinguish them. Any confusion in the *Treatise* is nicely resolved in the *Enquiry*, however, where Hume presents the two arguments in different sections. By getting clear on the structures of these two arguments we will be in a better position to evaluate the three objections that I have just noted.

1. THE ARGUMENTS IN SECTIONS IV AND VII OF THE *ENQUIRY*

The first argument I want to look at is from Section IV of the *Enquiry*. It will be remembered that we have already seen the argument in

Chapter 2, where it was portrayed as an argument for skepticism about the future. But the real point of the argument is that there is no knowledge of any matter of fact that is not observed. Future matters of fact are just one example of unobserved matters of fact.

As we saw in Chapter 2, the argument centers on the claim that there is a crucial assumption in all of our reasoning concerning what is not observed. Namely, all reasoning about unobserved matters of fact involves the "regularity principle," or the principle that unobserved cases will be similar to observed cases. Another way to state the principle is to say that nature will continue to be regular. Hume argues that the regularity principle cannot be supported, and that therefore all of our beliefs concerning unobserved matters of fact rest on an unsupported supposition. Here is how Hume states the argument in the *Enquiry*.

> All reasonings may be divided into two kinds, namely, demonstrative reasoning, or that concerning relations of ideas, and moral reasoning, or that concerning matter of fact and existence. That there are no demonstrative arguments in the case seems evident: since it implies no contradiction that the course of nature may change, and that an object, seemingly like those which we have experienced, may be attended with different or contrary effects. . . .
>
> If we be, therefore, engaged by arguments to put trust in past experience, and make it the standard of our future judgement, these arguments must be probable only, or such as regard matter of fact and real existence, according to the division mentioned. But that there is no argument of this kind, must appear, if our explication of that species of reasoning be admitted as solid and satisfactory. We have said that all arguments concerning existence are founded on the relation of cause and effect; that our knowledge of that relation is derived entirely from experience; and that all our experimental conclusions proceed upon the supposition that the future will be conformable to the past. To endeavor, therefore, the proof of this last supposition by probable arguments, or arguments regarding existence, must be evidently going in a circle, and taking that for granted, which is the very point in question. (pp. 35–36)

In this passage Hume argues that neither demonstrative nor moral reasoning can justify the regularity principle. But his intended conclusion is that the principle cannot be justified at all. Hume's suppressed premise here is that the regularity principle must be justified by reasoning if it is to be justified at all. I take it that Hume does not make the premise explicit because he thinks that it is obvious. The only other sources of justification besides reasoning for Hume are present sense, intuition, and memory. Since it is clear that these are inadequate for the justification of the principle, Hume explicitly considers only moral and demonstrative reasoning. Here is a reconstruction of Hume's wider argument, with the suppressed premise in brackets.

(UMF1)
1. All reasoning is either demonstrative reasoning or moral reasoning.
2. The principle that unobserved cases will be like observed cases cannot be justified by demonstrative reasoning, since its denial is not a contradiction. It does not merely state a relation of ideas.
3. The principle cannot be justified by moral reasoning, since moral reasoning presupposes the very thing in question, and so such a justification would be circular.
[4. Neither can it be justified by intuition, present sense, or memory, since none of these is relevant to a factual supposition about unobserved cases.]
5. Therefore, the supposition that unobserved cases will resemble observed cases cannot be justified at all. (1,2,3,4)
6. All of our beliefs about unobserved matters of fact depend on that supposition for their justification.
7. Therefore, all beliefs about unobserved matters of fact are themselves unjustified, since they depend on an unjustified supposition. (5,6)

Hume's second argument appears in Section VII. In this section Hume considers the proper understanding of our ideas of necessary connection and cause and effect. He concludes that the idea of cause and effect contains the idea of necessary connection, so that when we say that X is the cause of Y, part of what we mean is that there is a necessary connection between X and Y. But the only idea of necessary connection that we have is that of (a) two objects (or events) constantly appearing together in experience, together with (b) an expectation in the mind that the two objects (or events) will continue to go together in the future:

The first time a man saw the communication of motion by impulse, as by the shock of two billiard balls, he could not pronounce that the one event was *connected*: but only that it was *conjoined* with the other. After he has observed several instances of this nature, he then pronounces them to be *connected*. What alteration has happened to give rise to this new idea of *connexion*? Nothing but that he now *feels* these events to be *connected* in his imagination, and can readily foretell the existence of one from the appearance of the other. When we say, therefore, that one object is connected with another, we mean only that they have acquired a connexion in our thought, and give rise to this inference, by which they become proofs of each other's existence: A conclusion which is somewhat extraordinary, but which seems founded on sufficient evidence. (pp. 75–6)

Hume does not say so explicitly in Section VII, but it is easy to see how this analysis of cause and effect has skeptical consequences. For if this is all that is contained in the idea that X is the cause of Y, then we cannot know that in the future X's occurring will result in Y's occurring. This is because the fact that two things have gone together in the past, together with the fact that we expect them to go together in the future, does not guarantee that the things *will* go together in the future. Here is a loose outline of the argument in Section VII, extended so as to explicitly include the skeptical conclusion:

(UMF2)   1. All beliefs about unobserved matters of fact depend for their justification on inferences involving the relation of cause and effect.
2. The only idea we have of this relation is that of two objects being constantly conjoined in the past, together with an expectation in the mind that the two objects will continue to go together in the future.
3. There is no argument that objects conjoined in the past and expected to go together in the future *will* go together in the future.
4. Therefore there is no rational basis for such an inference. (1,2,3)
5. Therefore no knowledge can be acquired via such an inference. (4)
6. Therefore there can be no knowledge of unobserved matters of fact. (1,5)

2. OBJECTION (a): HUME RELIES ON AN INADEQUATE
THEORY OF IDEAS

Let us understand Hume's empiricist theory of ideas as involving two main theses: (i) that ideas and beliefs can be analyzed in terms of sensations and (ii) that sensations are to be understood as essentially unrelated, simple particulars. We may call the first thesis "empirical reductionism" and the second thesis "empirical atomism." The present objection charges that Hume's skeptical arguments regarding unobserved matters of fact depend on this empiricist theory of ideas. But since this theory is false or otherwise inadequate, Hume's reasoning is without force. This kind of objection to Hume is associated with Dewey:

> The philosophic empiricism initiated by Locke was thus disintegrative in intent. It optimistically took it for granted that when the burden of blind custom, imposed authority, and accidental associations was removed, progress in science and social organization would spontaneously take place.... But after Hume with debonair clarity pointed out that the analysis of beliefs into sensations and associations left "natural" ideas and intuitions in the same position in which the reformers had placed "artificial" ones, the situation changed. The rationalists employed the logic of sensationalistic-empiricism to show that experience, giving only a heap of chaotic and isolated particulars, is as fatal to science and to moral laws and obligations as to obnoxious institutions; and concluded that "Reason" must be resorted to if experience was to be furnished with any binding and connecting principles. The new rationalistic idealism of Kant and his successors seemed to be necessitated by the totally destructive results of the new empirical philosophy.[1]

In this passage Dewey is blaming the empiricist assumptions of Locke and Hume for "destructive" skeptical results. But it is not clear which aspect of modern empiricism is to blame. At the start of the passage Dewey picks out "the analysis of beliefs into sensations and associations" as the culprit. But by the end of the passage the problem is the conception of experience as a "heap of chaotic and isolated particulars." So it is not clear whether Dewey thinks reductionism or atomism is the root of skepticism. A few pages later Dewey emphasizes the latter diagnosis.

> When experience is aligned with the life-process and sensations are seen to be points of readjustment, the alleged atomism of sensations totally disappears. With this disappearance is abolished the need for a synthetic faculty of super-empirical reason to connect them. Philosophy is not any longer confronted with the hopeless problem of finding a way in which separate grains of sand may be woven into a strong and coherent rope – or into the illusion and pretense of one.[2]

I will pause to note that the two passages from Dewey are inconsistent. The first implies that empirical reductionism is sufficient for skepticism, and the second implies that empirical atomism is necessary for skepticism. But on the assumption that reductionism does not imply atomism (which it does not), the two diagnoses of skepticism contradict each other.

Waving this aside, the more important point is that both of Dewey's objections are ineffective against Hume's skeptical reasoning. This is

---

1 John Dewey, *Reconstruction in Philosophy* (Boston: Beacon Press, 1957), pp. 82–83.
2 Ibid., p. 90.

because the argument from Section IV presupposes neither an atomistic conception of experience nor a reductionist account of belief. Both of these components of the empiricist theory of ideas are inessential to Hume's reasoning in argument (UMF1). That is not to say that Hume did not accept both atomism and reductionism. Hume did accept these, and his arguments are largely couched in the vocabulary of his empiricist theory of ideas. The present point is that the argument from Section IV need not be couched in such terms. Accordingly, Dewey's critiques focus on inessential aspects of Hume's reasoning.

In fairness to Dewey we may observe that the argument from Section VII does depend on Hume's reductionism. Specifically, premise (2) of argument (UMF2) is driven by Hume's analysis of necessary connection, and this analysis depends on Hume's position that every idea must be traced back to some original impression or impressions. The reason Hume thinks (2) is true is that he thinks there must be some impression behind our idea of necessary connection, and the only one he can find for the job is the expectation "we feel in the mind" when two things are observed to be constantly conjoined.

> Every idea is copied from some preceding impression or sentiment; and where we cannot find any impression, we may be certain that there is no idea. In all single instances of the operation of bodies or minds, there is nothing that produces any impression, nor consequently can suggest any idea, of power or necessary connexion. But when many uniform instances appear, and the same object is always followed by the same event; we then begin to entertain the notion of cause and connexion. We then *feel* a new sentiment or impression, to wit, a customary connexion in the thought or imagination between one object and its usual attendant; and this sentiment is the original of that idea which we seek for. (p. 78)

So Hume's argument in Section VII does presuppose his empiricist theory of ideas. But how is the argument of Section IV supposed to depend on that theory?

Here is one way that it might be thought to do so. It might be charged that Hume's reductionism is implicit in premises (1) through (3) of (UMF1). Those premises invoke the distinction between moral and demonstrative reasoning, and these two concepts are defined in terms of matters of fact and relations of ideas. Therefore, the distinction between moral and demonstrative reasoning implies the distinction between matters of fact and relations of ideas. But this latter distinction, the present objection goes, involves empirical reductionism, and therefore (UMF1) really does depend on Hume's theory of ideas.

It should be conceded that Hume's distinction between matters of fact and relations of ideas does involve empirical reductionism. Without going into details of Hume scholarship, the distinction presupposes the notion that complex ideas are built up out of simple ideas, and exist in various kinds of relations. But what is important to recognize is that (UMF1) can be reconstructed without the distinction between matters of fact and relations of ideas, and without its reductionist presuppositions. For that reason (UMF1) does not depend on Hume's theory of ideas in any essential respect.

What Hume needs to run his argument is not the distinction between matters of fact and relations of ideas, but the distinction between contingent and necessary truths. More exactly, Hume requires a distinction between contingent truths arrived at by empirical reasoning and necessary truths arrived at by *a priori* reasoning. It is true that Hume's theory of ideas provides one way of cashing out the relevant distinction. But it is not the only way or even the most plausible way, and therefore (UMF1) does not essentially involve that theory.[3]

Another way in which (UMF1) might be supposed to involve Hume's theory of ideas is in premise (4). That premise makes reference to the notion of "present sense," and so it might be thought that Hume's atomism about experience plays an essential role in the argument here. But again, the notion of "present sense" need not be understood in Hume's atomistic way. The relevant meaning of "present sense" in the context of (UMF1) is empirical observation. In this regard premise (4) claims only that a principle about unobserved occurrences cannot be *observed* to be true, and therefore cannot be established by empirical observation alone. If such a principle is to be justified at all, then its evidence must involve some other source of knowledge, and presumably some kind of *inference* from what is empirically observed. That claim seems plausible enough, and certainly does not require the theory of ideas in general or Hume's atomistic conception of experience in particular.

Taking all of this into account, we can reconstruct argument (UMF1) as follows, purging it of any remnants of Hume's theory of ideas.

---

3   In fact, Hume does not even need this distinction. What he needs is the assumption that the regularity principle must be justified by empirical reasoning, together with the assumption that empirical reasoning always involves the regularity principle. However, I will continue to employ the present distinction in reconstructing Hume's argument, since this more closely parallels Hume's argument in the text.

(UMF1B) 1. All reasoning is either empirical reasoning about contingent truths or *a priori* reasoning about necessary truths.
2. The regularity principle cannot be justified by *a priori* reasoning about necessary truths, since its denial is not a contradiction. It does not state a necessary truth.
3. The principle cannot be justified by empirical reasoning about contingent truths, since all such reasoning presupposes the very thing in question, and therefore such a justification would be circular.
[4. Neither can the principle be justified by intuition, empirical observation, or memory alone, since none of these can give direct knowledge of a factual supposition about unobserved cases.]
5. Therefore, the supposition that unobserved cases will resemble observed cases cannot be justified at all. (1,2,3,4)
6. All of our beliefs about matters of fact that go beyond current empirical observation and memory depend on that supposition for their justification.
7. Therefore, all of our beliefs about unobserved matters of fact are themselves unjustified, since they depend on an unjustified supposition. (5,6)

We may conclude that Hume's skeptical argument in Section IV does not essentially involve his empiricist theory of ideas, considered either as a theory of experience or as a theory about the analysis of ideas and beliefs. For this reason objection (a) is ineffective against Hume's reasoning. The objection focuses on superficial aspects of Hume's arguments as they happen to appear in the text, and not on anything essential in Hume's reasoning.

3. OBJECTION (b): HUME REQUIRES ABSOLUTE CERTAINTY FOR KNOWLEDGE

The next objection charges that Hume's arguments require absolute certainty for knowledge. If so, Hume's skepticism is without force, since knowledge requires only some lesser degree of positive epistemic status.[4] We may reply on behalf of Hume by again focusing on the argument from Section IV of the *Enquiry*. According to (UMF1), the problem

---

4 For an example of this kind of objection see Rescher, *Scepticism: A Critical Appraisal*, esp. Ch. II. We may also include here Dewey's railings against the quest for certainty and Peirce's insistence on fallibilism.

with our beliefs about unobserved matters of fact is that they lack any positive epistemic status whatsoever; it is not that they lack absolute certainty.

We can see this by looking at the basic structure of (UMF1). In premises (2) through (4) Hume identifies five possible sources of justification and declares four of the five to be irrelevant to the supposition that unobserved cases will resemble observed cases. That supposition is a contingent truth about unobserved cases. Memory deals with the past, and empirical observation deals with present *observed* cases. Demonstrative reasoning and intuition deal with necessary truths. The only relevant source of justification for the supposition would be moral reasoning, but moral reasoning so employed would be circular.

The problem with circular reasoning, however, is not that it fails to provide absolute certainty. Rather, the problem is that circular reasoning provides no support *at all* for conclusions drawn from it. If Hume's argument is sound, then our beliefs about unobserved matters of fact are wholly lacking in positive epistemic status. Absolute certainty is not the issue.

II. The Standard Objection against Hume

Objection (c) charges that Hume is a deductivist. That is, the objection claims that Hume assumes that only deductive inferences can generate knowledge and justified belief, and so Hume's skeptical arguments can be avoided by simply recognizing the role of inductive inferences in empirical matters. This is perhaps the most widely accepted critique of Hume's skepticism about unobserved matters of fact. Barry Stroud calls it "the standard interpretation" of Hume, and D. C. Stove says that important aspects of it are "nearly common property among philosophers."[5] In Chapter 3, I rejected the charge of deductivism as a dismis-

---

5 See Barry Stroud, *Hume* (London: Routledge and Kegan Paul, 1977), p. 56, n. 11; D. C. Stove, *Probability and Hume's Deductive Scepticism* (Oxford: Clarendon Press, 1973), p. 51. Versions of the objection to Hume can be found in Reid and Peirce, but it has been more recently articulated and further developed by Stove in several essays and in his book just cited. Some form of the objection is defended in P. Edwards, "Bertrand Russell's Doubts about Induction," in Anthony Flew, ed., *Logic and Language, First Series* (Oxford: Blackwell, 1951); P. F. Strawson, *Introduction to Logical Theory* (London: Methuen, 1952); Stroud, *Hume;* and Anthony Flew, *David Hume* (Oxford: Blackwell, 1986), among others.

sive response to Hume's skepticism about the world. But as a response to the argument in Section IV of the *Enquiry* the objection has some plausibility. To see why, we will have to take a closer look at the objection and at Hume's argument.

1. THE OBJECTION

At first glance the objection seems wrong. For Hume clearly distinguishes between demonstrative and moral reasoning and then argues that neither of these can justify our beliefs about unobserved matters of fact. If we make the plausible assumption that Hume's "moral reasoning" roughly corresponds to what we mean by "inductive reasoning," then Hume cannot be said to *assume* that inductive reasoning is not epistemically efficacious. On the contrary, Hume has given an argument for that position: such reasoning always employs the regularity principle, but that principle is unjustified and must remain unjustified. In particular, inductive reasoning cannot justify the principle because such reasoning presupposes it, and so that would be going in a circle.

How, then, does Hume assume that only deductive inferences give rise to knowledge and justified belief? At this point the objection gets interesting. Why, it is asked, does Hume think that all moral reasoning presupposes the regularity principle? The answer, according to the present objection, is that Hume thinks that the principle is needed to make moral reasoning deductively valid. So although Hume explicitly makes a distinction between demonstrative and moral reasoning, he implicitly assumes that only deductive reasoning is epistemically respectable. Hume's assumption that the regularity principle must be involved in moral reasoning is really an assumption that moral reasoning must be deductive.

Stove articulates the objection nicely in the following passages.

Sometimes when we say of an argument from p to q, that it presupposes r, our meaning is as follows: that, as it stands, the argument from p to q is not valid, and that, in order to turn it into a valid argument, it would be necessary to add to its premises the proposition r. I believe that this is the sense in which "presuppose" occurs in . . . Hume's argument.

Hume's argument in stage 2 may therefore be summed up in the following way: from premises which prove at most the invalidity of predictive-inductive inferences, along with the unstated premiss that an inference is unreasonable if it is invalid, Hume concluded that predictive-inductive inferences are unreasonable.[6]

This objection is sophisticated and interesting, and as was already noted, it is popular as well. If the objection trades on an accurate understanding of Hume's argument, then it is also devastating, since the rationalist assumption that only deductive inferences are reasonable is no longer taken seriously in philosophy, and rightly so. But in my opinion Hume's argument can be reconstructed so as to avoid the present objection. For that reason the objection misses the real force of Hume's skeptical reasoning.

I will not argue that Hume's text forces the reconstruction I will propose. Rather, I claim only that the text is consistent with it. But then the principle of charity warrants my interpretation insofar as it makes what Hume says not obviously wrong. More importantly, whether or not the proposed interpretation is an accurate account of Hume's intentions, the substantive point holds: Hume's reasoning *can* be reconstructed so that it does not presuppose deductivism. A close analysis of Hume's argument teaches a more important lesson than is usually supposed.

How, then, should Hume's argument be reconstructed? My strategy is to distinguish three kinds of inferential support. Thus the relationship between the premises and the conclusion of an argument can be deductive-supportive, inductive-supportive, or nonsupportive. My thesis will then be as follows: Hume does not assume that inductive inferences cannot generate knowledge or reasonable belief. Rather, he makes the weaker assumption that non-supportive inferences cannot. If this is right, then Hume's argument is far more powerful than is generally acknowledged. For it is not at all obvious that non-supportive evidence can be epistemically efficacious; many philosophers would agree with Hume on *that* point. If Hume is granted this weaker assumption, however, then the rest of his argument is flawless.

In Sections II.2 and II.3 of this chapter, I show how Hume's argument can be reconstructed along these lines. In the final section (Section II.4), I focus on the real lesson of Hume's argument for positive epistemology. That lesson is not that our knowledge of unobserved matters of fact rests on inductive inferences. Rather, it is the more surprising conclusion that such knowledge rests on nonsupportive inferences, or inferences that are not even inductive-supportive.

---

6 Stove, *Probability*, p. 43, p. 51.

2. DEDUCTIVE, INDUCTIVE, AND NONSUPPORTIVE INFERENCES

In the *Treatise* and the *Enquiry* Hume employs the concepts of demonstrative and moral (or "probable") reasoning, whereas I have also been using the concepts of deductive and inductive inference. It is now necessary to say more about how Hume understands the former and I am understanding the latter.

First, we should observe that Hume's concepts of demonstrative and moral reasoning are multifaceted. Some of the descriptive and epistemic dimensions of demonstrative and probable reasoning can be extracted from the following passages:

All the objects of human reason or enquiry may naturally be divided into two kinds, to wit, *Relations of Ideas*, and *Matters of Fact*. Of the first kind are the sciences of Geometry, Algebra, and Arithmetic; and in short, every affirmation which is either intuitively or demonstratively certain.... Propositions of this kind are discoverable by a mere operation of thought, without dependence on what is anywhere existent in the universe.... Matters of fact, which are the second objects of human reason, are not ascertained in the same manner; nor is our evidence for their truth, however great, of a like nature with the foregoing. The contrary of every matter of fact is still possible; because it can never imply a contradiction.... (*Enquiry*, p. 25)

All reasoning may be divided into two kinds, namely, demonstrative reasoning, or that concerning relations of ideas, and moral reasoning, or that concerning matters of fact and existence. (Ibid., p. 35)

Descriptively, we learn that moral reasoning deals with matters of fact, whereas demonstrative reasoning deals with necessary truths, or truths the contrary of which imply a contradiction. We also learn that demonstrative reasoning may proceed "by a mere operation of thought" or "reasonings *a priori*," whereas later we learn that all probable reasoning "arises entirely from experience" (ibid., p. 27).

The concepts of demonstrative and moral reasoning also involve epistemic dimensions. Demonstrative reasoning gives rise to knowledge that is "certain." The evidence gained by probable reasoning, however great, is not "of a like nature." In the *Treatise* Hume speaks of "degrees of evidence." Demonstrative reasoning gives knowledge in the strict sense of the term. Moral reasoning gives only a lesser degree of evidence, although "in common discourse we readily affirm, that many arguments from causation exceed probability, and may be receiv'd as a superior kind of evidence" (*Treatise*, p. 124).

The terms "deductive inference" and "inductive inference" are not Hume's but ours. The terms have a variety of meanings, many of which include descriptive and epistemic dimensions that are similar to those implied by Hume's concepts of demonstrative and moral reasoning. But there is also a common understanding of deductive and inductive inference that is neither descriptive nor epistemic, but semantic. On this understanding an inference is deductive just in case, necessarily, if the premises are true then the conclusion is true. This understanding of deductive inference implies nothing descriptive of the premises or conclusion, nor does it imply that any of them are known or certain or even reasonable. As I said, the concept so understood is semantic rather than descriptive or epistemic. It is semantic in the sense that it concerns a necessary relation between the truth of the premises and the truth of the conclusion. This is the understanding of deductive inference that is used in logic and mathematics.

The semantic notion of deductive inference may be opposed to a semantic notion of inductive inference. On this understanding an inference is inductive just in case, necessarily, the truth of the conclusion is likely in relation to the truth of the premises. Here "likely" is to be understood in a non-epistemic sense, meaning something close to statistically probable, as opposed to epistemically probable or reasonable. The concept is semantic in the relevant sense; it concerns a relation between the truth of the premises and the truth of the conclusion, and that relation is necessary. This relation is different from that which is involved in deductive inferences, however. First, unlike entailment, inductive support can change by adding premises. Second, inductive support is weaker than entailment. It might be understood as a kind of partial entailment, in that it does not preserve truth but it does preserve likelihood of truth.[7]

Examples of inductive inferences so defined are as follows:

---

7 Ian Hacking attributes a similar concept to Jeffreys and Keynes. "[I]n the early decades of this century, there was much interest in the theory advanced by Harold Jeffreys and J. M. Keynes, according to which the probability conferred on a hypothesis by some evidence is a logical relation between two propositions. The probability of *h*, in the light of *e*, is something like the degree to which *h* is logically implied by *e*." Ian Hacking, *The Emergence of Probability* (Cambridge: Cambridge University Press, 1975), pp. 13–14.

i. Ninety-five percent of the dogs that live in New York City bite.
   Fido is a dog that lives in New York City.
   Therefore, Fido bites.
ii. Patent attorneys usually make good money.
    Joe is a patent attorney.
    Therefore, Joe makes good money.
iii. People who make promises they can't keep tend to regret it.
     Therefore, if you make a promise you can't keep you will regret it.
iv. The grocery store used to be on Main Street.
    Things haven't changed much around here.
    Therefore, the grocery store is still on Main Street.

In each of these arguments there is a relationship of inductive support between the premises and the conclusion in the sense defined; in each argument, it is necessarily true that the conclusion is likely in relation to the premises. This is not to say that in each argument the conclusion would remain likely in relation to the premises if others were added to the ones already stated. As was noted earlier, inductive support is unlike deductive entailment in that adding premises can change the relationship of support between the premises and the conclusion.

From what has been said it should be clear that arguments may be divided into three categories: those that involve deductive inferences, those that involve inductive inferences, and those that involve neither. Alternatively, we may say that arguments can be deductive-supportive, inductive-supportive, or nonsupportive. We may talk about evidence for a conclusion in the same way. Thus evidence for a conclusion can be deductive-supportive, inductive-supportive, or nonsupportive.

It is important to note that none of this concedes or denies anything to the skeptic. This is because "supportive" is here understood as a semantic notion, not an epistemic one. It remains an open question whether epistemic grounding requires semantic support, and, if it does, whether inductive support is sufficient.

Now that we have established a vocabulary, we may consider the standard objection against Hume's skeptical argument. In our terminology the objection is that Hume assumes that only deductive-supportive reasoning can give rise to knowledge and reasonable belief. Another way to put the objection is that Hume thinks all evidence must be deductive-supportive, so that if one's evidence does not entail what is concluded from it then that conclusion cannot amount to knowledge or even reasonable belief. The objection, of course, insists that evidence which is inductive-supportive can be sufficient for grounding knowledge. Therefore, Hume's argument rests on a false assumption about what kind of support is required for knowledge.

We get our first clue that the standard objection is misguided when we look at various of Hume's characterizations of the regularity principle. In all of these Hume states the principle in completely general terms. Hume always characterizes the principle as affirming that there are (in general) regularities in nature, but never as affirming that some particular regularity holds.

> [A]ll our experimental conclusions proceed upon the supposition that the future will be conformable to the past. (*Enquiry*, p. 35)

> [A]ll inferences from experience suppose, as their foundation, that the future will resemble the past, and that similar powers will be conjoined with similar sensible qualities. (Ibid., p. 37)

> If reason determin'd us, it wou'd proceed upon that principle, *that instances, of which we have had no experience, must resemble those, of which we have had experience, and that the course of nature continues always uniformly the same.* (*Treatise*, p. 89)

But if the regularity principle mentions no particular regularities, then adding the principle to arguments from observed cases to unobserved cases will *not* make those arguments deductive-supportive. And so we cannot say that Hume is insisting on deductive-supportive reasoning when he insists on the need for supposing the regularity principle.

Consider the argument that, in all past cases, bread has nourished me, and that therefore this bread will nourish me as well. Using Hume's second formulation we have,

> v. In the past, in all observed cases bread has nourished me.
> The future will resemble the past; similar powers will be conjoined with similar sensible qualities.
> Therefore, this bread will nourish me as well.

Because Hume's regularity principle does not say *how* the future will resemble the past, or which powers will be conjoined with which sensible qualities, the argument is not turned into a deductive one by adding the principle. Of course, a principle affirming a *particular* regularity between bread and nourishment would yield a deductive argument to the targeted conclusion. But as we can see from the various statements of the principle just quoted, Hume never characterizes the regularity principle as affirming particular regularities. For Hume the regularity principle is general in this sense.[8]

If Hume does not insist that we need the regularity principle for the purpose of making our reasoning deductive-supportive, then what is his point? My suggestion is that Hume thinks the principle is needed to make our reasoning inductive-supportive. That this is Hume's intention is suggested by the following passage from the *Enquiry*:

> If there be any suspicion that the course of nature may change, and that the past may be no rule for the future, all experience becomes useless, and can give rise to no inference or conclusion. (pp. 37–38)

In this passage Hume is arguing that if the regularity principle is not supposed, then our present and past observations become irrelevant to future events. Without the assumption of regularity, premises about the past and present would be irrelevant to – that is, wholly nonsupportive of – conclusions about the future. And in the sense in which we have been understanding "support," Hume is right. For it is not necessarily true that, given observations of a past constant conjunction, that conjunction will likely continue in the future. If the universe is chaotic rather than regular, then a past constant conjunction does not make a future conjunction even likely.

The present point is not that past observations do not entail conclusions about future conjunctions. That is obvious. The point is that, without the assumption that nature is regular, past observations do not give even inductive support to conclusions about the future. However, if we add the regularity principle to past observations, then our evidence does become inductive-supportive. For this principle is equivalent to the proposition that, in general, constant conjunctions in the past will continue. On this interpretation the role of the regularity principle is to make the premises of probable reasoning inductively relevant to their conclusions. The principle is needed to make probable reasoning inductive-supportive rather than nonsupportive.

It must be admitted that the passage just quoted from Hume does not force the interpretation I have given it. But on the interpretation I am suggesting, key passages from both the *Treatise* and the *Enquiry* become

---

8 Some commentators on Hume have noticed that adding the regularity principle (as Hume formulates it) to one's evidence for unobserved matters of fact does not indeed generate deductive inferences. But they have missed the significance of this, taking it to be a criticism of Hume rather than an objection to their interpretation. See, e.g., Strawson, *Introduction to Logical Theory*.

not only coherent but plausible. For example, the main argument from Section IV of the *Enquiry* can now be read as follows:

(UMF3)
1. Reasoning can provide justification for its conclusion only if it is supportive, either deductively or inductively, and its assumptions are themselves justified or reasonable to suppose.
2. Demonstrative reasoning is deductive-supportive, but it is not relevant to matters of fact.
3. Therefore, beliefs about unobserved matters of fact must be justified, if at all, by moral reasoning that is inductive-supportive. (1,2)
4. Moral reasoning is inductive-supportive only if it supposes the regularity principle.
5. That principle cannot be justified by demonstrative reasoning, since the principle does not state a relation of ideas.
6. The principle cannot be justified by moral reasoning, since moral reasoning already supposes it as a premise, and so that would be circular.
[7. Neither can the principle be justified by intuition, present sense, or memory, since none of these is relevant to a factual supposition about unobserved cases.]
8. Therefore, the regularity principle cannot be justified at all. (5,6,7)
9. Therefore, moral reasoning cannot provide justification for beliefs about unobserved matters of fact. (1,4,8)
10. Therefore, beliefs about unobserved matters of fact cannot be justified at all. (3,9)

The present interpretation of Hume runs the argument on premises (1) and (4) rather than on the dubious assumption that only deductive inferences are justification conferring. This is an advantage over the standard interpretation of Hume insofar as it is more charitable. The present interpretation, in fact, saves Hume from an embarrassing blunder.

The interpretation I am suggesting also does very well with the following passage of the *Treatise*:

[T]he next question is Whether experience produces the idea by means of understanding or of the imagination; whether we are determin'd by reason to make the transition, or by a certain association and relation of perceptions. If reason determin'd us, it wou'd proceed upon that principle, *that instances, of which we have had no experience, must resemble those, of which we have had experience, and that the course of nature continues always uniformly the same.* In order therefore to clear up this matter, let us consider all the arguments upon which such a proposition may be suppos'd to be founded. (pp. 88–89)

Suppose that by "reason" Hume means any reasoning that is either deductive-supportive or inductive-supportive, and by "imagination" he means any transition that is wholly non-supportive. Then a natural interpretation of the passage is as follows: "We have already established that the transition from observed matters of fact to unobserved is not by demonstrative reasoning. Therefore, if it is by reasoning that we make this transition, it will have to be by moral reasoning, or reasoning that is inductive-supportive. Now our reasoning here is inductive-supportive only if it proceeds on the regularity principle. But that is the case only if that principle is itself well founded, and so let us investigate that issue." Any number of passages in the *Treatise* and the *Enquiry* can be given a quite natural interpretation along similar lines.

3. AN OBJECTION CONSIDERED (AGAINST OUR INTERPRETATION OF HUME)

I now want to consider the objection that the present interpretation of Hume is only marginally more charitable than the standard one, and that therefore (UMF3) is only marginally more plausible than the argument commonly refuted. I have made (UMF3) run on the assumption that only inductive and deductive inferences can confer justification on their conclusions. One might argue that this is only slightly more plausible than the assumption that only deductive inferences can confer justification. This is because I have defined inductive support in such a way that almost none of our reasoning involves inductive inferences. That is, almost none of our reasoning is such that, necessarily, the truth of the conclusion is likely in relation to the truth of the premises.

To see the force of this objection we may note that even arguments (i) through (iv) in Section 2 would not stand up to the standards I have Hume endorsing, since the question of the reasonableness of their premises arises, and it is clear that there is no inductive-supportive argument that will establish those premises and that does not itself depend on some form of the regularity principle. The reasonableness of some of those premises can be attributed to sense perception or memory, but other premises would require an inference from sense perception and memory, and there is no inductive-supportive argument available to do the job. It might be thought that argument (i) is an exception, but even here the point holds. If the first premise of that argument is supported by observing all of the dogs in New York City, then Fido was observed, and so the conclusion does not go beyond observed cases. If the first premise is not supported by observing all dogs, then it must be arrived at via an argument involving the regularity principle or else via an argument that is nonsupportive.

What this objection recognizes is that Hume's skeptical argument runs as nicely on the assumptions I have attributed to him as it does on the dubious assumption that only deductive inferences are justification conferring. However, the objection goes, the assumptions I have put in Hume's argument are just as implausible as the rationalist deductivism others have attributed to him. That is the point I want to address now. I do so by articulating a non-rationalist motivation for the assumption that all evidence must be deductive-supportive or inductive-supportive. I argue that the assumption arises quite naturally out of considerations about what knowledge requires, and that rejecting the assumption threatens results that many have found counterintuitive. My conclusion is that rejecting the assumption amounts to a substantive and even surprising position regarding the nature of evidence.[9]

The assumption that I have been attributing to Hume amounts to this: An inference can confer justification on its conclusion only if there is a necessary relation of support between the premises and the conclusion. Alternatively, evidence can confer justification on a belief only if it is deductive-supportive or inductive-supportive. Why might one think that such an assumption is plausible? We can answer that question by considering some cases of reasonable and unreasonable belief.

First, consider a mathematician who knows that certain axioms are true and who proves a theorem on the basis of those axioms. By seeing that the theorem is entailed by the axioms, the mathematician comes to know the theorem. Contrast this situation with that of a novice who also knows that the axioms are true but who merely guesses that the

---

9 The assumption that good inductive inferences should necessarily confer probability is manifested in Carnap's attempt to formalize inductive logic and in Bayesian attempts to reduce inductive reasoning to the laws of probability. See, e.g., Rudolf Carnap, *Logical Foundations of Probability* (Chicago: University of Chicago Press, 1950), and Paul Horwich, *Probability and Evidence* (Cambridge: Cambridge University Press, 1982). It is perhaps also behind Peirce's attempts to prove that the scientific method necessarily discovers the truth in the long run. An informative historical overview of different concepts of probability and induction, but in somewhat different categories, is provided by Hacking, *The Emergence of Probability*.

theorem is true. Obviously the novice does not come to know the theorem, and a reasonable explanation is that he has no awareness of the relationship between the axioms and the theorem. If the novice knew that the axioms entailed the theorem, then he too would know the theorem.

Next consider a case of reasoning about a matter of fact. A mechanic sees green liquid dripping from underneath the front of a car and infers that the car's radiator is leaking. The mechanic's belief is at least reasonable and may even amount to knowledge. Surely one relevant feature of the case is that the mechanic knows that dripping green liquid is a reliable indication of a leaking radiator. Again, the mechanic is aware of the relationship between the truth of her premises and the truth of her conclusion. Suppose that someone not very familiar with automobiles observes green liquid leaking from his car. If the person does not understand that this is a reliable indication that his radiator is leaking, then surely he cannot know on the basis of his observation that his radiator is leaking. Or suppose that dripping green liquid were not a reliable indication of a leaking radiator. Then even if a person thought that it was, the observation of dripping liquid could not allow him to know that his radiator was leaking.

These examples support two conclusions about the nature of evidence. First, a body of evidence E can confer justification on a conclusion C only if the truth of E is a reliable indication of the truth of C. Second, a body of evidence E can confer justification on a conclusion C for a person S, only if S is sensitive to the fact that the truth of E is a reliable indication of the truth of C.[10]

The following question now arises: How is it that in cases of knowledge and reasonable belief, S becomes sensitive to the fact that the truth of her evidence is a reliable indication of the truth of her conclusion? In cases where the evidence is deductive-supportive or inductive-supportive a possible answer is that S can just "see" that the truth of the conclusion is entailed or made likely by the truth of the evidence. The "seeing" here is not literal seeing, but a kind of intuitive seeing associated with the knowing of self-evident necessary truths. The idea is that

---

10   Compare Richard Fumerton, *Metaepistemology and Skepticism* (Lanham, MD: Rowman and Littlefield, 1995). According to Fumerton, the following "Principle of Inferential Justification" is a platitude: To be justified in believing one proposition P on the basis of another proposition E, one must be (1) justified in believing E and (2) justified in believing that E makes probable P.

deductive-supportive and inductive-supportive reasoning involves such a logical intuition. When we employ either kind of argument, we can "see" that, necessarily, the truth of the conclusion is indicated by the truth of the premises.

Now suppose that there are inferences that are justification conferring but that are neither deductive nor inductive in the senses we have defined. That would amount to supposing that there are inferences where the truth of the evidence is a reliable indication of the truth of the conclusion, but where that fact is contingent rather than necessary. It is plausible that the reasoning about the leaky radiator involves an inference of just this kind. In fact, it is plausible that *all* of our reasoning about unobserved matters of fact involves inferences of just this kind. Indeed, this latter conclusion is what I take to be the import of Hume's argument concerning unobserved matters of fact. More exactly, Hume's argument establishes that if our reasoning about unobserved matters of fact is reliable at all, then it is only contingently reliable. Such reasoning is neither deductive-supportive nor inductive-supportive, and this is equivalent to saying that it is not necessarily reliable.

So again, suppose that this is what our inferences are like. Why is that a problem? The problem is that we are now at a loss to say how we could be sensitive to the reliability of those inferences. The examples we have considered naturally gave rise to two intuitions: that inferences must be reliable to confer justification, and that we must be aware of that reliability. If the reliability of our inferences is necessary, then we can account for our sensitivity to their reliability by invoking our ability to know self-evident necessary truths. But this account is blocked if our inferences are only contingently reliable. If they are contingently reliable, then their reliability cannot be self-evident. And if it is not self-evident then how can it be evident at all? Of course one might begin to look for an argument that our inferences are reliable, but that would only raise all of the same questions regarding the reliability of *that* argument.

I will now summarize the main point of this section: The objection was raised that (UMF3) is only marginally more plausible than the argument from Hume that is commonly refuted. This is because (UMF3) runs on the assumption that only supportive inferences can be justification conferring, but given the notion of support employed, that assumption is only slightly more plausible than the assumption that only deductive inferences can be justification conferring. On the present understanding, an inference is supportive only if it is necessarily reliable, and so premise (1) of (UMF3) amounts to the assumption that only necessarily reliable inferences are justification conferring. In response, I have tried to motivate the assumption that only necessarily reliable inferences are justification conferring. The argument is that it is a requirement of knowledge and reasonable belief that one be sensitive to the reliability of any inference that is involved. But if an inference is not necessarily reliable, then it is hard to see how one could be sensitive to its reliability. Therefore, there is a strong motivation for thinking that only necessarily reliable inferences can generate knowledge and reasonable belief.

4. THE LESSON OF HUME'S SKEPTICAL ARGUMENT

I have been arguing that skeptical arguments serve as heuristic devices for driving positive epistemology. As such, skeptical arguments teach us lessons about the nature of knowledge and evidence. What is the lesson that Hume's argument teaches?

If Hume is granted the assumption that only logically supportive inferences are justification conferring, then the rest of his argument goes through and we must conclude that we have no knowledge or reasonable belief about unobserved matters of fact. To see that this is so we need only review the argument. If the assumption is granted, then any reasoning about unobserved matters of fact must be deductive-supportive or inductive-supportive. That there are no deductive-supportive arguments about unobserved facts from past and present observations is now almost universally acknowledged, and I think Hume must be conceded that point. Therefore our reasoning about unobserved matters of fact will have to be inductive-supportive. But now such reasoning will be inductive-supportive only if its premises include something like the regularity principle; without some such principle it will not be necessarily true that the conclusions of such reasoning are likely in relation to their premises. Furthermore, such a principle cannot be supported by either deductive or inductive arguments. Once again, we should concede the point that there are no deductive arguments. But neither can the regularity principle be supported by inductive arguments, and for just the reason Hume tells us. If all inductive reasoning already assumes the regularity principle, then using inductive reasoning to support it would be "going in a circle" in the most obvious sense; it would be assuming as a premise that which is supposed to be the conclusion.

So if we grant Hume the assumption that only supportive inferences are justification conferring, then the rest of his skeptical argument goes through. Therefore, one lesson of Hume's argument is straightforward: we must conclude that nonsupportive inferences can be justification conferring. Put another way, any adequate epistemology will have to countenance evidence about unobserved matters of fact that is neither deductive-supportive nor inductive-supportive. Providing the details about how this is possible constitutes one condition of an adequate theory of evidence.

But that raises another problem. We saw that the motivation for accepting Hume's assumption was that knowledge seems to require that one be sensitive to the reliability of one's inferences, and it is hard to see how one could be sensitive to the reliability of inferences that are only contingently reliable. An adequate epistemology will have to solve this problem as well.

One way to solve the problem is to make the case that one need not be sensitive to the reliability of one's inferences. This is the strategy that simple reliabilism adopts. According to simple reliabilism, S is justified in believing p just in case the cognitive process that generates S's belief is in fact reliable. Thus if S's believing p is the result of some inferential cognitive process, S need not be aware that the process or the inference it involves is reliable; all that counts is that the process is in fact reliable. Here we have an example of an epistemology that countenances non-supportive inferences in the sense that any adequate epistemology must. But it does so at the cost of denying one of our strongest intuitions about the nature of evidence: namely, it denies that S need be sensitive to the reliability of her evidence. Simple reliabilism has been widely criticized on just this point.[11]

Moreover, simple reliabilism is not the only theory with this kind of problem. Consider Robert Audi's view of indirect justification in his book *The Structure of Justification*.[12] According to Audi, a person S is justified in believing p on the basis of r only if there is some support relation C, and S believes C to hold between r and p. Audi calls this last belief a "connecting belief." A trilemma arises, depending on how we think of connecting beliefs and the support relation they involve. If connecting beliefs express contingent reliability relations, then the problem of their justification arises as we have noted: their justification will have to be inferential, and so will involve either a circle or a regress of

---

11 For example, see BonJour, *The Structure of Empirical Knowledge*, and Fumerton, *Metaepistemology and Skepticism*.

12 See esp. Ch. 8.

further connecting beliefs. If connecting beliefs express necessary relations, then their justification can be non-inferential, but a different problem arises for either of two further possibilities. If the beliefs express a semantic relation implying reliability, then Humean problems arise as before: r and p are semantically related only if r involves something like the regularity principle, and so we encounter problems about the justification of r. If connecting beliefs express a non-semantic relation, perhaps about some kind of epistemic justification that does not imply reliability, then Audi's position fails to accommodate the intuition above: that knowledge requires that a person be sensitive to the reliability of her evidence.[13]

This suggests that an adequate epistemology ought to adopt a different strategy for solving the problem at hand. Such an epistemology must give some account of how we can be sensitive to the reliability of our inferences, even when those inferences are not necessarily reliable, and even if we do not have beliefs about those inferences. How such an account would go is an open question, and the Humean considerations we have just rehearsed should convince us that it is a difficult one. In any case, Hume's skeptical argument suggests this further condition of an adequate theory of evidence.

To sum up, in this chapter I have offered a reconstruction of Hume's skeptical reasoning that is consistent with the text, and that avoids the standard objection that Hume assumes only deductive inferences can be justification conferring. Second, I have argued that the resulting skeptical argument is a powerful one, and that rejecting it forces us to adopt a substantive and even surprising position in our positive account of the nature of knowledge and evidence. Finally, I have argued that Hume's skeptical reasoning suggests two conditions for an adequate theory of evidence. Specifically, any adequate theory will have to explain (a) how contingently reliable inferences can be justification conferring and (b) how knowers can be sensitive to the reliability of such inferences.

In Chapter 7, I defend a theory of knowledge and evidence that does just this. The theory is a version of reliabilism, because it holds that knowledge arises from the reliable cognitive powers of believers. As such, the theory adopts the strategy of simple reliabilism in making the reliability of empirical reasoning contingently reliable. But the theory goes beyond simple reliabilism by affirming that knowledge requires a

---

13 A similar trilemma arises for Fumerton, since he accepts the Principle of Inferential Justification. See my note 11.

sensitivity to the reliability of one's inferences. The trick is to understand such sensitivity in a way that both (a) avoids Humean circularity problems and (b) is psychologically plausible.

The main idea is as follows. First, inference patterns that give rise to reliable reasoning are manifested in the cognitive behavior of intellectually virtuous agents, but not in a way that requires agents to have *beliefs* about their inferences. Rather, intellectually virtuous agents are sensitive to the reliability of their inferences in the sense that they are disposed to engage in such inferences when they reason carefully. Put differently, intellectually virtuous agents have a disposition to try to believe the truth, and a disposition to reason in certain ways when so motivated. In that sense, they recognize (are sensitive to) the reliability of those ways in achieving the aim of that motivation.

Second, the cognitive dispositions that give rise to reliable empirical reasoning allow inferences from observed cases to unobserved cases without first justifying anything like the regularity principle. Such dispositions make us reliable because *in fact* nature is regular, and therefore inferences based on observed cases will be in fact reliable. Understanding the notion of an intellectual virtue in this way – that is, as a disposition to reliably form true beliefs and with that motivation – we can say that virtuous agents are sensitive to the reliability of their reasoning, but not in a way that gives rise to circularity or that is psychologically implausible.

This broad theory of knowledge also accommodates the lessons of Chapters 3, 4, and 5, explaining why not all evidential relations are inferential, how perceptual knowledge can be based directly on sensory appearances, and how knowledge not based on justifying reasons is possible. The idea is that the cognitive dispositions manifested by virtuous agents include both inferential and non-inferential dispositions. Cognitive powers such as mathematical and empirical reasoning involve dispositions to make certain inferences, but non-inferential powers such as memory, intuition, and perception involve dispositions of a different kind. For example, perception disposes us to form beliefs about objects in the world immediately (i.e. non-inferentially) on the basis of sensory appearances. In all cases the cognitive dispositions that virtuous agents manifest make them reliable in relevant environments – that is, such dispositions make virtuous agents contingently reliable. But they are reliable nonetheless.

The ideas of the preceding two paragraphs are developed in Chapter

7. Accordingly, in that chapter we move from negative to positive epistemology; I defend a positive account of knowledge and evidence on the grounds that it explains *why* certain skeptical assumptions are false. The theory also captures our pre-theoretical intuitions about which cases count as knowledge, and is psychologically plausible as well.

7

Agent Reliabilism

We are looking for a theory of knowledge and evidence that confirms and explains the conclusions of Chapters 2 through 6. More specifically, we are looking for a theory that explains (a) why not all evidential relations are inferential; (b) how sensory evidence in particular can be non-inferential (or how beliefs about the world can be evidentially grounded in sensory appearances yet not inferred from sensory appearances); (c) how some knowledge can be foundational (or how some knowledge can be based on evidence which is not itself in need of further justifying reasons); and (d) how inferences that are only contingently reliable can nevertheless give rise to knowledge. Our theory should also explain (e) how knowers can be sensitive to the reliability of their inferences, and even though such inferences are only contingently reliable, so knowers cannot just "see" that they are reliable by a kind of logical intuition into necessary relations.

I have already suggested that agent reliabilism does all of these things. In this chapter I develop and defend that claim. The argument occurs in two stages. In Part I, I argue that reliabilist theories in general confirm all of the conclusions noted in (a) through (d). In other words, "simple" or "generic" reliabilism explains *why* the skeptical assumptions rejected in Chapters 2 through 6 are false. In Part II, I argue that agent reliabilism is the best version of reliabilism. This is because, in part, agent reliabilism explains (e), or how knowers can be sensitive to their contingent reliability without falling into Humean circularity problems.

In the next chapter, I continue to show how agent reliabilism addresses skepticism by revisiting argument (D3) from Chapter 2. This is the version of Descartes' skeptical argument that I claimed was susceptible to a relevant possibilities approach. In Chapter 8, I develop an account of what makes a possibility relevant, or what makes a possibility such that it must be ruled out in order that one have knowledge, and I show how agent reliabilism can provide a theoretical explanation of that account. In other words, the theory explains why some possibilities need to be ruled out to have knowledge, and why other possibilities are irrelevant and can be ignored.

If a theory of knowledge can do all of these things, then that is powerful evidence in its favor. Such a theory would capture a wide range of our pre-theoretical intuitions about which particular cases count as knowledge, would explain why skepticism is false, and would be psychologically plausible. In the final chapter of the book, Chapter 9, I argue that agent reliabilism also gives us insight into the possibility of moral and religious knowledge. A consideration of various skeptical arguments suggests that empirical knowledge is grounded in the faculties and habits of cognitively virtuous agents, and teaches us something about the nature of the cognitive virtues involved. This puts us in a position to consider whether similar virtue is possible regarding religious and moral beliefs. For example, we may consider the possibility of moral perception in the light of our conclusions about the nature of empirical perception. Traditional arguments against moral perception, it turns out, are no longer persuasive in the context of our more adequate understanding of empirical perception. Progress in moral and religious epistemology would constitute further evidence in favor of the theory of knowledge being defended.

I. *Simple Reliabilism*

I now turn to the argument that reliabilism provides a theoretical explanation for the conclusions of Chapters 2 through 6. I begin by sketching the view and then turn to the concerns of (a) through (d) just reviewed.

1. SIMPLE RELIABILISM: THE BIG IDEA

Simple reliabilism is the view that knowledge arises from reliable cognitive processes. Here "reliable" cannot mean "reliable in producing knowledge." That would be to give a circular account of knowledge. Rather, reliable cognitive processes are ones that are reliable in arriving at *truth*.

Note that we need not load much into the word "truth" here. For example, we need not think of truth as correspondence with reality. Although most reliabilists do endorse a correspondence theory of truth, that theory is not part of reliabilism as such. Plug in your favorite notion of what truth is, or better yet, just remain commonsensical about it. The main idea is that knowledge is produced by cognitive processes that "get things right" or are "accurate" a good deal of the time.

The following passage from Alvin Goldman expounds this simple but powerful idea.

> We can gain insight into this problem by reviewing some faulty processes of belief-formation, i.e., processes whose belief-outputs would be classed as unjustified. Here are some examples: confused reasoning, wishful thinking, reliance on emotional attachment, mere hunch or guesswork, and hasty generalization. What do these faulty processes have in common? They share *unreliability*: they tend to produce *error* a large proportion of the time. By contrast, which species of belief-forming (or belief-sustaining) processes are intuitively justification-conferring? They include standard perceptual processes, remembering, good reasoning, and introspection. What these processes seem to have in common is *reliability*: the beliefs they produce are generally true. My positive proposal, then, is this. The justificational status of a belief is a function of the reliability of the process or processes that cause it, where (as first approximation) reliability consists in the tendency of a process to produce beliefs that are true rather than false.[1]

A number of points warrant consideration. First, by a "reliable" process Goldman does not mean an infallible one – he says that a reliable cognitive process has a "tendency" to produce or sustain beliefs that are true rather than false. The greater the reliability, the greater the degree of justification or positive epistemic status, and Goldman implies that a very high degree of reliability would be required for knowledge.

Suppose Jones believes he has just seen a mountain-goat. Our assessment of the belief's justifiedness is determined by whether he caught a brief glimpse of the creature at a great distance, or whether he had a good look at the thing only 30 yards away. His belief in the latter sort of case is (*ceteris paribus*) more justified than in the former sort of case. And, if his belief is true, we are more prepared to say he *knows* in the latter case than in the former. The difference between the two cases seems to be this. Visual beliefs formed from brief and hasty scanning, or where the perceptual object is a long distance off, tend to be wrong more often than visual beliefs formed from detailed and leisurely scanning, or

---

1 Alvin Goldman, "What Is Justified Belief?", in Moser, p. 179.

where the object is in reasonable proximity. In short, the visual processes in the former category are less reliable than those in the latter category. ²

Second, whether an inference gives rise to true belief depends on the premises one starts with, and so Goldman needs to introduce the idea of conditional reliability. A reasoning (or inferential) process is conditionally reliable just in case, given true premise-beliefs, the process tends to produce true conclusions. In this sense valid deduction is perfectly reliable, while good inductive reasoning is also reliable though not perfectly so.³ The theory that results is what Goldman calls a "historical" or "genetic" theory, because it makes positive epistemic status depend on the history of the belief in question. "The theory says, in effect, that a belief is justified if and only if it is '*well-formed*,' i.e., it has an ancestry of reliable and/or conditionally reliable cognitive operations."⁴

2. WHY SKEPTICAL ARGUMENTS GO WRONG

With this sketch in place we can see that simple reliabilism confirms the conclusions of Chapters 2 through 6. In other words, simple reliabilism gives us a theory of knowledge and evidence that explains *why* the skeptical assumptions rejected in those chapters are false. Let us take a closer look.

a. Why Not All Evidence Is Inferential

First, simple reliabilism explains why not all evidential relations are inferential. I suggested in Chapter 4 that the most general characterization of the evidential relation is as follows: A cognitive state (such as a belief or experience) is evidence for another cognitive state if and only if being in the first state tends to confer positive epistemic status on the second state. If reliabilism is true, then the way that this works is through reliable cognitive processes. Such processes take an initial cognitive state

---

2 Ibid., p. 180.
3 If we define "deduction" as a cognitive process that employs valid (truth-preserving) reasoning, then deduction is perfectly (conditionally) reliable. However, we will need to define another process, a pseudodeduction, to recognize cases where mistakes are made. Alternatively, we may use "deduction" to designate a process whereby one intends to reason validly, in which case not even deduction will be perfectly reliable. Compare Sosa, *Knowledge in Perspective*, pp. 227–233.
4 Goldman, "What Is Justified Belief?", p. 183.

such as experience or belief, and produce an additional state in a reliable (i.e., truth-conducive) way.

Now let us say that an inference is a movement from a premise-belief or premise-beliefs to a conclusion-belief on the basis of their contents and according to a general rule. According to reliabilism, this is one way in which a belief can be evidentially grounded, since using an inference-rule can be one way in which a belief may be reliably formed. But if reliabilism is true, then that is not the only way that an evidential relation can be manifested. For there might be other cognitive processes – that is, processes other than employing an inference rule from belief to belief – that ground one cognitive state in another in a reliable way. Put differently, not every movement in thought constitutes an inference from premise-belief to conclusion-belief according to a general rule. Moreover, these other kinds of movement might nevertheless be reliable or conditionally reliable.

It might be objected that the present point is merely a verbal one; the way in which we make room for evidential relations that are non-inferential is by employing a restricted sense of "inference." But the idea is more important than that. The real point is that not all movements in thought can be evaluated by the criteria governing inferences in the narrower sense defined earlier. *Some* movements of thought may be evaluated by considering the truth of initial premises together with the conditional reliability of an inference-rule employed. If we have both true premises and a conditionally reliable inference-rule then the reasoning in question is deductively or inductively sound. But what if there is no adequate inference involved, deductive or inductive? Or what if there are not adequate "premises," in the sense of true or justified *beliefs* from which we are starting? Does that entail that the movement in thought is inadequate for generating knowledge or justified belief? Only if we insist on using the criteria for good inferences where such criteria are out of place. This is exactly the mistake that many skeptical arguments make, and that many non-skeptical philosophers make as well. It is, for example, the mistake of the hermeneutical school, which holds that all good evidence must be from within the circle of belief.[5]

---

5 A similar critique of the hermeneutical school is made by Ernest Sosa in "Philosophical Scepticism and Epistemic Circularity," *Proceedings of the Aristotelean Society* (1994): 263–290, esp. pp. 264–266. There he cites Heidegger, Gadamer, Habermas, Foucault, and Derrida as holding the position that "a belief can be justified and amount to knowledge only through the backing of reasons or arguments." He attributes the same position to Davidson, Rorty, BonJour, and Michael Williams. In earlier work Sosa calls this position the "Intellectualist

b. *Why Knowledge of the World Need Not Be Inferred from Sensory Appearances*

If not all evidential relations are inferential, what might be an example of a non-inferential evidence relation? This brings us to our second conclusion from previous chapters: sensory appearances can be good evidence for beliefs about the world, even though such beliefs are not inferred from appearances. Reliabilism accounts for this, since it holds that appearances are good evidence so long as they reliably cause true beliefs, whether by employing good inferences or in some other way. The present question is, What is that other way?

I have already suggested in Chapter 4 that the process is more direct than inference. On this view, the way things appear is interpreted as being of certain objects with certain properties. I am appeared to in a characteristic way by a tree bearing apples by a brook, and I interpret that, quite directly and without anything like an inference, as a tree bearing apples by a brook. I say that there is nothing like an inference involved because I do not first form other beliefs — for example, beliefs about how things appear — and then construct a clever argument to the conclusion that what I see is a tree. Certainly I do not do any such thing explicitly, but there is no reason to think that I do so implicitly either. And as we have seen, there is good reason to think that I do not.

At this point it might be useful to address a possible misconception. To say that perception does not depend on inference is *not* to say that it does not depend on prior assumptions, prejudices, conceptual schemes, and the like. Quite the contrary: such things are what make at least many perceptions possible. But the point here is that such things do not function as premises in an inference: they do not function as grounds of which we are aware, and from which we draw conclusions on the basis of sensitivity to their content and according to a general inference-rule. Rather, they shape perception in other ways. To put things too vaguely, they function as the causal antecedents of belief by creating perceptual dispositions: they cause us to see one way rather than another, to discriminate some of an infinite number of patterns, to recognize some information while filtering out other information.[6] But to evaluate these

---

Model of Justification" and subjects it to similar critique. See, e.g. his essay "The Raft and the Pyramid," in *Knowledge in Perspective*, esp. pp. 169–173. Compare also James VanCleve, "Epistemic Supervenience and the Circle of Belief," *Monist* 68 (1985): 90–104.

6 In Chapter 9, I invoke schema theory in psychology to make these claims about non-

dispositions the way one evaluates discursive reasoning is to miss their nature altogether. According to reliabilism, the relevant criterion for evaluation is whether the dispositions governing our perceptions make those perceptions reliable. Do our assumptions, prejudices, and schemes serve to put us in better touch with the world or do they merely obscure it? If the former, then perceptual beliefs have positive epistemic status and can even amount to knowledge.[7]

Accordingly, to ask whether there is a good inference from appearance to reality misunderstands the way that appearances function as evidence for the world. This mistake is manifested both in the skeptical demand for such an inference and in the non-skeptical philosopher's attempt to reconstruct one.

c. Why Some Knowledge Is Not in Need of Justifying Reasons

From what has already been said we can see how simple reliabilism explains the possibility of foundational knowledge, or knowledge not based on further justifying reasons. If we conceive of justifying reasons as evidential *beliefs* from which knowledge is to be *inferred*, then not all knowledge needs further reasons, because some knowledge is based directly on sensory appearances. In this way the regress of justifying reasons comes to an end. In the preceding discussion we have already seen the theoretical explanation for this. According to simple reliabilism, positive epistemic status is a function of the reliability of cognitive processes, and therefore so long as perceptual processes are reliable they generate positive epistemic status. This is so even though such processes involve no justifying reasons from which perceptual beliefs are inferred.

So if reliabilism is true, then not all knowledge is based on justifying reasons. This is because we are conceiving reasons as further beliefs from

---

inferential perception less vague. The main idea is that perception involves "scripts" or stories through which sensory appearances are processed. The perceptual dispositions that result are theoretically loaded, to be sure. But they are best understood, I argue, as being non-inferential – they ground a process very different from inferring conclusions from premises.

[7] Goldman discusses work in empirical psychology which shows that background assumptions and other contextual features can increase reliability in perception. See *Epistemology and Cognition*, esp. pp. 188–191. There he cites G. Reicher, "Perceptual Recognition as a Function of Meaningfulness of Stimulus Material," *Journal of Experimental Psychology* 81 (1969): 275–280; E. Tulving, G. Mandler, and R. Baumal, "Interaction of Two Sources of Information in Tachistoscopic Word Recognition," *Canadian Journal of Psychology* 18 (1964): 62–71; and D. D. Wheeler, "Processes in Word Recognition," *Cognitive Psychology* 1 (1970): 59–85.

which knowledge is inferred, and the evidence of sensory appearances does not work in that way. But we may ask a further question about evidential *grounds*, where these are understood to include any kind of justifying evidence whatsoever. Must all knowledge be based on evidential grounds, where we understand grounds to include sensory appearances, and perhaps other cognitive states, as well as beliefs?

If reliabilism is true, then not all knowledge need be based on evidential grounds. For what is essential on that theory is that beliefs be reliably formed, and it remains an open question whether there are cognitive processes that are both reliable and involve no evidential grounds whatsoever. It is possible that memory works in this way. Logical intuition might be another candidate for such a process.

To elaborate, we may define three possible kinds of cognitive process. First, a process is *inferential* if it takes initial beliefs as inputs and generates other beliefs as outputs by employing some inference-rule. Second, a process is *experiential* if it takes sensory appearances or other kinds of experience as inputs and generates beliefs on that basis, but not by employing some inference from input states. I have argued that sensory perception is best understood as a process of this kind. Finally, a cognitive process is *groundless* if it does not operate on reliable grounds at all.[8] Now it is an empirical question whether human cognition includes this third kind of process. As we have just noted, it is possible that memory or logical intuition work this way. But that is not obvious, since these might involve their own phenomenology, and in a way that is consistent with their involving reliable grounds.[9]

For present purposes we may keep the question open, since the point is only that the third kind of process is possible. If such a process is also reliable, then it would confer positive epistemic status according to simple reliabilism. This would provide a different kind of foundational belief from what we have seen so far. Such beliefs would have positive epistemic status or even amount to knowledge, even though they are not grounded in any evidence whatsoever.[10]

---

8 Here we must make a distinction between cognitive states that serve as truth-indicating grounds for a belief, and those involved in a belief's production in some other manner. E.g., some beliefs might serve merely as background assumptions governing cognition; others might act as defeaters of counter-evidence.

9 For useful discussions of this question with regard to memory and logical intuition, see Plantinga, *Warrant and Proper Function*, esp. pp. 57–64 and pp. 103–110.

10 The phenomenon of blindsight might offer an example of the third kind of cognitive process. Individuals with certain kinds of brain injury lack the normal phenomenology of

d. How Contingently Reliable Inferences Can Give Rise to Knowledge

Simple reliabilism accounts for contingently reliable inferences in a straightforward manner. According to simple reliabilism, positive epistemic status is generated by reliable cognitive processes. If the use of an inference constitutes a reliable process, it does not matter that the inference is only contingently reliable. Put differently, simple reliabilism makes *de facto* reliability the grounds of positive epistemic status; it makes no difference whether the inference is contingently reliable or necessarily reliable. Neither does it matter whether a believer knows that her inference is reliable, or is justified in believing that it is, or is even aware that it is. Much less does it matter that she knows this to be a necessary truth.[11]

If simple reliabilism is correct, then this solves the problem of induction. That problem can be characterized as follows. In order to have inductive knowledge one must first know that inductive reasoning is reliable. But because any knowledge that inductive reasoning is reliable must rely on such reasoning itself, one cannot know that inductive reasoning is reliable. In short, you need to know that induction is reliable, but you can't. But as James Van Cleve has argued, if reliabilism is true then the skeptical argument is wrong on both counts: to have inductive knowledge you need not know that induction is reliable, but you can.[12]

First, one need not know that induction is reliable, because *de facto* reliability is what matters, not knowledge of reliability. But second, one can know that induction is reliable, because now an inductive argument to that conclusion is available. Specifically, it is now possible to do an induction on inductive arguments without falling into circularity. To

---

vision. However, testing shows that they can retain the ability to detect spatial locations of objects and can even improve it with practice. The explanation is that information about light hitting the retina is successfully carried to relevant parts of the brain, even though the information now bypasses parts of the brain associated with the production of visual imagery. However, the evidence for a third kind of cognitive process is ambiguous here. Even in cases of blindsight people report an odd kind of phenomenology, although it is not that of visual appearances.

11 For excellent discussions on the relationship between reliabilism and induction, see Plantinga, *Warrant and Proper Function*, esp. Ch. 7; Hilary Kornblith, *Inductive Inference and Its Natural Ground* (Cambridge, MA: MIT Press, 1993); and James Van Cleve, "Reliability, Justification, and the Problem of Induction," *Midwest Studies in Philosophy* 9 (1984), 555–567.

12 Van Cleve, "Reliability, Justification, and the Problem of Induction."

see why this is so, remember that reliabilism countenances contingently reliable inferences. Accordingly, these inferences need not include some premise to the effect that nature is regular or that induction is reliable; one will be able to argue directly from observed cases of induction to induction in general. But if such premises are not needed in inductive arguments, then an inductive argument that concludes that induction is reliable will not involve circular reasoning – that is, will not involve its conclusion as a premise.

The following example of enumerative induction illustrates the point:

(EI) 1. In the past, in many observed cases, enumerative induction has been reliable.
      2. Therefore, in general, enumerative induction is reliable.

This argument amounts to an enumerative induction on enumerative induction. But the argument is not circular, because the conclusion is not used as a premise, even implicitly.

Now (EI) *would* be circular if enumerative inductions had to include a premise about their reliability. (EI) would also run into circularity problems if inductive arguments required the regularity principle as a premise. For then the justification of that principle would be at issue, and any inductive argument in its favor would, by hypothesis, have to include the principle itself. But if simple reliabilism is true then enumerative inductions require neither the regularity principle nor a premise about their own reliability. For again, what matters is *de facto* reliability, and enumerative induction is in fact reliable even without such premises. That is because the world is in fact regular, and that is all that is needed for enumerative induction to be *de facto* reliable.

We have seen that according to simple reliabilism reasoning need only be contingently reliable to confer positive epistemic status on its conclusions. We have also seen that this characteristic of the theory allows it to answer the problem of induction. Before leaving this section I want to make one more general point. According to simple reliabilism, *all* evidential relations require only contingent reliability, and therefore the relationship between sensory appearances and the beliefs they cause need only be contingently reliable for perceptual knowledge. This is a fortunate result, since it is implausible that this relation *could* be any more than contingent.

Consider that the perceptual faculties of other species are very different from our own. As such, very different sensory appearances may indicate the same physical realities for these creatures; the way that a tree appears to a bat using sound-based sonar is nothing like the way the same tree appears to a human being using light-based vision. Consider also that the way things appear to us now could have indicated different physical realities. For that matter, we could have been built so that visual appearances reliably indicated nothing at all about objects in the world. The point is that there is no necessary relation between the way things appear and the way things are. That certain appearances reliably indicate certain real properties is merely a contingent fact.

This means that there is an important analogy between perceptual evidence and our evidence for unobserved matters of fact: namely, in each case our evidence for the relevant kind of belief is only contingently reliable. We saw in Chapter 6 that this creates a problem for any adequate understanding of inductive evidence. On the one hand, knowledge seems to require that the knower be sensitive to the reliability of her evidence. On the other hand, it is hard to see how one could be sensitive to this if one's evidence is only contingently reliable. I am now suggesting that exactly the same problem arises for a theory of perceptual evidence as well.

Finally, we should note that the problem cannot be avoided by thinking of sensory appearances as having representational content. This is because it remains a contingent matter whether sensory appearances having a particular representational content are reliable indications of the truth of beliefs having that same content. For example, in normal circumstances and in normal perceivers, there seeming visually to be a tree bearing apples by the brook is a reliable indication that there is a tree bearing apples by the brook. But this is a contingent fact about human visual perception rather than a necessary truth. Just as it could have been the case that visual phenomenal *qualia* do not reliably indicate anything about objects in the world, it could have been the case that thick visual seemings do not either.

3. FROM PROCESSES TO VIRTUES

We have seen that simple reliabilism has much in its favor. The theory explains why each of the conclusions in (a) through (d) is correct and therefore explains why the skeptical arguments in Chapters 2 through 6 are mistaken. It is, therefore, the kind of theory that we are looking for. But simple reliabilism is not quite right. It is on the right track, to be sure, but it is in need of some revision to bring it into better shape.

One problem with simple reliabilism has already been mentioned in Chapter 6, and again just now. Namely, the theory fails to explain how knowers can be sensitive to the reliability of their evidence. In this regard, simple reliabilism says that evidence must in fact be reliable for it to give rise to knowledge and justified belief. There is no further requirement that the knower realize that her evidence is reliable, or that she know this, or that she be sensitive to this in some other way. A second, related problem with simple reliabilism may be called "The Problem of Strange and Fleeting Processes." Put simply, simple reliabilism is too weak, because some reliable processes (strange and fleeting ones) do not give rise to knowledge and justified belief. In the remainder of this section I explore this second problem, and I argue that agent reliabilism can solve it. In Part II of the chapter, I argue that agent reliabilism solves the first problem as well.

Here are three examples of reliable yet epistemically inefficacious processes. First, consider "The Case of the Epistemically Serendipitous Lesion."[13] Imagine that there is a rare sort of brain lesion, one effect of which is to cause the victim to believe he has a brain lesion.

Suppose, then, that S suffers from this sort of disorder and accordingly believes that he suffers from a brain lesion. Add that he has no evidence at all for this belief: no symptoms of which he is aware, no testimony on the part of physicians or other expert witnesses, nothing. (Add, if you like, that he has much evidence *against* it; but then add also that the malfunction induced by the lesion makes it impossible for him to take appropriate account of this evidence.) Then the relevant [cognitive process] will certainly be highly reliable; but the resulting belief – that he has a brain lesion – will have little by way of warrant for S.[14]

As a second example, consider "The Case of the Absurd Reasoner." Having little understanding of biology, but fascinated by deterministic explanations of human behavior, Charles reasons as follows. If he witnesses two people ordering the same fruit drink on the same day, he concludes on that basis that they are genetically related. As it turns out, his whimsical reasoning process is perfectly reliable, since everyone is genetically related.

Finally, consider "The Case of the Helpful Demon." René thinks he can beat the roulette tables with a system he has devised. Reasoning according to the Gambler's Fallacy, he believes that numbers which

---

13 This case is from Alvin Plantinga, "Positive Epistemic Status and Proper Function," p. 28, and from *Warrant: The Current Debate* (Oxford: Oxford University Press, 1993), p. 199.
14 Plantinga, *Warrant: The Current Debate*, p. 199.

have not come up for long strings are more likely to come up next. However, unlike Descartes' demon victim, our René has a demon helper: every time René forms a belief that a number will come up next, the demon arranges reality so as to make the belief come out true. Given the ever present interventions of the helpful demon, René's belief-forming process is highly reliable. But this is because the world is made to conform to René's beliefs, rather than because René's beliefs conform to the world.

These examples of strange but reliable processes show that simple reliabilism is too weak. More exactly, it would seem that not just any reliable cognitive process can give rise to positive epistemic status. That, in turn, raises the question of what the appropriate restriction should be. How can simple reliabilism be revised so as to exclude these strange cases as counting for knowledge and justified belief? The answer is suggested in the following passage from Sosa, where he is considering how a certain move in ethics might fruitfully be applied to epistemology:

> In what sense is the doctor attending Frau Hitler justified in performing an action that brings with it far less value than one of its accessible alternatives? According to one promising idea, the key is to be found in the rules that he embodies through stable dispositions. His action is the result of certain stable virtues, and there are no equally virtuous alternative *dispositions* that, given his cognitive limitations, he might have embodied with equal or better total consequences, and that would have led him to infanticide in the circumstances. The important move for our purpose is the stratification of justification. Primary justification attaches to virtues and other dispositions, to stable dispositions to act, through their greater contribution of value when compared with alternatives. Secondary justification attaches to particular acts in virtue of their source in virtues or other such justified dispositions.
>
> The same strategy may also prove fruitful in epistemology. Here primary justification would apply to *intellectual* virtues, to stable dispositions for belief acquisition, through their greater contribution toward getting us to the truth. Secondary justification would then attach to particular beliefs in virtue of their source in intellectual virtues or other such justified dispositions.[15]

Relevant to present purposes is Sosa's suggestion for a restriction on reliable cognitive processes: it is those processes that have their bases in the stable and successful dispositions of the believer that are relevant for knowledge and justification. Just as the moral rightness of an action can be understood in terms of the stable dispositions or *character* of the moral

---

15 Sosa, "Raft and Pyramid," pp. 167–168.

agent, the epistemic rightness of a belief can be understood in terms of the intellectual character of the cognizer.

Sosa names this approach "virtue epistemology," since the stable and successful dispositions of a person are appropriately understood as virtues.

For example, it may be one's faculty of sight operating in good light that generates one's belief in the whiteness and roundness of a facing snowball. Is possession of such a faculty a "virtue"? Not in the narrow Aristotelian sense, of course, since it is no disposition to make deliberate choices. But there is a broader sense of "virtue," still Greek, in which anything with a function – natural or artificial – does have virtues. The eye does, after all, have its virtues, and so does a knife. And if we include grasping the truth about one's environment among the proper ends of a human being, then the faculty of sight would seem in a broad sense a virtue in human beings; and if grasping the truth is an intellectual matter then that virtue is also in a straightforward sense an intellectual virtue.[16]

In this regard Sosa cites Book 1 of Plato's *Republic*, where Plato says that vision is the virtue of the eyes and hearing the virtue of the ears.[17] But whatever the terminology we adopt, the important point is that the move solves the problem of strange and fleeting processes. For the cognitive faculties and habits of a believer are neither strange nor fleeting. They are not strange, because they make up the person's intellectual character – they are part of what make her the person that she is. They are not fleeting, because faculties and habits by definition are *stable dispositions* – they are not the kind of thing a person can adopt on a whim or engage in an irregular fashion.

On the present view, knowledge and justified belief are grounded in stable and reliable cognitive character. Such character may include both a person's natural cognitive faculties and her acquired habits of thought. Accordingly, innate vision gives rise to knowledge if it is reliably accurate. But so can acquired skills of perception and acquired methods of inquiry, including those involving highly specialized training or even advanced technology. So long as such habits are both stable and successful, they make up the kind of character that gives rise to knowledge.

We may now explicitly revise simple reliabilism as follows: A belief p has positive epistemic status for a person S just in case S's believing p results from stable and reliable dispositions that make up S's cognitive character. I will call this position "agent reliabilism," since the disposi-

---

16   Sosa, *Knowledge in Perspective*, p. 271.
17   For example, at 342 and 352.

tions referred to in the definition are dispositions of cognitive agents. Accordingly, the definition makes the reliability of agents central to the analysis of knowledge and justified belief.

I have been arguing that agent reliabilism solves the problem of strange and fleeting reliable processes, and as such constitutes an improvement over simple reliabilism. We may briefly note that the position has the same advantage over several other versions of reliabilism, such as method reliabilism, social practice reliabilism, and evidence reliabilism. For with each of these other views, it is possible to imagine cases where the specified seat of reliability is fleeting, and therefore cases where the view rules incorrectly that there is knowledge. For example, we can imagine cases where a person bases her belief on evidence that is perfectly reliable, but where there is no corresponding disposition to form beliefs on evidence of a relevant kind. In the isolated case where the person happens to use evidence that is in fact reliable, it seems incorrect to call the result knowledge. Similarly, we can imagine that a person adopts a perfectly reliable method, but on a whim. Where there is no corresponding disposition to employ the method, it seems wrong to say that the person obtains knowledge by employing it in an isolated incident. This is because in each case the method, or the practice, or the adoption of particular evidence amounts to a fleeting process. The belief is formed by a reliable process, but there is a sense in which the reliability of the process is accidental from the believer's point of view.

In each case the problem can be solved if the view is revised so as to require a disposition to use the process in question. But then the view would become a version of agent reliabilism. Since the relevant dispositions would be properties of agents, such a revision would have the effect of requiring agent reliability. For example, consider William Alston's social practice reliabilism.[18] If social practices are defined independently of people's dispositions to engage in them, then the view is subject to counterexamples as just described: it will be possible that agents adopt practices in isolated incidents, on a whim, and so forth. But if social practices are by definition *dispositions* to act in certain ways, then it will be impossible for an agent to engage in a reliable social practice without having a reliable cognitive character.[19] On this second version

---

18   William Alston, "A 'Doxastic Practice' Approach to Epistemology," in Marjorie Clay and Keith Lehrer, eds., *Knowledge and Skepticism* (Boulder: Westview, 1989); and Alston, *Perceiving God* (Ithaca: Cornell University Press, 1991), esp. Ch. 4.
19   It is clear that Alston means to define a practice in the second way. He writes, "A doxastic

of the view, social practice reliabilism becomes a version of agent reliabilism, but with further details about the nature of cognitive dispositions. In effect, it says that knowledge and justified belief are grounded in the reliable dispositions of agents, and that these are to be understood in terms of reliable social practices.

This means that agent reliabilism is sufficiently general to admit of many versions, depending primarily on how one fills in the details regarding the nature of reliable character. Understood thus generally, the position is widely popular in contemporary analytic epistemology.[20] Historically, the theory has its roots in the Aristotelian–Thomistic conception of the person as the seat of intellectual powers, and in Reid's anti-skeptical faculty epistemology.[21]

But despite current popularity and excellent historical credentials, agent reliabilism is by no means uncontroversial. In Part II of the chapter, I want to look at one major issue facing the position and to address some objections that arise within that context. The issue is how to address the concern of (e) at the beginning of the chapter – that is,

---

practice can be thought of as a system or constellation of dispositions or habits, or to use a currently fashionable term, 'mechanisms,' each of which yields a belief as output that is related in a certain way to an 'input'." *Perceiving God*, p. 153.

20 In addition to Sosa and Alston, Plantinga has developed a detailed position around the thesis that knowledge is grounded in the stable and reliable faculties of believers, where "faculties" are understood to include both natural and acquired dispositions. For the most recent statement of Plantinga's position, see *Warrant and Proper Function*. Goldman, in his most recent work, moves away from his earlier process reliabilism to a version of agent reliabilism, calling his own view a "virtues theory" and comparing it sympathetically with Sosa's. See "Epistemic Folkways and Scientific Epistemology" in *Liaisons*, esp. p. 163. Each of these authors defends a different position. My claim here is that all are versions of the core position that I call "agent reliabilism." Linda Zagzebski also understands knowledge and justified belief as deriving from intellectual virtue, making the analogy to Aristotelian virtue ethics even stronger than Sosa would have it. Early versions of Zagzebski's position were instances of agent reliabilism. However, in the latest statement of her views Zagzebski explicitly rejects the requirement that knowers have a reliable cognitive character. Therefore, although her latest position is a version of virtue epistemology, it is not a version of agent reliabilism. For the earlier view, see Linda Zagzebski, "Religious Knowledge and the Virtues of the Mind," in Linda Zagzebski, ed., *Rational Faith: Catholic Responses to Reformed Epistemology* (Notre Dame: University of Notre Dame Press, 1993), and "Intellectual Virtue in Religious Epistemology," in Elizabeth Radcliffe and Carol White, eds. *Faith in Theory and Practice: Essays on Justifying Religious Belief* (La Salle: Open Court, 1993). For the later view, see *Virtues of the Mind* (Cambridge: Cambridge University Press, 1996). For a criticism of Zagzebski's later position, see my "Two Kinds of Intellectual Virtue," *Philosophy and Phenomenological Research*, forthcoming.

21 See Plantinga, *Warrant: The Current Debate*, p. v and pp. 183–184, and Jonathan Kvanvig's useful discussion in *The Intellectual Virtues and the Life of the Mind* (Savage, MD: Rowman and Littlefield, 1992), esp. pp. 11–27.

how to explain the kind of sensitivity to one's own reliability that is required for knowledge. Another way to put the question is in terms of subjective justification: In what sense must knowledge be well formed from the knower's own point of view, as opposed to objectively well formed, or *de facto* reliable? My claim will be that agent reliabilism has the resources to successfully address these issues.

II. Agent Reliabilism and the Question of Subjective Justification

Agent reliabilism makes *de facto* reliability an important condition on knowledge. In this sense a belief counts as knowledge only if it is objectively well formed. But it would seem that knowledge has to be subjectively appropriate as well as objectively reliable. As we have noted, one way in which the subjective side of knowledge manifests itself is in regard to the concern raised in (e): inductive evidence, and evidential grounds in general, seem capable of generating knowledge only if the believer has some insight into the reliability of those grounds. The novice mathematician who does not "see" that her axioms entail her theorem, we said, does not know the theorem on that account. So far we have not seen how agent reliabilism can account for this strong intuition regarding the requirements for knowledge.

The issue of subjective appropriateness is often discussed in terms of epistemic justification. The question then becomes: How can agent reliabilism understand epistemic justification? The question threatens to turn into an objection. For our concept of knowledge does seem to involve a subjective requirement, and if agent reliabilism cannot account for this, then the view fails on that ground. But at this point the objection that threatens has not been adequately stated. For we have not articulated well just what *kind* of subjective justification is required for knowledge. In what sense, exactly, must knowledge be well formed from the knower's point of view? Or, in terms of (e), in what sense must knowers be sensitive to their own reliability?

In Sections II.1 through II.3 I review several senses of subjective justification which should *not* be required for knowledge. In each case, requiring this kind of sensitivity on the part of knowers would make knowledge impossible. I then argue in Section II.4 that agent reliabilism has the resources for understanding a different sense of subjective justification, and that this sort of justification is required for knowledge. In this way, agent reliabilism explains (e) as well as (a) through (d), and in general accounts for the intuition that knowledge must be subjectively appropriate as well as objectively reliable.

1. KNOWING THAT ONE KNOWS

One way to articulate the problem of subjective justification is in terms of the internalism–externalism debate in analytic epistemology. Internalism is the position that the conditions for justification must be appropriately internal to the knower's perspective. Roughly, something is internal to S's perspective so long as S is aware of it or could be aware of it merely by reflecting. Externalism is simply the denial of internalism, holding that the conditions for justification need not be within the knower's perspective. In this terminology, agent reliabilism is a form of externalism. For example, whether a person's perception is functioning reliably might not be something of which he is aware or could be aware just on reflection. The present issue is whether externalist theories like agent reliabilism can account for the kind of subjective justification that knowledge requires.

In the following passages BonJour reflects on the significance of cases like that of Norman the clairvoyant. Due to his highly reliable power of clairvoyance, Norman believes that the president is in New York City – despite the fact that Norman has considerable evidence otherwise, and has no suspicion that he has the power of clairvoyance. By hypothesis, Norman's belief about the president is caused by a reliable cognitive process: his little-used and completely unrecognized clairvoyance. But according to BonJour, it is counterintuitive to suppose that his belief is justified, and neither do we want to say that it is a case of knowledge:[22]

> We are now face-to-face with the fundamental – and obvious – intuitive problem with externalism: *why* should the mere fact that such an external relation obtains mean that Norman's belief is epistemically justified when the relation in question is entirely outside his ken? As I noted earlier, it is clear that one who knew that [the externalist's] criterion was satisfied would be in a position to construct a simple and quite cogent justifying argument for the belief that the President is in New York City: if Norman has property H (being a completely reliable clairvoyant under the existing conditions and arriving at the belief on that basis), then he holds the belief in question only if it is true; Norman does have property H and does hold the belief in question; therefore,

---

22 The example is from BonJour, *The Structure of Empirical Knowledge*, p. 41.

the belief is true. Such an external observer, having constructed this justifying argument, would be thereby in a position to justify *his own* acceptance of a belief with the same content.... But none of this seems in fact to justify Norman's *own* acceptance of the belief, for Norman, unlike the hypothetical external observer is *ex hypothesi* not in a position to employ this argument. . . .[23]

One reason why externalism may seem initially plausible is that if the external relation in question genuinely obtains, then Norman will in fact not go wrong in accepting the belief, and it is, *in a sense*, not an accident that this is so. . . . But how is this supposed to justify Norman's belief? From his subjective perspective, it *is* an accident that the belief is true. And the suggestion here is that the rationality or justifiability of Norman's belief should be judged from Norman's own perspective rather than from one which is unavailable to him.[24]

BonJour's complaint is that Norman's reliability is "outside his ken" or external to his "subjective perspective": thus the name "externalism" for theories of justification and knowledge of this general kind. But in what sense is Norman's reliability external to his perspective, and why is that a problem? This is what we have to get straight if we are to judge the force of BonJour's objection against externalism in general and agent reliabilism in particular.

We might interpret BonJour's argument as follows: First, knowledge is transparent: no one knows unless he knows that he knows, or at least can know that he knows. But if externalism is true, then no one ever does know that he knows. And therefore, if externalism is true, the skeptic is right when he says that no one knows.

Whether or not this is what BonJour intends, there is something natural about the argument. Many philosophers have explicitly affirmed the principle that knowledge entails knowing that one knows, and such a position is at least implied in many reactions to externalism.[25] But for all its naturalness the argument is confused. For one thing, there is no reason why one cannot know that she knows on agent reliabilism. On that theory, one knows that one knows in the same way one knows anything – by believing so as the result of reliable cognitive character.

Another problem with the current argument is that its first premise is false. That premise expresses the principle that one knows only if one

---

23 Ibid., p. 43.   24 Ibid., pp. 43–44.
25 For endorsement of this principle and ones like it see Roderick Chisholm, "Knowing That One Knows," in *The Foundations of Knowing*; Carl Ginet, *Knowledge, Perception and Memory* (Dordrecht: Reidel, 1975); and H. A. Prichard, *Knowledge and Perception* (Oxford: Clarendon Press, 1950).

knows that one knows (Kp only if KKp). But this principle cannot be right, since it leads directly to total skepticism; if the principle were correct, then I could not know even that I exist, and no matter what theory of knowledge is correct. This is because, according to the principle, I know that I exist only if I know that I know that I exist. But by a second application of that principle, I know that I know that I exist only if I know that I know that I know that I exist. Kp implies KKp, which in turn implies KKKp, which implies KKKKp, which implies KKKKKp, and so forth. But sooner or later I will reach propositions which I cannot even grasp, much less know. So if the principle is right, I do not know even that I exist. But of course I do know that I exist, and so the principle does not state an actual condition on knowledge.[26]

Let us consider a second interpretation of BonJour's objection. The passages from BonJour strongly suggest the following argument: In order to know, it is not sufficient that one's belief be reliably formed; one must also *know* that one's belief is reliably formed. But if this is BonJour's meaning, then his objection is again misguided. For like the principle just discussed, such a requirement generates an infinite regress and leads directly to skepticism. To see why, consider the conditions for knowledge that the objection suggests:

S knows that p only if
  i. S believes that p is true;
  ii. p is true;
  iii. S's belief is reliably formed; and
  iv. S knows that her belief is reliably formed.

The problem here is with condition (iv). Not only does it make the conditions for knowledge circular – it makes them impossible to fulfill. For on this suggestion S must know p': that p is reliably formed. But knowing this will generate (through (iv)) the condition that S know p": that p' is reliably formed. And the regress goes on. But since no one is capable of knowing an infinite number of increasingly complex propositions, a total skepticism is entailed. What this shows is not that total skepticism is true, but that the present objection to externalist theories is misguided.

---

26 The same argument applies if we take a weaker version of the principle: that one knows only if one can know that one knows. For more extended arguments that this principle and ones like it should be rejected, see William Alston, "Level Confusions in Epistemology," *Midwest Studies in Philosophy* 5 (1980): 135–150; and my "Internalism and Epistemically Responsible Belief," *Synthese* 85 (1990): 245–277.

BonJour does not say so, but someone might think that the need to know about one's own reliability is grounded in the following principle: To have knowledge, one must know that the conditions for having knowledge are fulfilled. This is another version of the idea that knowledge is transparent, so I will call it the "transparency principle." Since the transparency of knowledge has been such an attractive position, it is worth noting that the principle is not merely false but borders on being incoherent. For to say that conditions X, Y, and Z are sufficient conditions for knowing p is just to say that *nothing else* is required for knowing p. To go on to require that one must also *know* that conditions X, Y, and Z are satisfied is to give up the original contention that X, Y, and Z are sufficient conditions.[27] Of course, one might think that knowing p requires knowing that the conditions for knowing p are satisfied, because one thinks that knowing implies knowing that one knows. But we have already seen that this last assumption is false.

Finally, it is important to note that the transparency principle would have disastrous consequences for any theory of knowledge whatsoever, and not just for agent reliabilism. Suppose, for example, that we adopt a crude relativism, endorsing the theory that knowledge is what society agrees upon. According to the transparency principle, one can know that p is true only if one also knows that society agrees that p is true. And by a second application of the principle, one must also know that society agrees that society agrees that p, and so on *ad infinitum*. Again, since it is impossible to believe an infinite number of increasingly complex propositions, the transparency principle directly entails total skepticism, even for the theory that knowledge is what society agrees upon. Clearly the principle is either incoherent or false.

2. UNDERSTANDING THAT ONE KNOWS

So far we have seen three ways *not* to understand the subjective requirement on knowledge. Before moving on to something better, I want to look at a related objection against agent reliabilism. The objection is raised by Stroud and may be stated in the form of the following argument: If agent reliabilism is true, then no one can *understand* that the conditions for having knowledge are satisfied, since no one can reason without circularity that one's cognitive faculties and habits are reliable.

---

27 Here I am indebted to James Van Cleve. See his "Foundationalism, Epistemic Principles, and the Cartesian Circle," *Philosophical Review* 88 (1979): 77.

But if one cannot understand that the conditions for having knowledge are satisfied, then one cannot understand that one has knowledge. Therefore, agent reliabilism does not give us an adequate understanding of our knowledge. Moreover, since the task of epistemology is to understand how we know what we know, agent reliabilism cannot be a satisfactory epistemology.[28] More formally, we have the following argument.

(STR)
1. A person can understand that she has knowledge only if she understands that she fulfills the conditions for having knowledge.
2. If agent reliabilism is true, then a condition for knowing anything is that one's cognitive powers (i.e., faculties and habits) are reliable.
3. Therefore, if agent reliabilism is true, then one can understand that she has knowledge only if she understands that her cognitive powers are reliable. (1,2)
4. But if agent reliabilism is true, then one cannot understand that one's cognitive powers are reliable.
5. Therefore, if agent reliabilism is true, then no one can understand that she has knowledge. (3,4)

Remember that the support for premise (4) is as follows:

(STR4)
1. If agent reliabilism is true, then one can understand that one's cognitive powers are reliable only by reasoning in a circle.
2. Understanding cannot be based on circular reasoning.
3. Therefore, if agent reliabilism is true, then one cannot understand that one's cognitive powers are reliable. (1,2)

Like BonJour's, Stroud's argument has a certain intuitive pull. However, a closer look reveals that it has several problems. First, premise (4) of (STR) is false. According to agent reliabilism, one can know that one's cognitive powers are reliable so long as one's belief to this effect is itself grounded in reliable cognitive powers. But then the agent reliabilist can say the same thing about understanding: so long as one's belief is in fact well formed by virtuous faculties and habits, one understands what one believes. Stroud insists that understanding involves having reasons, but this added requirement on understanding is not a problem for agent reliabilism. On any plausible account, one *will* have reasoned to the

---

28 See Barry Stroud, "Understanding Human Knowledge in General," in Clay and Lehrer; and again in "Scepticism, 'Externalism,' and the Goal of Epistemology," *Proceedings of the Aristotelean Society* (1994): 291–307.

belief that one's powers are reliable. So long as the reasoning is in fact virtuous, understanding results.

(STR4) charges that any such reasoning would be circular, but that too seems to involve a confusion. Specifically, to understand that one's cognitive powers are reliable one must *use* those very powers, and in particular one must use one's reasoning faculties. But one need not reason from the reliability of one's powers *as a premise*. That would be circular, reasoning to a conclusion that one is reliable from a premise that one is reliable. But agent reliabilism requires no such circles.

For example, to know that your vision is in good working order you might visit an eye doctor. And certainly your vision will be involved in learning from the doctor that your vision is in fact in good working order – you will need to read a report, or at least identify the doctor as the person you are talking to. So will reasoning be involved, since you will have to infer the reliability of your vision from the evidence gathered. But at no time during this process would you reason from the assumption that your vision and reasoning are reliable. Again, you learn that your vision is reliable by using it and by using your reason, not by reasoning from assumptions about the reliability of your vision or your reason. Similar things can be said about other cognitive powers. For example, cognitive scientists learn about the reliability of human inference by inferring their conclusions from relevant observations. But that is the point: they infer the reliability of inference from observations, not from some premise to the effect that inference is reliable.

Premise circularity is vicious, but it is not involved in determining the reliability of one's cognitive faculties and habits. What about "faculty circularity," or the process of using one's faculties to determine the reliability of those same faculties? First, we should note that in general one cannot escape using one's cognitive powers to determine the reliability of those very powers – for, by definition, one's cognitive powers are that by which one cognizes. But to see that this fact is benign, consider that it is the condition of any cognizer whatsoever. Although skepticism is presented by Stroud and others as a problem for the human condition, it is true of *any* cognizer, God included, that one must think by the ways that one thinks.[29] Finally, if Stroud's objection were effective against agent reliabilism, a similar line of reasoning would preclude understanding that we know on any theory of knowledge whatsoever.

---

29 I am indebted to Keith DeRose for this last point, which he made in a paper presented at Fordham University.

For no matter what conditions on knowledge are laid down by a theory, we will have to use our thinking to determine that our thinking satisfies those conditions.

3. SOSA'S PERSPECTIVISM

We have seen three ways not to understand subjective justification and a related misplaced objection from Stroud. Nevertheless there seems to be something right about BonJour's general point, acknowledged in (e) at the start of the chapter: Even if knowledge does not require knowing that one knows, or knowing that one's cognitive powers are reliable, it does seem to require some kind of sensitivity to one's own reliability. As BonJour put the point, one's belief ought to be well formed from one's "subjective perspective." The trick is in how to understand that notion, if not in any of the ways we have considered so far.

Sosa is one agent reliabilist who has tried to tackle exactly this problem. According to him subjective justification is to be understood in terms of a reliable perspective on one's own faculties. The central idea is that for reflective knowledge (as opposed to mere "animal knowledge"), one must have a true grasp of the fact that one's belief is grounded in a reliable cognitive faculty. This grasp must in turn result from a faculty of faculties, which gives rise to the required epistemic perspective:

> For one is able to boost one's justification in favor of P if one can see one's belief of P as in a field F and in circumstances C, such that one has a faculty (a competence or aptitude) to believe correctly in field F when in conditions C. ... One thereby attributes to oneself some intrinsic state such that when there arises a question in field F and one is in conditions C, that intrinsic state adjusts one's belief to the facts in that field so that one always or very generally believes correctly.[30]

According to Sosa, to "see" one's belief of P as in a field and circumstances is to have true beliefs to that effect, where those true beliefs are themselves products of a cognitive virtue.

It is clear how this position can be applied to the case of Norman mentioned in Section II.1. Sosa can say that Norman has animal knowledge but not reflective knowledge, since Norman does not see himself

---

30 Sosa, *Knowledge in Perspective*, p. 282. Sosa develops this strategy in "Intellectual Virtue in Perspective" and in "Reliabilism and Intellectual Virtue," both in *Knowledge in Perspective*.

as believing from a reliable faculty of clairvoyance. Further, Sosa can say that Norman's belief is reflectively unjustified, since his belief actually conflicts with his epistemic perspective on his faculties. Remember we said that Norman has good evidence against his belief that the president is in New York City, and so from his own perspective he ought not to believe what he does.

Therefore Sosa's view correctly handles the cases of Norman the clairvoyant: our intuition is that Norman does not have knowledge, and Sosa's position has that result. However, a different problem arises for the view, concerning its psychological plausibility. Specifically, it would seem that we seldom have the perspective on our faculties that Sosa requires for justification. In the typical case we have no beliefs *at all* about the source of our beliefs. Much less do we have beliefs about our reliability in particular fields and circumstances, or about whether a belief is in such a field, or we in such circumstances.

Or at least we do not have occurrent beliefs like these. Is it plausible that we typically have such beliefs dispositionally? Where we do have such a dispositional perspective, the field and circumstances that our perspective specifies are probably the wrong ones. To the extent that I dispositionally attribute to myself certain cognitive faculties, those faculties are specified much too broadly to be of any use. For example, consider my belief that there is a glass of water on the table. In the typical case I have no occurrent beliefs about the source of this belief in a given cognitive virtue. Let me now consider any dispositional beliefs I might have. After considering the issue for a moment, it occurs to me that my belief about the glass is the result of sight. But if you ask me to get very specific about a field of propositions F, or a set of circumstances C, such that I am highly reliable in that field when in those circumstances, I am at a loss. I simply do not have very specific beliefs in this area, nor is it plausible that such beliefs are available dispositionally if only I think about it a little more. But if I do not have such a perspective in the typical case, then on Sosa's criteria I will not have justification and knowledge either. As we have seen, psychologically implausible conditions on knowledge lead directly to skepticism.

In reply to a similar objection Sosa writes the following:

[A person judging shapes on a screen] is justified well enough in taking it that, in his circumstances, what looks to have a certain shape does have that shape. He implicitly trusts that connection, as is revealed by his inferential 'habit' of moving from experiencing the look to believing the seen object to have the corresponding shape. So the 'belief' involved is a highly implicit belief, manifested chiefly in such a 'habit.' Habits, too, can be assessed as intellectually or cognitively proper or improper, 'justified' or not. And they can even be assessed for 'correctness.' Thus the habit of moving from 'looks round' to 'is round' is strictly correct if, in the relevant circumstances, anything that looked round would in fact be round (and we can view the 'habit,' alternatively, as a belief that, in the circumstances, anything that looked round would in fact be round)....

Since 'inferential habits' can be assessed as 'correct' or 'incorrect' in the senses specified, and as 'justified' or 'unjustified,' (not just *any* habit, no matter how acquired, being proper), *therefore* there is some motivation to view such habits as implicit beliefs (that can be thus correct and justified) in the corresponding conditionals, as suggested above.[31]

Sosa's strategy for meeting the psychological implausibility objection is to stress the implicit nature of the perspective on our faculties. The knower's perspective is "highly implicit" and is "manifested chiefly" in his habits of inference rather than in any explicit acceptance or judgment on the knower's part. But notice an ambiguity in Sosa's notion of a "perspective" and then a shift in his position. The ambiguity is between (a) dispositional beliefs and (b) dispositions to believe. In the passages quoted Sosa begins by understanding our epistemic perspective in the first way, but ends by understanding it in the second way. Let us take a closer look.

In the beginning of the first passage the required perspective on our faculties is constituted by highly implicit dispositional beliefs. These beliefs are "revealed by" and "manifested in" our habits of inference. But at the end of the first passage and in the second, our perspective on our faculties is *identified* with the habits. Sosa writes, "[W]e can view the 'habit,' alternatively, as a belief," and "[T]here is some motivation to view such habits as implicit beliefs." Sosa talks as if these alternatives are equivalent, or at least equivalent for relevant purposes. But they are not. To have a belief, even an implicit one, is not the same as having a disposition to form beliefs.[32]

The distinction is important because it is not at all implausible that we have habits of inference, or dispositions to form certain beliefs on

---

31 Ernest Sosa, "Virtue Perspectivism: A Response to Foley and Fumerton," in Enrique Villanueva, ed., *Philosophical Issues 5: Truth and Rationality* (Atascadero CA: Ridgeview, 1994), pp. 42–43. Sosa is responding to an objection from Richard Foley, "The Epistemology of Sosa," same volume.

32 For an extended discussion of the present distinction, see Audi, "Dispositional Beliefs and Dispositions to Believe."

certain bases and in certain circumstances. But it is highly implausible that we have beliefs about the details of belief production. For even implicit beliefs are intentional – they are beliefs *about* something. Accordingly, the view that we have an implicit perspective on our faculties implies that in some sense we think *about* our first-level beliefs, the details of how they are produced, and whether beliefs so produced are reliable in the circumstances in which we find ourselves. As we have seen, there is simply no evidence that such thinking takes place in the typical case, and plenty of evidence against it.

Therefore we should conclude that Sosa's perspectivism does not capture what it is to be subjectively justified – not if a perspective is intentional, so that a perspective on one's faculties is a perspective about those faculties. But we said that the passages from Sosa contained a shift in position – a shift from thinking of our perspective as dispositional beliefs to thinking of it as dispositions to believe. It seems to me that the second position is the more fruitful one. Let us pursue it further.

4. FROM PERSPECTIVES TO DISPOSITIONS

My proposal is that we can understand subjective justification in terms of the knower's dispositions to believe. More exactly, subjective justification can be understood in terms of the dispositions a person manifests when she is thinking conscientiously – when she is trying to believe what is true as opposed to what is convenient, or comforting, or fashionable. Something like this is perhaps Sosa's considered position, but then we should drop the terminology of "epistemic perspective," "reflective knowledge," and "seeing one's belief," since all of this implies intentional attitudes that we do not typically have – that is, thoughts about one's beliefs and the sources of those beliefs. None of that is implied here.

The proposal then is this:

(VJ) A belief p is subjectively justified for a person S if and only if S's believing p is grounded in the cognitive dispositions that S manifests when S is thinking conscientiously.

A few comments are in order. First, by "thinking conscientiously" I do not mean thinking with an explicitly voiced purpose of finding out the truth. Neither do I mean thinking with this as one's sole purpose. Rather, I intend the usual state that most people are in as a kind of default mode – the state of trying to form one's beliefs accurately. One might say "thinking honestly" instead, and this is intended to oppose such modes as trying to comfort oneself, trying to get attention, and being pigheaded. The latter, we might say, reflect epistemic vices rather than virtues.

Second, (VJ) does not equate justified belief with conscientious belief. This is because a person might be conscientious in believing that something is true without manifesting the dispositions she usually does in conscientious thinking. For example, a father might sincerely try to discover the truth about a son accused of bad behavior and yet nevertheless violate norms of good reasoning that he would usually manifest when thinking conscientiously: in this case his good judgment is undermined by affection for his child, and despite himself. In a similar fashion, someone might try too hard to get at the truth, thereby failing to manifest the good habits that he typically does. In such cases we say that the person outthinks himself, much as players can press too hard in sports.

Third, the dispositions that a person manifests when she is thinking conscientiously are stable properties of her character and are therefore in an important sense hers. Accordingly, in an important sense a belief produced from such dispositions will be well formed from the person's own point of view. The current proposal is that this fact solves the problem posed in (e) at the beginning of the chapter: namely, it explains in what sense knowers must be sensitive to the reliability of their own inferences. The relevant sense is that inferences that generate knowledge are appropriately grounded in the knower's cognitive character – specifically, the character she manifests when thinking conscientiously. This same line of reasoning addresses the requirement that knowers be sensitive to the reliability of their evidence in general, whether or not that evidence is conceived as inferential. Just as knowers are disposed to form beliefs on the basis of inferences from other beliefs, they are disposed to form perceptual beliefs directly on the basis of sensory appearances. The fact that they do this in some ways and not others constitutes a kind of sensitivity to the reliability of their evidence, whether that evidence be inferential or experiential.

This way of understanding subjective justification is quite natural on a virtue theory, since intellectual virtues are stable dispositions constituting a person's cognitive character. A long tradition suggests that virtuous belief is also properly motivated. This is captured in the present proposal by the reference to conscientious thinking. A person's intellectual virtues are identified with the dispositions she manifests when she is sincerely trying to believe what is true.

Finally, the view proposed in (VJ) does not have the problem we saw for the first interpretation of Sosa's perspectivism. This is because we require for justification that a belief be grounded in one's character, but not that one have beliefs *about* one's character. In this respect good thinking is like good hitting; when a baseball player swings the bat, he manifests dispositions that are a product of both innate capacities and acquired learning. If he is a good hitter then these dispositions will generate success in relevant conditions. But even so, the most successful player need not be a good coach; he may not have any beliefs at all, or may even have incorrect beliefs, about the nature and character of the dispositions that he himself manifests when batting conscientiously. What makes for a good hitter is that he hits well, and what makes for a good thinker is that he thinks well. Accordingly, (VJ) makes no requirement concerning a perspective on one's faculties or character, implicit or otherwise, and for this reason escapes the charge of psychological implausibility.

5. THE PLACE OF EPISTEMIC NORMS

We may further explore the present proposal by considering the question of epistemic norms. A natural way to understand subjective justification is in terms of conformance to the norms of good thinking, and the question arises whether (VJ) is consistent with this. The idea that subjective justification can be understood in terms of conformance to norms is suggested by John Pollock:

Norms are general descriptions of the circumstances under which various kinds of normative judgments are correct. Epistemic norms are norms describing when it is epistemically permissible to hold various beliefs. A belief is justified if and only if it is licensed by correct epistemic norms. . . . The concept of epistemic justification can be explained by explaining the nature and origin of the epistemic norms that govern our reasoning.[33]

Pollock stresses that epistemic norms govern our behavior without our having beliefs about them. Like most other action-guiding norms, epi-

---

33 Pollock, *Contemporary Theories of Knowledge*, pp. 124–125.

stemic norms influence our behavior without our thinking about them at all:

> Now let us apply this to epistemic norms. We know how to reason. That means that under various circumstances we know what to do in reasoning. This can be described equivalently by saying that we know what we should do. Our epistemic norms are just the norms that describe this procedural knowledge. . . . They describe an internalized pattern of behavior that we automatically follow in reasoning, in the same way we automatically follow a pattern in bicycle riding.[34]

We are presently considering whether this view of justification is consistent with (VJ). In another place I have argued that it is, suggesting that the dispositions a person manifests when she is thinking conscientiously have their basis in her conformance to countenanced norms.[35] On this view justified belief is grounded in cognitive dispositions, which in turn are grounded in conformance to correct epistemic norms. But although this position is possibly correct, it now seems to me that whether it is correct is an empirical question. Specifically, it is an empirical question whether cognition is governed by norms, and therefore an empirical question whether cognitive virtues have their bases in conformance to norms.

This issue arises due to the nature of norms. In particular, I am thinking of norms as rules that *govern* behavior, as opposed to rules that merely describe behavior. As such, norms in this sense play a causal role in the production of behavior. We may think of such norms as conditionals with antecedents stating certain conditions and consequents directing behavior in those conditions. For example, a rule of the relevant kind might have the structure, "In conditions C, believe B." Furthermore, C must state conditions to which we have cognitive access, since a rule can be followed only if we can be aware that its antecedent conditions are fulfilled.[36] An example of such a norm in perception would be, "Given such and such sensory experience, believe that there is a cat on the couch." But now it is an empirical question whether human cognition can be understood in this way – whether all human thought can be understood as governed by such rules. Evidence is mounting that it cannot be.

---

34 Ibid., p. 131.
35 John Greco, "Internalism and Epistemically Responsible Belief," and "Virtues and Vices of Virtue Epistemology," *Canadian Journal of Philosophy* 23 (1993): 413–432.
36 On this point I follow Pollock, *Contemporary Theories of Knowledge*, p. 133.

The problem is not that we do not *explicitly* follow such rules in our thinking, or even that implicit norms are exceedingly hard to articulate. Rather, the problem is that at least some parts of human cognition might not be rule governed at all. This would be the case, for example, if connectionist theories of perception and memory are correct. Let us take a moment to consider this last possibility, and to consider the consequences for understanding cognition as rule governed.

We can think of connectionism as a theory for modeling cognitive processing.[37] Unlike models of cognition suggested by traditional rule-based theories, connectionist systems are made up of numbers of simple but connected units that can be "activated" or excited to some degree. The units are set up so that the activation of each affects the activation of others to which it is immediately connected. In the most interesting models the interaction among units affects connection "strengths" over time, so that the effect of one unit on another is increased or inhibited on the basis of prior interaction between the two units. Processing takes place in a connectionist system when an initial pattern of activation is supplied to input units. This original activation sets off activity among the various units of the system until stability in the system is achieved. The pattern of activation over the output units then represents the system's "answer" to a proposed problem.

What is important for our purposes is that processing in a connectionist system does not take place according to programmed rules. Rather, the interaction among the units of the system is governed only by the laws of thermodynamics – initial activation together with initial connection strengths cause a pattern of activity that eventually settles the system into the state of highest entropy.[38]

An example will illustrate. James McClelland, David Rumelhart and Geoffrey Hinton have proposed a model for the perception of obscured letters in visually presented words.[39] Words are presented in partially degraded condition, and the system is supposed to identify the obscured letter. For example, the word WORK is presented so that the fourth

---

37 William Bechtel, "Connectionism and the Philosophy of Mind: An Overview," in William Lycan, ed., *Mind and Cognition* (Oxford: Blackwell, 1990), p. 253.
38 Ibid., p. 254.
39 The model is described in James McClelland, David Rumelhart, and Geoffrey Hinton, "The Appeal of Parallel Distributed Processing," in Brian Beakley and Peter Ludlow, eds., *The Philosophy of Mind* (Cambridge, MA: MIT Press, 1992). Reprinted from James Rumelhart, David McClelland, and the PDP Research Group, *Parallel Distributed Processing: Explorations in the Microstructure of Cognition*, vol. 1 (Cambridge, MA: MIT Press, 1986).

letter is partially obscured, and the problem for the system is to correctly identify the letter as a K. Here is how it works.

The model assumes that there are units that act as detectors for the visual features which distinguish letters, with one set of units assigned to detect the features in each of the different letter-positions in the word. . . . There are also four sets of detectors for the letters themselves and a set of detectors for the words.

In the model, each unit has an activation value, corresponding roughly to the strength of the hypothesis that what that unit stands for is present in the perceptual input. The model honors the following important relations which hold between these 'hypotheses' or activations: First, to the extent that two hypotheses are mutually consistent, they should support each other. Thus, units that are mutually consistent in the way the letter T in the first position is consistent with the word TAKE, tend to excite each other. Second, to the extent that two hypotheses are mutually inconsistent, they should weaken each other. . . . [I]nconsistencies operate in the word perception model to reduce the activations of units. Thus, the letter units in each position compete with all other letters in the same position, and the word units compete with each other. This type of inhibitory interaction is often called *competitive inhibition*. In addition, there are inhibitory interactions between incompatible units on different levels. This type of inhibitory interaction is simply called *between-level inhibition*.[40]

The present model does not operate like classical artificial intelligence models, where a system calculates outputs from inputs according to programmed rules. Nevertheless, the system works so as to give the right answer. In the following illustration the letters W, O, and R are presented as completely visible and enough of a fourth letter is shown to rule out all letters other than R and K.

Before onset of the display, the activations of the units are set at or below 0. When the display is presented, detectors for the features present in each position become active (i.e., their activations grow above 0). At this point, they begin to excite and inhibit the corresponding detectors for the letters. In the first three positions, W, O, and R are unambiguously activated, so we will focus our attention on the fourth position where R and K are both equally consistent with the active features. Here, the activations of the detectors for R and K start out growing together, as the feature detectors below them become activated. As these detectors become active, they and the active letter detectors for W, O, and R in the other positions start to activate detectors for words which have these letters in them and to inhibit detectors for words which do not have these

---

40 McClelland et al., pp. 273–275.

letters. A number of words are partially consistent with the active letters, and receive some net excitation from the letter level, but only the word WORK matches one of the active letters in all four positions. As a result, WORK becomes more active than any other word and inhibits the other words, thereby successfully dominating the pattern of activation among the word units. As it grows in strength, it sends feedback to the letter level, reinforcing the activations of the W, O, R, and K in the corresponding positions. In the fourth position, this feedback gives K the upper hand over R, and eventually the stronger activation of the K detector allows it to dominate the pattern of activation, suppressing the R detector completely.[41]

Here we have an illustration of perception without rules or norms. More exactly, we have a model of how perception might work without norms, since a machine does not literally perceive anything. The important point is that the model opens up this possibility for human perception. Whether human perception really does work this way is an empirical question.

An interesting feature of connectionist systems is that their behavior manifests regularities *as if* governed by inferential and other rules. But it is only "as if," since no such rules play any causal role in the mechanisms that generate those regularities.[42] Moreover, connectionist systems do not mimic rule following perfectly: exceptions occur, and so even the appearance of rule following is only approximate. This is in fact an attractive feature of connectionist models, because humans also behave as if their thinking is rule governed, but only approximately and with exception. If connectionist models produce the appearance of rule following, but also the same kind of *divergence* from rules that we see in human cognition, then that is good evidence for the thesis that human cognition is connectionist, and so also merely "as if" by rules or norms.

A further example illustrates how this treatment of rules is suggested by connectionist models. McClelland, Rumelhart, and Hinton describe a model for learning the past tenses of English verbs through repeated examples of root forms paired with past-tense forms. The model consists of two pools of units, one for representing root forms and the other for representing their past tenses. Training takes place when units for the root forms are activated and a learning rule adjusts connection strengths with the units for past-tense forms.

---

41   Ibid., p. 275.
42   Jerry Fodor and Zenon Pylyshyn, "Connectionism and Cognitive Architecture: A Critical Analysis," in Beakley and Ludlow (1992), p. 298. Reprinted from *Cognition* 20 (1988).

The model is trained initially with a small number of verbs that children learn early in the acquisition process. At this point in learning, it can only produce appropriate outputs for inputs that it has explicitly been shown. But as it learns more and more verbs, it exhibits two interesting behaviors. First, it produces the standard *ed* past tense when tested with pseudo-verbs or verbs it has never seen. Second, it "overregularizes" the past tense of irregular words it previously completed correctly. Often, the model will blend the irregular past tense of the word with with the regular *ed* ending, and produce errors like CAMED as the past of COME. These phenomena mirror those observed in the early phases of acquisition of control over past tenses in young children.[43]

The eerie similarity to the behavior of young children cannot help but suggest that they learn the past tenses of verbs in the same way.

The model learns to behave in accordance with the rule, not by explicitly noting that most words take *ed* in the past tense in English and storing this rule away explicitly, but simply by building up a set of connections in a pattern associator through a long series of simple learning experiences. The same mechanisms of parallel distributed processing and connection modification which are used in a number of domains serve, in this case, to produce implicit knowledge tantamount to a linguistic rule. The model also provides a fairly detailed account of a number of specific aspects of the error patterns children make in learning a rule. In this sense, it provides a richer and more detailed description of the acquisition process than any that falls out naturally from the assumption that the child is building up a repertoire of explicit but inaccessible rules.[44]

But as Fodor and Pylyshyn emphasize, it is misleading to put the point in terms of implicit versus explicit rule acquisition. For on a connectionist model rules on the cognitive level do not govern *at all*. The point is not that rules governing learning (or interpretation, or inference) are not "explicitly noted" or "explicitly stored away"; it is that no such rules play *any* causal role in cognition. Again, on a connectionist model it is only "as if" such rules are being followed; in actuality they do not do any work.[45]

The preceding discussion has consequences for how we should understand epistemic justification. Specifically, the discussion shows that (VJ) is more general than a theory of justification in terms of epistemic norms. The basis of our best cognitive dispositions might be conformance to epistemic rules or norms, but it might not be. Accordingly, whether the details of (VJ) are to be cashed out in terms of epistemic

---

43   McClelland et al., p. 287.   44   Ibid.
45   Fodor and Pylyshyn, p. 293.

norms is therefore at least partly an empirical question, to be decided by what empirical investigation into human cognition reveals.

This way of proceeding is in keeping with the methodology of strong particularism. If connectionism turns out to be true and human perception is not governed by norms, then it would be misguided to require conformance to norms for perceptual knowledge. It is obvious that I do know by perception that there is a computer in front of me, and that there is a cat on the couch. If a theory of knowledge and justification has built into it presuppositions about human perception that are inconsistent with this, then so much for that theory and its presuppositions. It will have turned out that a longstanding way of understanding subjective justification – that is, as conformance to correct intellectual norms – was just wrong.

Let us suppose that connectionism is true and that important areas of human cognition are not governed by norms. Would this mean that there is no place for epistemic norms whatsoever? Not at all, since there are several ways in which norms might still be relevant to justification. First, even if human thinking is not governed by norms, it might still be the case that good thinking is *describable* by norms. In other words, even if norms play no causal role in the production and regulation of belief, good human thinking might nevertheless be characterized by a set of rules describing how good thinking proceeds. Second, from the fact that not all human cognition is governed by norms it does not follow that none is. Perhaps connectionism is true for some areas of cognition, such as perception and memory, but not others. Third, even where cognition is not produced by norm-governed processes in its details, the beliefs that result may nevertheless be covered by more general epistemic norms. For example, even if connectionism is correct regarding the mechanisms of perception, perceptual beliefs might come under some such norm as "Trust your perception unless you have specific reason not to." Such a norm might be involved in perception and relevant to the justification of perceptual beliefs, even if perception is not norm governed in its details.

Finally, cognitive norms might emerge from processes that are not originally norm governed. For example, over a period of time perception might give rise to the norm, "Do not trust visual perception regarding small objects at large distances." Or memory might produce the norm, "Do not trust ostensible memories of emotionally charged events." Such norms might serve to refine perception or memory, making them reliable in conditions or fields where they otherwise would not be. If so, then conformance to emergent norms can constitute a significant if partial basis of reliable dispositions. In a similar way, norms governing good reasoning might be successfully adopted through informal or formal training. For example, empirical research shows that training in statistical rules can improve inductive reasoning.[46]

But even if there is ample place for epistemic norms in human cognition, we still should not *define* subjective justification in terms of conformance to norms. First, it remains an empirical question whether cognition is governed even by very general covering norms, or refined by emergent or learned norms. Second, not all beliefs in conformance with these would be justified. For example, suppose that unknown to me my perception is malfunctioning, causing me to believe that there is a cat on the couch on the basis of sensory appearances that would not normally cause this belief. In such a case my belief would be in conformance with the norm, "Trust your perception unless you have specific reason not to," but it would not be produced by any stable disposition usually in place when I am thinking conscientiously. Would such a belief nevertheless be subjectively justified? In a weak sense yes, since the belief would violate no norm that I countenance. But it would not be subjectively justified in a further sense that all knowledge requires: the belief would not be appropriately grounded in my cognitive character.

Perhaps we should endorse the following relations between subjective justification and countenanced norms. Let it be stipulated that a belief is in *conformance* with a norm just in case the norm plays a relevant causal role in the production of the belief. A belief is in *accordance* with a norm just in case the belief is consistent with the conditional rule that the norm specifies, even if the rule plays no causal role in the actual production of the belief.

(NJ1) A belief p is subjectively justified for a person S only if S's believing p is in conformance with the norms that S countenances when S is thinking conscientiously.

(NJ2) A belief p is subjectively justified for a person S only if S's believing p is in accordance with norms that correctly describe S's dispositions when S is thinking conscientiously.

---

46 John Holland, Keith Holyoak, et al. "Learning Inferential Rules," in Hilary Kornblith, ed., *Naturalizing Epistemology*, 2nd ed. (Cambridge, MA: MIT Press, 1994).

Note that (NJ1) and (NJ2) state only necessary conditions for justification, not sufficient ones. Second, (NJ1) applies only when there are norms which govern S's thinking. If no such norms exist, (NJ1) will be an empty condition on subjective justification.

6. THE PLACE OF EPISTEMIC RESPONSIBILITY

It has also been common to understand subjective justification in terms of epistemic responsibility, where responsibility is conceived in terms of either praiseworthiness or freedom from blame.[47] Should we agree that knowledge requires epistemic responsibility? Not if epistemic praise and blame are to be understood along Kantian lines. For Kant, the moral versions of these notions are intimately tied to duty, and duty to conformance to the moral law. But as we have seen, it is an empirical question whether cognition is governed by laws. Therefore, we should not make Kantian responsibility a necessary condition of knowledge.

What about Aristotelian responsibility? Aristotle's discussion of moral praise and blame lays down two major conditions for responsible action: knowledge of particular circumstances and freedom from compulsion. Discussion of the latter "control" condition contains two themes, which Aristotle does not seem to distinguish. First, responsible action must be such that "the moving principle" is at least partly within the agent. This is opposed to cases where the agent is coerced by external forces; "[T]hat is compulsory of which the moving principle is outside, being a principle in which nothing is contributed by the person who acts."[48] Second, responsible action must be such that the agent could have acted otherwise in a strong sense. Aristotle writes, "Now the man acts voluntarily; for the principle that moves the instrumental parts of the body in such actions is in him, and the things of which the moving principle is in a man himself are in his power to do or not to do."[49] Let us call this power to do or not to do an action "strong control."

Now the first aspect of control, that the principle of action is within the agent, fits well with the idea that justified belief is grounded in cognitive character. For if a belief arises from character, clearly the cause

---

47 See, e.g., BonJour, Chisholm, and Ginet in the works previously cited. I have defended responsibilist conceptions of epistemic justification in "Internalism and Epistemically Responsible Belief" and "Virtues and Vices of Virtue Epistemology."
48 Aristotle, *The Nicomachean Ethics*, trans. David Ross (Oxford: Oxford University Press, 1980), 3.1.
49 Ibid.

of the belief is partly the knower herself. Problems arise, however, regarding the second aspect of control. Specifically, it is not clear whether knowledge is always such that the knower could have believed otherwise.

To be sure, Aristotle does not require direct or immediate strong control for moral responsibility. Thus he says that persons can be responsible for their states of character because they can be "part-causes" of such.[50] For example, a person can be blameworthy for ill health even if it is not in his power now to be healthy. This will be so if earlier voluntary actions were part-causes of his present illness. Similarly, one might hold that we have at least indirect control over our doxastic lives. For example, we can decide to gather more evidence before drawing conclusions about some matter. Moreover, we can strive to develop better cognitive habits or work to alleviate cognitive vices.

But still, the issue of strong control can be pressed. Is it realistic to think that all human cognition is at least within our indirect strong control? For example, is it in my power (in any relevant sense) to refrain from believing that there is a truck bearing down on me when I see that there is? The issue is complicated, since the ways in which our choices and actions can affect even perception are not fully understood. But perhaps this point alone is sufficient reason to reject any such condition on subjective justification or knowledge: namely, it is largely an empirical question whether we have strong control over our cognition, and to what extent. Therefore, it is an empirical question whether all human knowledge can satisfy this strong Aristotelian condition on praiseworthiness and blameworthiness. This being the case, we should not say that strong Aristotelian responsibility is a condition on knowledge. As in the case of cognitive norms, we do not want to build into our theory of knowledge conditions that we may in fact not satisfy.

Another consideration confirms the conclusion that knowledge does not require this kind of epistemic responsibility. Suppose it turns out that human perception is not within our strong control, even indirectly. Suppose also that, nevertheless, our perception is as reliable as we ordinarily assume that it is. Would we hesitate to say that we can know what we clearly see to be the case? For example, would we say that I cannot know that there is a truck bearing down on me because, as it turns out, I cannot help but believe that there is, given the truck that I see? Or suppose that we come across alien beings who have far more

50   Ibid., 3.5.

accurate and reliable perception than we do, but who do not have the power to believe otherwise than how they perceive. It seems wrong to say that, for lack of control in this strong sense, such beings do not have perceptual knowledge. These considerations suggest that epistemic responsibility, in any sense that requires the ability to believe otherwise, is not a part of our concept of knowledge. Even if, as a matter of fact, all of our cognition is within our strong control and so all knowledge is praiseworthy, such praiseworthiness is not a necessary condition on knowledge.

However, there remains a weaker sense of praiseworthiness in which it is correct to say that knowledge requires epistemic responsibility: namely, there is a sense in which something is praiseworthy just in case (a) it is properly motivated and (b) the principle of action is within the agent. The way that agent reliabilism understands subjective justification guarantees that these weaker conditions are fulfilled in cases of knowledge.[51]

7. CONCLUSIONS

We have seen that reliabilism in general can provide a theoretical explanation of the conclusions expressed in (a) through (d), and that agent reliabilism can account for the concern in (e) as well. In other words, agent reliabilism provides a principled refutation of all of the skeptical arguments that we have considered and also explains in what sense knowers must be sensitive to the reliability of their inferences. The theory also has resources for defining an important sense of subjective justification. In this way, it accounts for our persisting intuition that knowledge ought to be well formed from the knower's point of view, or that knowledge must be subjectively appropriate as well as objectively reliable. Finally, the theory does all of this in a way that is psychologically plausible, and that captures our pre-theoretical intuitions about what cases do and do not count as knowledge.

---

51 Matthias Steup argues that cognitive control can be fruitfully understood in terms of sensitivity to one's evidence. Just as some philosophers have attempted to define "could have done otherwise" as "would have done otherwise if choice had been different," Steup suggests that we might define "could have believed otherwise" as "would have believed otherwise if evidence had been different." Perhaps this describes another sense in which knowledge can be understood to involve epistemic responsibility. "Epistemic Obligation and the Freedom to Believe Otherwise," typescript.

In the next chapter I continue the defense of agent reliabilism by showing how it gives a theoretical explanation of what it is for an alternative possibility to be epistemically relevant. That is, the position explains which alternative possibilities to one's belief need to be ruled out to have knowledge and which do not, and why this is so.

8

Agent Reliabilism and the Relevant Sense of "Relevant Possibility"

Recall the skeptical argument (D3) from Chapter 2. The major premise of that argument was that good evidence must discriminate among alternative possibilities. In other words, my evidence for a belief p can give me knowledge only if it would cause me to believe that p is true in cases where p is true, and also would not cause me to believe that p is true in cases where p is false and some alternative is true. But, the argument continues, since sensory appearances do not discriminate in this way between what we believe and various skeptical scenarios, sensory evidence cannot give rise to knowledge of the material world.

I suggested that a solution to (D3) is to deny the assumption that evidence must rule out all alternative possibilities to generate knowledge. The idea was that evidence must discriminate among *relevant* possibilities, but not all possibilities are relevant. In particular the possibilities that I am a brain in a vat or the victim of an evil demon do not seem to be relevant ones. Of course if I *were* a brain in a vat or the victim of a deceiving demon, then I would not know what I think I do, but so long as these remain mere possibilities they fail to undermine my knowledge.

This strategy against (D3) gave rise to (D4). That argument ran as follows:

(D4)   1. S can know that p is true on the basis of evidence E only if E discriminates p's being true from all *relevant* possibilities that are inconsistent with p's being true.
2. My evidence for my belief that I am sitting by the fire is my sensory experience.
3. It is a relevant possibility that I am not sitting by the fire but only dreaming that I am.

4. Therefore, I can know that I am sitting by the fire only if my sensory experience discriminates my sitting by the fire from my only dreaming that I am. (1,2,3)
5. But my sensory experience does not discriminate these possibilities for me.
6. Therefore, I do not know that I am sitting by the fire. (4,5)

Since (D4) concedes that evidence need only rule out relevant possibilities, its first premise becomes unassailable. But now premises (3) and (5) of (D4) become problematic. Specifically, the idea of dreaming in (3) is ambiguous between normal dreams that occur in sleep and "philosophical" dreams involving evil demons and brains in vats. The problem is that on either interpretation the argument contains a claim that is less than wholly plausible.

If we interpret (D4) as making claims about normal dreams, then premise (5) seems false. Perhaps it is at times a relevant possibility that I am dreaming in the everyday sense of "dreaming," but in such cases my evidence does discriminate that possibility from waking life; if I pay close attention, or perhaps pinch myself, I can tell that I am not dreaming. On the other hand, if (D4) is about philosophical dreams, then premise (3) seems false, or at least less than obvious. Intuitively it is not a relevant possibility that I am the victim of a deceiving demon, or that I am a brain in a vat. These are possibilities in some broad sense, but not in any sense that seems to present a problem for my knowing. Therefore, on either interpretation of dreaming, the skeptical argument contains a premise that we need not accept.

1. TWO TASKS FOR WORKING OUT THIS APPROACH

The relevant possibilities approach has been a popular one, but it needs to be worked out further. First, we want an account of what makes a possibility relevant and why the skeptical hypotheses do not constitute relevant possibilities. In other words, we need an account of "relevant possibility" that (a) accords with our pre-theoretical intuitions about which possibilities need to be ruled out and which do not in ordinary cases of knowledge and (b) rules that the skeptical possibilities do not need to be ruled out. Second, we do not want our account to be *ad hoc*. What we would like is an account of knowledge which explains why our account of relevant possibility has the content that it does.

a. Providing an Account of "Relevant Possibility"

It has been popular to attempt an account of relevant possibility in terms of objective probability.[1] The problem with this solution is that we lack an adequate account of "objectively probable." The most natural way to understand that notion is in terms of percentage of a reference class. However, it is hard to see how a reference class could be specified in the present case, or even what a reference class would begin to look like here. For this reason attempts to define relevant possibility along these lines have failed.[2]

I propose that we understand relevant possibility in a different way, making use of the "possible worlds" semantics of modal logic. The idea is that it is a *logical* possibility that I am a brain in a vat hooked up to a supercomputer programmed to deceive me. In other words, there are possible worlds in which this is the case. But such possible worlds are "far away" from the actual world. There are no close possible worlds in which I am a brain in a vat, where "closeness" is to be understood, roughly, in terms of overall world similarity. The current proposal, then is, this: a possibility is relevant if it is true in some close possible world, irrelevant if not. This proposal explains many of our pre-theoretical intuitions about which possibilities need be ruled out and which do not in order to know, and it explains why the skeptical possibilities do not need to be ruled out.

More work needs to be done, of course. Most importantly, the proposed account of relevant possibility is too weak as it stands; more possibilities are epistemically relevant than those that are true in close possible worlds. Also, we will have to say more about what constitutes world closeness in order to make the account more informative. But this is the main idea for completing the first task. The details presented in Sections 2 and 3 will fix up the account by making it stronger in the required way and by making the notion of world closeness more informative.

---

1   See, e.g., Fred Dretske, "Epistemic Operators," *Journal of Philosophy* 67 (1970): 1007–1023; Alvin Goldman, "Discrimination and Perceptual Knowledge"; and Marshall Swain, "Revisions of 'Knowledge, Causality, and Justification,' " in Pappas and Swain (1978). For objections to these views see, Sosa, "Knowledge in Context, Skepticism in Doubt," in James Tomberlin, ed., *Philosophical Perspectives 2: Epistemology* (Atascadero, CA: Ridgeview, 1988). The account I offer here avoids Sosa's objections by making the notion of objective likelihood more informative, and by adding subjective conditions to the account of "relevant possibility."
2   Sosa makes this point in "Knowledge in Context, Skepticism in Doubt."

b. *Providing an Account of Knowledge to Support Our Account of Relevant Possibility*

I have already said that agent reliabilism can provide a theoretical understanding of what makes a possibility relevant. In other words, the theory can explain why some possibilities need to be ruled out to have knowledge and why others do not. In the present context, this is equivalent to explaining why evidence must discriminate among possibilities that are true in close possible worlds, but not among possibilities that are true only in far-off worlds.

The main idea is as follows. Cognitive virtues are a kind of power or ability. Abilities in general are stable and successful dispositions to achieve certain results under certain conditions. But abilities cannot be defined in terms of actual conditions only. Rather, when we say that someone has an ability we mean that she would be likely to achieve the relevant results in a variety of conditions similar to those that actually obtain. In the language of possible worlds, someone has an ability to achieve some result under relevant conditions only if the person is very likely to achieve that result across close possible worlds. But if knowledge essentially involves having cognitive abilities, and if abilities are dispositions to achieve results across close possible worlds, then this explains why possibilities are relevant only when they are true in some close possible world. Specifically, only such possibilities as these can undermine one's cognitive abilities. In an environment where deception by demons is actual or probable, I lack the ability to reliably form true beliefs and avoid false beliefs. But if no such demons exist in this world or similar ones, they do not affect my cognitive faculties and habits.

The remainder of the chapter develops this main idea. In Section 2 I present and defend a more detailed account of relevant possibility. In Section 3 I further explore the idea of a cognitive virtue by offering a possible worlds analysis for abilities in general and cognitive abilities in particular. In Section 4, I show how agent reliabilism explains the account of relevant possibility presented in Section 2.

2. THE RELEVANT SENSE OF "RELEVANT POSSIBILITY"

Our first task is to provide an account of relevant possibility such that (a) knowledge requires only that our evidence rule out (discriminate) that kind of possibility and (b) the skeptical possibilities involving brains in vats and evil demons turn out not to be relevant possibilities. As a first try consider the following account of relevant possibility, which I believe comes close to meeting these two criteria. Let us say that a possible world W is close to a possible world W' if and only if, roughly, W is very similar to W'. Then,

> q is a relevant possibility with respect to S's knowing that p is true if and only if
> i. If q is true, then S does not know that p is true, and
> ii. In some close possible world, q is true.

What is important to notice is that this account effectively disallows that evil demons and brains in vats are relevant possibilities. So long as the actual world is anything like we think that it is, there are no close worlds in which we are disembodied spirits or brains in vats. Accordingly, the account has significant consequences for the force of (D4). Premise (3) of that argument implies that the skeptical scenarios are relevant possibilities. On the current account this amounts to saying that the skeptical possibilities are true in some close possible world. But of course there is no reason whatsoever to accept that claim. Presumably such scenarios are logically possible, so that each is true in some far-off possible world. But we have no reason to believe that either is true in any close possible world.

Therefore, if the current account of relevant possibility is correct, then it seriously undermines the force of the skeptical argument. The claim that the account is correct is supported by reflection on two further examples. First, imagine that you see Tom Grabit take a book from a library shelf and put it in his bag.[3] On the basis of this evidence you form the belief that Tom Grabit took a library book. Unknown to you, however, Tom has a twin brother Jack, who was also in the library at the time you saw Tom take the book. Intuitively, you do not know that it was Tom who took the book, since if Jack had taken the book you would have been fooled into thinking that Jack was Tom. In order for you to know that Tom took the book you must be able to rule out the possibility that it was Jack who took the book. But consider the case where Tom does not have a twin brother. Must you still be able to rule out the possibility that it was his twin brother who took the book, in

---

3 Tom Grabit cases were first introduced by Lehrer and Paxson. See Keith Lehrer and Thomas Paxson, "Knowledge: Undefeated Justified True Belief," *Journal of Philosophy* 66 (1969): 225–237, reprinted in Pappas and Swain (1978).

order to know that Tom took the book? Intuitively the answer is no. In the case where there is no twin brother it is enough that you saw Tom take the book.

As a second example, consider the case of the barn facades. You are driving through a part of the country where, unknown to you, the local residents have constructed sides of barns in order to fool passers-by into thinking that the community is wealthier than it actually is. You drive by a real barn and form the belief that there is a barn ahead. In this case the proposition that you see a barn facade rather than a barn is a relevant possibility. You do not know the latter if you cannot rule out the former. But must you *always* be able to rule out the possibility of a barn facade before you can know that you see a barn from the highway? Intuitively the answer is no, and this is in fact how the account rules.[4]

The proposed account of relevant possibility handles these two cases well. However, it is not quite right and some revisions are necessary. This is because there are possibilities that are not true in any close possible world, but that nevertheless need to be ruled out in order for someone to have knowledge. Consider a revised version of the Tom Grabit example. Everything is as before, except that Tom Grabit has no twin brother. However, S *believes* that Tom does have a twin brother. It seems to me that S's evidence must rule out the possibility that Tom's twin brother took the book, even though the possibility is not true in any close possible world (since Tom in fact has no twin brother). Another version of the Tom Grabit example raises a different problem. Suppose that Tom does not have a twin brother and S does not believe that Tom has a twin brother, but S ought to believe that Tom has a twin brother – S has good reason for believing that Tom has a twin brother. Again, it seems to me that in such a case the possibility that Tom's twin took the book must be ruled out by S's evidence. In these cases the problem is not that the possibility is true in some close possible world, but that S believes, or ought to believe, that the possibility is likely to be true. Fortunately the account can easily be revised to accommodate both of the these cases. Thus we have,

> (RP) q is a relevant possibility with respect to S's knowing that p is true if and only if
>   i. If q is true, then S does not know that p is true; and
>   ii. Either (a) in some close possible world q is true, or

---

4 The example is from Goldman, "Discrimination and Perceptual Knowledge."

(b) S believes that q is likely to be true, or
(c) S ought to believe that q is likely to be true.

I believe that (RP) covers all and only those possibilities that must be ruled out in cases of knowledge. Secondly, (RP) continues to exclude the skeptical scenarios as relevant possibilities, assuming that there are no brains in vats or victims of evil demons in our environment, and assuming that we neither believe nor ought to believe that there are.

Before moving on we should address a possible misconception. Namely, one might think that the present strategy against (D4) merely ends in a stalemate with the skeptic. This is because the skeptic will insist that, for all we know, some skeptical hypothesis is true in some close possible world, perhaps because it is true in the actual world. But this kind of objection is misguided in two respects. First, there is no skeptic with whom we are debating and with whom we could fall into such a stalemate. Rather, what we have is a skeptical argument and we are evaluating its force so as to root out any mistaken assumptions that it might contain. We are trying to learn a lesson about what knowledge does and does not require, and how we might fulfill those requirements.

Second, the objection misunderstands the dialectic of the investigation so far. We deemed Descartes' original argument to have force precisely because it claimed only that the skeptical scenarios were in some sense possibilities, and it does seem that we have to allow that assumption. But we have now pushed the argument so that premise (3) of (D4) claims that the scenarios are *relevant* possibilities, and on the present interpretation this amounts to the claim that in some close possible world I *am* a brain in a vat or the victim of an evil deceiver. But now the argument is flawed if it depends on that premise. We will have found an assumption that we need not accept, and that in fact there is no reason whatsoever to accept.

In effect this shows that there is only one way to challenge the present strategy against (D4): namely, one must challenge the account of relevant possibility in (RP). For if that account is right, clearly the claim that the skeptical scenarios are relevant is implausible. I will now go in the other direction, however; that is, I will now defend the account in (RP) by showing how it is explained by agent reliabilism.

3. A THEORY OF VIRTUES AND A VIRTUE THEORY OF KNOWLEDGE

The central idea of agent reliabilism is that knowledge arises from cognitive abilities or powers. An ability, in turn, is a stable and successful disposition for achieving some result under appropriate conditions. What we need now is a more detailed account of what this amounts to. I will proceed by offering an account of abilities in general and then an account of cognitive abilities in particular. After that it will be relatively easy to see how the resulting theory explains the proposed account of relevant possibility in (RP).

a. What Is an Ability?

Roughly, an ability in general is a stable disposition to achieve some result under appropriate conditions. For example, we say that Don Mattingly has the ability to hit baseballs. By this we mean that Mattingly has a disposition to hit baseballs under normal conditions for playing baseball. Notice that we do not require that Mattingly have perfect success, nor do we require that he have a disposition for hitting baseballs under just any conditions. In general, how high a success rate is required will depend on the kind of ability in question. Likewise, what conditions are appropriate will depend on the kind of ability in question, as well as on other contextual matters.

These remarks might suggest the following account of having an ability to achieve a result:

(A1) S has an ability to achieve result R in conditions C if and only if S has a high rate of success achieving R when S is in C in actual cases.

The current proposal, however, is both too weak and too strong. First, (A1) does not distinguish between having an ability to achieve R and having success achieving R due to good luck. Thus it is possible that in all actual cases of swinging at baseballs, I hit the ball due to amazingly good luck. My bat just happens to be where it ought to be on every pitch. In that case I would have great success hitting baseballs in actual cases, but it would be false that I have an ability to hit baseballs. Or consider the case of Mr. Magoo. Magoo in fact is highly successful in avoiding harm, meaning that in the actual world Magoo rarely comes to harm. But we would not say that Magoo has an ability to avoid harm, since he avoids harm only by amazingly good luck. (An inch to the left and that anvil lands on his head!)

For a similar reason the current proposal is also too strong. For it might be that S does have an ability to achieve R but fails in nearly all actual cases due to amazingly bad luck. Just as it is possible to have an ability to achieve R and yet fail in some actual case, it is possible (even if improbable) to have the ability and yet fail in nearly all actual cases. Finally, it makes sense to say that S has an ability to achieve R even if S never achieves R because S never comes under the appropriate conditions. Thus it makes perfect sense to say that you have the ability to count by fives to one thousand, even if you never do so because no actual situation ever calls for it. And so we have several reasons why (A1) fails to capture what it is to have an ability in general.

These last considerations suggest that having an ability is not a function of what S does in actual cases, but of what S would do in possible cases. And this suggests the following subjunctive account of having an ability:

(A2) S has an ability to achieve result R in conditions C if and only if, if S were in C, then S would achieve R with a high rate of success.

But this account is also both too weak and too strong, and for somewhat similar reasons as with (A1). First, consider the case where S is often in C and has success achieving R in actual cases due to good luck. Then the subjunctive conditional in (A2) is true, but S does not have an ability to achieve R. Second, consider the case where S is often in C but fails to achieve R in actual cases due to bad luck. Then the subjunctive conditional in (A2) is false, but it is possible that S does have an ability to achieve R.

I suggest that the following account avoids all of the problems that we have raised for (A1) and (A2):

(A3) S has an ability to achieve result R in conditions C if and only if, across the range of close possible worlds where S is in C, S achieves R in C with a high rate of success.

Two examples will help to explain the motivation for (A3). First, consider that in some close possible world a fair coin will come up heads one hundred times in one hundred tosses. However, across a range of close possible worlds, the coin will come up heads 50 percent of the time, since improbable strings of heads will be offset by improbable strings of tails. Now let us consider an example of an ability. There is a close possible world where Mattingly hits .000 for the month of April, due to an improbable string of bad luck. But across the range of close possible worlds, Mattingly presumably hits near .300, since strings of bad luck are offset by strings of good luck. The current proposal is that this is why Mattingly has the ability to hit baseballs; he in fact hits near .300 in the actual world, but, more importantly, he hits near .300 across the range of close possible worlds.

The current proposal, then, does not equate abilities with actual successes, since it requires that S have a high rate of success across close possible worlds. For this reason (A3) handles the case of Mr. Magoo. Although Magoo avoids harm in the actual world, there are close possible worlds (large numbers of them in fact) where Magoo is harmed at every step. Further, the proposal does not rule out abilities where there is no actual high rate of success. Thus where S has little actual success achieving R, but only due to strings of bad luck, it will still be the case that S has a high rate of success through close possible worlds. The case in which S never finds herself in the relevant conditions is also handled nicely by the current account. For even if S is never in C in the actual world, it will still be either true or false that, across the range of close possible worlds, S has a high rate of success with respect to R when under the relevant conditions. (In the close worlds where you must count by fives to one thousand to save your life, you do it.)

Finally, consider how the current proposal distinguishes Mattingly from the lucky batter. We say that Mattingly has an ability to hit baseballs. Not only does he have good success hitting baseballs in the actual world, but presumably he has a high rate of success across close possible worlds. Thus in worlds where the pitch comes in a little lower, Mattingly adjusts his swing accordingly. Not so with the lucky batter. The lucky batter swings without an ability and just happens to connect with the pitch. If the pitch had come in a little lower, the lucky batter would have swung over it.

We may therefore accept (A3) as a correct account of what it is to have an ability in general. Of course (A3) is vague in many respects. It does not say how high the rate of success across close possible worlds must be, or which conditions are the relevant ones. But this is as it should be. First, which conditions are relevant will depend on the ability in question, as well as on context. For example, when we say that Mattingly can hit baseballs we obviously do not mean at night and without lights, but this is well understood in the context of a conversation about baseball. Similarly, contextual features set different boundaries when we say that Mattingly has the ability to hit baseballs and when we say that a Little Leaguer has the ability to hit baseballs.

Context does not eliminate vagueness completely, but this too is as it should be. This is because the concept of an ability is vague even within contexts. For example, when I claim that a rookie has the ability to hit baseballs, do I mean that he can hit in pressure situations? Do I mean that he can hit against the very best pitchers in the league? Normally my claim will be at least somewhat vague in these respects. Sometimes closer attention to context or further stipulation will eliminate such vagueness, and sometimes it will not.

Other kinds of vagueness are associated with the concept of world closeness, and these might seem more problematic. We said that closeness is a function of overall world similarity, but what kinds of similarity count, and what degree of similarity is important? Again, this will depend on the kind of ability in question, and it will depend on contextual features as well. But also again, fixing kind of ability and contextual features will not eliminate all of the vagueness involved.

Having said this, we can nevertheless give our concept of world closeness a substantial degree of content. First, what counts for world closeness is partly determined by our account as it stands. Specifically, since (A3) relativizes abilities to a range of relevant conditions, only worlds in which S is in such conditions will be relevant for consideration. Second, it seems clear that when we say that S has an ability, we mean that S has the ability as S is actually constituted. For example, when we say that Mattingly can hit baseballs, this does not become false because in some possible worlds Mattingly is injured or drugged or out of shape and therefore can no longer hit baseballs. For similar reasons it is clear that only worlds with the same laws of nature as hold in the actual world will count as close.

The issue can be pressed, however. Which aspects of S's constitution are relevant for determining world closeness, where the issue is whether S has the ability to achieve result R in conditions C? The answer seems to be that it is those aspects of S's constitution which, given the actual laws of nature and given conditions C, are relevant to whether S's actions in C result in producing R. In other words, we will want to keep constant any characteristics of S which, given the laws of nature and the relevant conditions, figure into whether the relevant results occur.

Two examples here should lend some clarity. First, we want to say that Mattingly has the ability to hit baseballs because, given Mattingly's actual constitution, the normal conditions for hitting baseballs, and the laws of nature which actually hold, Mattingly's actions result in a high ratio of hit baseballs. This occurs in the actual world, but it would also occur if the world were a little different: if the pitch came in a bit lower, Mattingly would still hit the baseball. On the other hand, it makes no sense to say that Mattingly lacks an ability to hit baseballs because in some possible worlds he is nearsighted. This is because the constitution of Mattingly's eyes figures importantly into the laws of nature that govern the occurrence of the result in question.

Let us consider a second example. Imagine that due to amazingly good luck my bat hits the baseball whenever I swing at a pitch in the actual world. It does not follow that I have the ability to hit baseballs. This is because, given the constitution of my eyes, and given the laws of nature that actually hold, if the world were a little different I would miss the baseball entirely. When the pitch comes in a little lower, Mattingly, constituted as he is, adjusts his swing. But when the pitch comes in a little lower to me, I see no difference and I swing over the ball.

We can now make the notion of world closeness more informative. Let us define S's R-constitution as those characteristics of S that, given the actual laws of nature, are relevant to whether S's actions result in producing R when S is in conditions C. Then we may say that a world W is close to the actual world (in the sense relevant to whether S has the ability to produce R in C) only if S has the same R-constitution in W as in the actual world, and only if the laws of nature that hold in W are the same as those that hold in the actual world. (A3) should be read with this characterization of world closeness in mind.

According to these suggestions, the conditions for S's having an ability involve four dimensions, three of which are kept constant and one of which is allowed to vary. To determine whether S has an ability in question, we keep constant the actual laws of nature, the set of conditions associated with the ability, and S's R-constitution associated with the ability. We then vary the other conditions of the environment, and we look at S's success rates in the worlds where such variations are kept relatively minor. What kind of environmental variations are important and what makes a variation relatively minor? This is left vague in (A3), but context will serve to eliminate much of that vagueness.

b. What Is a Cognitive Ability?

A cognitive ability has the form of an ability in general, but with the cognitive end of arriving at true beliefs and avoiding false beliefs. Therefore a cognitive ability, in the sense intended, is an ability to arrive at truths in a particular field and to avoid believing falsehoods in that field, under relevant conditions.

More formally,

(CA)   S has a cognitive ability A(C,F) with respect to proposition p if and only if there is a field of propositions F and a set of conditions C such that
  i. p is in F, and
  ii. Across the range of close possible worlds where S is in C, S has a high rate of success with respect to believing correctly about propositions in F.[5]

This account successfully distinguishes cognitive abilities such as vision, memory, and reliable reasoning from non-abilities such as dreaming, wishful thinking, and hasty generalization. Thus under normal conditions vision is a cognitive ability with respect to determining color properties of middle-sized objects. This is because in the actual world and across close possible worlds we have a propensity to believe correctly about such propositions when in normal conditions. In other words, across these worlds we have a high rate of success. However, we have no such propensity with respect to beliefs caused by dreaming. Even if by coincidence someone were to enjoy actual success in forming true beliefs through dreaming, there would be no high rate of success across close possible worlds, and so the lucky dreamer would not count as having a cognitive ability on the present account.

Similarly, (CA) correctly distinguishes between the two Tom Grabit cases and between the two barn facade cases. Thus in the case where Tom has no twin brother, S will very likely be correct about Tom taking the book in the relevant worlds. But in the case where Tom has an indistinguishable twin brother, S's rate of success will drop significantly in close worlds. Likewise, in the case where there are no barn facades in the environment, S will have a propensity to believe correctly about the existence of barns in the relevant worlds. But in the case where there are barn facades in the environment, S's rate of success will drop dramatically across close worlds.

---

5   Compare Sosa, *Knowledge in Perspective*, Ch. 16.

These cases also constitute examples of how our concept of world closeness sways with our concepts of a cognitive ability and of knowledge. For example, how far off must the nearest barn facade be before S has a cognitive ability with respect to beliefs about the existence of barns? If there are facades in the immediate environment, it is obvious that S has no ability. And if there are no such facades within one hundred thousand miles, then it seems that S does have the ability. I suggest that there are many cases in between where our intuitions are not sharp. The present point is that our intuitions about world closeness will sway with our intuitions about whether there is a cognitive ability and whether there is knowledge. If this is correct, then the vagueness in our accounts is a virtue rather than a vice. This is because our accounts of a cognitive ability and of knowledge capture a vagueness that already exists in those concepts and explain that vagueness by locating it at a deeper level of analysis.

With the present account of cognitive abilities in place we may now look at how agent reliabilism explains the account of relevant possibility in Section 2.

4. AGENT RELIABILISM AND RELEVANT POSSIBILITIES

The way that agent reliabilism explains clause (iia) of (RP) is straightforward. According to agent reliabilism, knowledge is true belief grounded in cognitive abilities. And according to our account of abilities, they are a function of S's rates of success across close possible worlds. But then possibilities that are true only in far-off worlds do not affect S's abilities in the actual world. If I were a brain in a vat in the actual world, then across close possible worlds I would lack a high rate of success with respect to forming true beliefs about my environment. But so long as I am not a brain in a vat, this mere possibility does not affect my success rate in the actual world and in close possible worlds. Therefore, the mere possibility that I am a brain in a vat is irrelevant to whether I know.

This result is obvious even when we grant that the concept of world similarity is vague, and that this vagueness infects our account of knowledge. This is because it is clear that the world in which I am a brain in a vat is a very far world from the actual world, given that the actual world is anything like we think it is. For although our concept of world similarity is vague, it is not vague in all respects. One stipulation that was made on world closeness was that a world W is close to the actual world only if S's constitution in W is similar to S's constitution in the actual world. This stipulation was well motivated in our account of what it is to have an ability in Section 3, and the same stipulation serves nicely here as well. For similar reasons, no skeptical scenarios which entail a change in the laws of nature will turn out to be relevant. Even if such scenarios count as logical possibilities, they do not count as relevant possibilities and so do not undermine our capacities for knowledge.

What about clauses (iib) and (iic) of (RP)? These clauses resulted from our intuitions that knowledge should be subjectively justified as well as objectively reliable. Put another way, knowledge requires that one's beliefs be appropriately formed from one's own point of view. Agent reliabilism recognizes these intuitions and can therefore explain these additional clauses of (RP). Because our cognitive abilities include ones governing the evaluation of counter-evidence, a virtuous believer will discriminate among alternative possibilities that she believes might be true. Moreover, she will discriminate possibilities that she ought to think might be true. Let us take a moment to elaborate on this idea.

We are presently working with the following account of knowledge:

(AR)   S knows p only if
   i. p is true;
   ii. S's believing p is the result of dispositions that S manifests when S is thinking conscientiously;
   iii. Such dispositions make S reliable in the present conditions, with respect to p.

The first point is that the dispositions referred to in (AR) will include ones that make S sensitive to counter-evidence to what seems to be the case. So, for example, my perceptual faculties will involve forming material object beliefs on the basis of sensory appearances, but will also involve a process of checking those beliefs against background beliefs that I have. This process need not be a conscious one. What is required is that appropriate revisions in my belief system are made as new evidence comes in; either the new evidence will issue in new beliefs and cause conflicting ones to be revised, or it will be resisted and previous beliefs will be maintained. This grounds clause (iib), which says that an alternative possibility is relevant if S believes that it might be true.

The second point is that in particular cases of knowledge a person must manifest the cognitive dispositions that make her reliable in general. Put another way, she must manifest the dispositions that she does when thinking conscientiously. But this grounds clause (iic), which says that a possibility is relevant if S ought to think that it might be true. In other words, if a possibility is such that S would believe that it is likely if S were thinking conscientiously, then S's evidence must rule it out for S to have knowledge. Only then would S be appropriately reliable in the particular case. Accordingly, the nature of our cognition together with the requirements of subjective justification and reliability explain the various clauses in (RP).

Finally, it is the nature of *our* cognition that explains the clauses – it is not an abstract truth about knowledge that (RP) has the content that it does. It is possible, for example, that some beings have perfectly reliable perception without any process for checking counter-evidence. But that is not how human cognition works, and so the need for clauses (iib) and (iic) in an account of what makes a possibility relevant for us.

9

Moral and Religious Epistemology

In this last chapter I want to sketch how the methodology of strong particularism can be extended to moral and religious epistemology. I do this by way of three illustrations. In Part I of the chapter, I look at work by Plantinga and Alston in religious epistemology, and I show how these authors effectively engage in an indirect application of the methodology. Both authors argue that objections to the rationality of religious belief trade on assumptions that, if true, would lead to skepticism in the empirical realm as well. As a result, the objections against religious belief are determined to be unsound. Also as a result, positive suggestions for the epistemology of religious belief emerge. We will see how Plantinga defends the general idea that beliefs about God might be non-inferentially justified, and how Alston develops this line of thought in a theory of religious perception. The general structure of Alston's discussion is as follows: Objections to religious perception trade on an inadequate understanding of perception in general; such objections, if sound, would make even empirical perception impossible. Once an adequate theory of empirical perception is in place, however, the possibility of perceiving God becomes a live option in religious epistemology.

In Part II of the chapter, I want to do for moral perception what Alston does for religious perception. Drawing on the results of Chapters 2 through 8, I argue that traditional objections to moral perception misunderstand the nature of perception in general. Again, if such objections were sound, then analogous ones would show that even empirical perception is impossible. However, a theory of empirical perception that is both epistemologically and psychologically adequate quite naturally suggests the possibility of moral perception. Drawing on some recent developments in empirical psychology, I argue that a particular model of empirical perception is especially suggestive along these lines.

I. Religious Epistemology

I have said that strong particularism can be applied to moral and religious epistemology either directly or indirectly. A direct application of the method requires us to assume that moral (or religious) beliefs have some kind of positive epistemic status. We might assume, for example, that some moral beliefs amount to knowledge, or that some religious beliefs are at least rational. We may then reject assumptions about knowledge and rationality that are inconsistent with the assumptions we are willing to make. If a skeptical argument leads to the conclusion that no one knows that any action is wrong, for example, then there must be something wrong with that argument. Progress in the epistemology of moral belief is made if we can identify what that mistake is. Further progress is made if we can replace it with something better.

As I have said, this seems to me to be a perfectly reasonable way to proceed in moral and religious epistemology. On the one hand, it seems outrageous to think that no one knows anything about what is right or wrong, or that no one's religious beliefs are even rational. On the other hand, some of the assumptions operative in discussions about moral and religious epistemology have these consequences. The implausibility of such assumptions is exposed by making their skeptical consequences explicit. That is, we want to make those consequences *fully* explicit, pressing the logic of a skeptical line of reasoning so as to display the full force and range of its skeptical conclusions. Moreover, we want to stress the counterintuitiveness of the more radical forms of skepticism that result. It is easy enough to say in the classroom that no one "really" knows right from wrong, but almost no one actually believes this. Clearly no such belief is manifested in the way that people actually make moral judgments, or in the way that people actually live.

It seems to me, therefore, that strong particularism can be extended directly to moral and religious epistemology. But the methodology can be applied indirectly as well. In this case we do not assume that moral or religious beliefs have some positive epistemic status, but that empirical beliefs do. We then look for arguments against moral (or religious) belief such that, if they were sound, would entail unwanted skeptical consequences for empirical belief as well. By rooting out the mistaken assumptions in such arguments, and by replacing them with something better, we again make advances in moral and religious epistemology. A paradigm example of this methodology is Plantinga's treatment of the evidentialist objection to belief in God. I turn to that now to illustrate the methodology I have in mind.

1. PLANTINGA'S REJECTION OF THE EVIDENTIALIST OBJECTION TO RELIGIOUS BELIEF

According to the evidentialist objection, belief in God is not rational unless it is based on good evidence.[1] But since there is no such evidence, belief in God is not rational. This kind of objection to the rationality of religious belief is widespread. In turn, many theists have tried to answer it, most often by trying to satisfy the demand for evidence. Recent work by Plantinga takes a different approach, however. Rather than focusing on the second premise of the argument, which states that there is no good evidence for belief in God, Plantinga addresses the first premise.

Why should one accept the premise that belief in God is rational only if it is based on good evidence? Proponents of the evidentialist objection do not require that all rational beliefs be based on other beliefs for their evidence, since this would issue in an infinite regress. They must be thinking, therefore, that beliefs about God are of a kind that need evidence. But this last is a substantive assumption, Plantinga argues. It depends on a theory of rationality which divides rational beliefs into those that need evidence and those that do not, and which places belief in God squarely in the former camp.

According to Plantinga, the evidentialist objection assumes some form of classical foundationalism. Classical foundationalism is a particularly strict version of foundationalism. Specifically, it is particularly strict about what kinds of belief are allowed to be foundational. According to ancient and medieval classical foundationalism, only beliefs that are self-evident or evident to the senses are foundational, with all other rational belief requiring support from these. Modern classical foundationalism is even more strict, allowing as foundational only self-evident beliefs and incorrigible beliefs about one's own experience. It is because beliefs

---

1 The discussion that follows is based on Alvin Plantinga, "Reason and Belief in God," in Alvin Plantinga and Nicholas Wolterstorff, eds., *Faith and Rationality* (Notre Dame: University of Notre Dame Press, 1983).

about God fall into none of these categories, Plantinga argues, that the objection to religious belief demands evidence. Beliefs about God are neither self-evident, evident to the senses, nor incorrigible, and so if they are rational at all they must be based on other beliefs that have such status.

The next move that Plantinga makes is the one that is most relevant for our purposes. Having identified classical foundationalism as a crucial assumption of the evidentialist objection, he goes on to reject the assumption precisely because it leads to broader skeptical consequences. If classical foundationalism were true, this would have implausible skeptical consequences for *other* kinds of belief, such as beliefs about the past and beliefs about other minds. And so classical foundationalism must be false.

> We should note first that . . . if these claims are true, then enormous quantities of what we all in fact believe are irrational. One crucial lesson to be learned from the development of modern philosophy – Descartes through Hume, roughly – is just this: relative to propositions that are self-evident and incorrigible, most of the beliefs that form the stock in trade of ordinary everyday life are not probable. . . . Consider all those propositions that entail, say, that there are enduring physical objects, or that there are persons distinct from myself, or that the world has existed for more than five minutes: none of these propositions, I think, is more probable than not with respect to what is self-evident or incorrigible for me.
>
> . . . . And now suppose that we add to the foundations propositions that are evident to the senses, thereby moving from modern to ancient and medieval foundationalism. Then propositions entailing the existence of material objects will of course be probable with respect to the foundations, because included therein. But the same cannot be said either for propositions about the past or for propositions entailing the existence of persons distinct from myself; as before, these will not be probable with respect to what is properly basic.[2]

Having rejected classical foundationalism's criteria for proper basicality, Plantinga goes on to suggest that belief in God might be properly basic. For example, such beliefs might be grounded in various kinds of experiences of God.

> Upon having experience of a certain sort, I believe that I am perceiving a tree. In the typical case I do not hold this belief on the basis of other beliefs; it is nontheless not groundless. My having that characteristic sort of experience . . . plays a crucial role in the formation of that belief. It also plays a crucial role in its *justification*. . . .

---

2   Ibid., pp. 59–60.

Now similar things may be said about belief in God. When the Reformers claim that this belief is properly basic, they do not mean to say, of course, that there are no justifying circumstances for it, or that it is in that sense groundless or gratuitous. Quite the contrary, Calvin holds that God "reveals and daily discloses himself in the whole workmanship of the universe," and the divine art "reveals itself in the innumerable and yet distinct and well ordered variety of the heavenly host." God has so created us that we have a tendency or disposition to see his hand in the world about us.[3]

The idea is that beliefs about God might be evidentially grounded in religious experience, much as beliefs about material objects can be evidentially grounded in sensory experience. The logical space for this kind of approach to the epistemology of religious belief is created by a rejection of classical foundationalism. That position is not rejected in an *ad hoc* manner, however. Rather, it is rejected by showing that the position has unacceptable skeptical consequences – that is, consequences that are unacceptable even for the person who thinks that beliefs about God are not rational.

The position that there might be a perception of God is developed further by Alston. Before turning to Alston's discussion, however, I want to consider some remarks that Plantinga makes about methodology in epistemology. According to Plantinga, the proper way to proceed in epistemology is by means of Chisholm's particularism. We are to consider a range of cases that seem to be instances of beliefs having some positive epistemic status, and a range of cases that seem not to be. We then look for theories of knowledge and evidence that explain our intuitions about these cases. A question arises, however, regarding cases where our intuitions conflict with those of others. What happens if religious believers think that a range of beliefs about God are rational, or even amount to knowledge, but non-believers refuse to grant those same beliefs about God any such status? Plantinga's response is to adopt a kind of methodological pluralism.

And hence the proper way to arrive at such a criterion is, broadly speaking, *inductive*. We must assemble examples of beliefs and conditions such that the former are obviously properly basic in the latter, and examples of beliefs and conditions such that the former are obviously *not* properly basic in the latter. We must then frame hypotheses as to the necessary and sufficient conditions of proper basicality and test these hypotheses by reference to those examples. . . .

But there is no reason to assume, in advance, that everyone will agree on

---

3 Ibid., pp. 79–80.

the examples. The Christian will of course suppose that belief in God is entirely proper and rational; if he does not accept this belief on the basis of other propositions, he will conclude that it is basic for him and quite properly so. Followers of Bertrand Russell and Madelyn Murray O'Hare may disagree; but how is that relevant? Must my criteria, or those of the Christian community, conform to their examples? Surely not. The Christian community is responsible to *its* set of examples, not theirs.[4]

It seems to me that we are not forced into any such pluralism, however. This is because a good theory of knowledge ought to explain why our intuitions disagree, when they do. That is, all parties to the dispute ought to look for a theory of knowledge that (a) explains clear and uncontroversial cases, (b) explains cases where our intuitions are vague, and (c) explains the cases where our intuitions disagree.

In a different essay, Plantinga himself provides us with a nice illustration of how this could work. There he defends a general theory of knowledge which is a version of agent reliabilism. According to that theory, a belief has the kind of positive epistemic status required for knowledge just in case, roughly, it is produced by reliable faculties functioning properly in an appropriate environment. On this view, someone who believes in God on the basis of religious experience can have knowledge thereby, so long as the belief is the product of some properly functioning faculty, in this case a *sensus divinitatus*, so to speak. But of course individuals will disagree over whether a given belief *is* such a product, or even could be. Religious believers, or at least some of them, will think that human beings are so designed and that therefore such beliefs are possible. Freudians and Marxists, or at least some of them, will think that we are not so designed, and that therefore such beliefs are not possible. Rather, beliefs about God must be the result of a cognitive *mal*function. But notice that this is a disagreement over the non-epistemological facts. Both the atheist and the theist could agree on Plantinga's agent reliabilism, and precisely because it explains everyone's intuitions involved, including such disagreements as arise.

Plantinga ends his discussion by noting that disputes over the rationality of religious belief are not merely epistemological – they involve an ontological or metaphysical dimensions as well:

What is rational depends upon what sort of beings human beings are; and what you properly take to be rational, at least in the sense in question, depends upon

---

4 Ibid., pp. 76–77.

what sort of metaphysical and religious stance you adopt; it depends upon what kind of beings you think human beings are, and what sorts of beliefs their noetic faculties will produce when they are functioning properly.[5]

I fully agree, but we must keep in mind exactly where the metaphysics comes in. It is not in determining which intuitions are to be explained, and it is not in determining which theory of knowledge and evidence best explains those intuitions. It does not even come in when we apply the theory to individual cases, so long as those cases are hypothetical ones that we can fully describe. Even a staunch atheist might agree that belief in God would have positive epistemic status *in cases where the universe is as the theist describes it*. And even a committed theist might agree that belief in God would lack positive epistemic status *in cases where the universe is as the atheist describes it*. Rather, one's metaphysics comes in only when one decides whether particular, actual beliefs satisfy the conditions that the preferred theory lays down. But again, that will not be an epistemological dispute, except in an extended sense. Therefore, people with quite different metaphysical positions can engage in strong particularism and can thereby come to agree on the essentially epistemological questions. Methodological pluralism is not warranted by a plurality of intuitions, or even by a plurality of metaphysical positions.[6]

2. ALSTON'S DEFENSE OF RELIGIOUS PERCEPTION

Alston develops systematically the idea that a perception of God is possible.[7] One objection to this idea that immediately arises is that religious experience is, in itself, a merely subjective phenomenon. In order for such an experience to justify one's beliefs about God, one must have some good argument for believing that the experience is veridical. In other words, one must have some good reason for believing that the experience is of what one takes it to be. But no such argument is

---

5 Plantinga, "Epistemic Probability and Evil," *Archivio di Filosofia* 56 (1988): 557–584, at p. 583. Reprinted in Daniel Howard-Snyder, ed., *The Evidential Argument from Evil* (Bloomington: Indiana University Press, 1996).
6 The point is less straightforward with respect to subjective justification, but I think that it can be made even here. So, e.g., disputes about what beliefs are subjectively justified might be explained in terms of different opinions regarding the availability and strength of counterevidence, or about what norms are typically countenanced, or what dispositions are typically manifested, in conscientious thinking.
7 In William Alston, "Christian Experience and Christian Belief," in Plantinga and Wolterstorff (1983), and *Perceiving God*.

forthcoming, the objection goes, since a putative experience of God could be explained in any number of other ways.

Alston responds to this objection by noting an analogous problem for empirical perception.

> Around about the seventeenth century someone had the bright idea of remarking that whereas we had all along been supposing that any normal adult human being could get plenty of empirical data of the form "This log is burning" or "I am seated before the fire in a dressing gown" just by opening her eyes, these supposed data are really hybrids. There is indeed a real datum of the form "I seem to see a log burning" or "A burning-logish sense datum is in my visual field" or "I am being appeared to log-burningly." This datum gets conjoined with an explanation, namely, that it is generated, by a psychological process we will pass over in discrete silence, by an actual physical log that is actually burning, to produce the hybrid we uncritically take as the datum. Hence, before we can use our experience as a ground for supposing that there are such things as burning logs, or that a particular log is burning at a particular time, we must find some way of justifying this particular way of explaining the occurrence of sense data.
>
> It is obvious that this familiar move in the epistemology of sense perception is exactly parallel to the challenge we are considering to the claims of religious experience. If we can figure out what to do in this case, it may help us with our original problem.[8]

Alston notes that attempts in the history of philosophy to meet the challenge head-on have failed miserably. A better approach in the epistemology of empirical perception is to hold that we perceive material objects directly.

> [O]ur only hope is to reject the bifurcation alleged in the challenge and seek to justify the claim that we do encounter independently existing physical objects in our experience. Put the matter in a somewhat different way. The question concerns the justifiability of a certain *practice* – the practice of forming physical-object beliefs directly on the basis of perception rather than as an explanation of what is perceived or experienced.[9]

An adequate (i.e., non-skeptical) theory of empirical perception requires that we think of perception as non-inferential: quite immediately and without anything like an inference, we take sensory experience to be

---

8 Alston, "Christian Experience and Christian Belief," p. 108.
9 Ibid., p. 109.

the experience of physical objects, and we form our beliefs accordingly. Alston suggests that we consider this model for religious perception as well. Just as we form beliefs about physical objects directly on the basis of sensory experience, some people form beliefs about God directly on the basis of religious experience.

The next question is whether this practice gives rise to beliefs that are epistemically respectable. Granting that Alston has correctly described the psychological process by which some people form some of their beliefs about God, does the practice of forming beliefs in that way give rise to justification and/or knowledge? Alston does not think that the analogy to empirical perception in itself shows that it does. Rather, it opens up the possibility. We have seen that thinking of empirical perception as inferential dooms one to skepticism about empirical perception. Likewise, thinking of the perception of God as inferential dooms one to skepticism about religious perception. In both cases, this is because there are unanswerable skeptical objections to the possibility of an adequate inference. But denying that there need be an inference from religious experience to divine reality opens up the logical space. As with empirical perception, it does not show that religious perception is actual, but it removes a skeptical obstacle that would otherwise show that it is impossible.

To take mystical experience as a form of perception is not to beg the question as to the upshot of the inquiry. It still could be true that sense perception is genuine perception of its putative objects, whereas mystical perception is not, and that sense perception provides justified belief and knowledge about its objects – whereas mystical perception yields no such results for any beliefs about anything. The point is only that the problems, both as to the nature of the perception and as to the epistemic status of the perceptual beliefs stemming therefrom, arise in the same form for both. Whereas on the widespread view that mystical experience is to be construed as purely subjective feelings, sensations, and the like, to which supernaturalistic causal hypotheses are added, the issues concerning the two modes of experience will look very different (unless one is misguided enough to treat sense perception in the same fashion).[10]

So far so good. But *is* the perception of God actual, in an epistemic sense of perception? In other words, do some people actually perceive God, and on this basis have justified beliefs and knowledge about God? In general, one perceives an object only if that object exists and one is appropriately related to it. For this reason it is impossible to argue that

---

10 Alston, *Perceiving God*, pp. 66–67.

some people actually perceive God without assuming that God exists and is experienced by people in the required way. But even without making such assumptions, there is still a lot that can be said about the epistemology of religious perception. We can look at the practice of forming beliefs about God directly on the basis of religious experience (call this RP, for "religious practice"), and we can compare this to the practice of forming beliefs about material objects directly on the basis of sensory experience (call this SP, for "sensory practice"). Alston's strategy throughout is to argue that the two kinds of perceptual practice are in the same epistemic boat.[11]

Consider first the question of whether the two practices are objectively reliable, or truth conducive. In both cases this will be a matter of what the facts are: it will depend on whether God (or the material world) exists, and whether beliefs formed on the basis of the practice hook up with the relevant reality in a reliable way. But in both cases, *if* the relevant reality exists, and *if* that reality is related to us in the right way, then the relevant practice is objectively reliable. Moreover, engaging in the relevant practice could constitute a reliable perception of the reality in question.

Consider next whether we can prove or establish that the practices are objectively reliable. Alston argues that, again, RP and SP are in the same boat. In both cases it is impossible to establish the reliability of the practice without engaging in a particular kind of circularity. Specifically, we cannot establish the reliability of the practice without using premises that are deliverances of the practice in question. Thus we can establish the reliability of empirical perception, but only by using empirical perception. If we want something more than this – for example, an argument that is independent of any empirical premise – then we will be disappointed. Alston takes it that the history of philosophy teaches us this lesson; we need only look at the litany of failed attempts to establish the reliability of empirical perception in this fashion.

The point is significant, because it blocks an otherwise plausible objection to the possibility of perceiving God. RP cannot be shown to be a reliable process, unless, of course, one is allowed to use beliefs resulting from the practice itself as premises. But this kind of epistemic circularity cannot count against the epistemic efficacy of RP. For if it

---

11 Alston tends to talk in terms of "Christian practice" and "Christian mystical practice," but as he notes himself, there is nothing particular about Christianity that figures into his account of religious perception. I therefore use the term "religious practice."

did, an analogous objection would be sound against SP as well. Since skepticism with regard to empirical perception is assumed to be false, we may draw the conclusion that epistemic circularity of the sort just described cannot ground a skeptical conclusion with regard to religious perception.

The reliability of SP cannot be established without epistemic circularity. On the other hand, there is no good reason to think that SP is unreliable. Alston argues that RP is once again in the same boat epistemically. His reasons for this are somewhat involved, and going into them in detail is beyond the scope of the present discussion. The important point for our purposes is the main structure of Alston's argument. Once again, his main idea is that an adequate understanding of religious perception should be based on an adequate understanding of empirical perception. In particular, we cannot reject the idea of religious perception on the basis of considerations which, if sound, would show empirical perception to be impossible as well.

The implicit assumption of Alston's entire discussion, of course, is that perceptual knowledge and justified belief in the empirical realm *are* possible. In other words, Alston's methodology is an instance of strong particularism: we assume for the sake of our investigation that empirical knowledge and justified belief are possible, and we quite appropriately reject assumptions about knowledge and evidence which are inconsistent with this.

Finally, throughout Alston's discussion he considers several objections to RP, all to the effect that the practice has some epistemically crippling defect. Some of these he classifies as instances of "epistemic imperialism." These objections reject RP for not having some feature of SP, thereby making the features of SP normative for all epistemically legitimate practices. Other objections, however, are classified as instances of a double standard. Here the idea is that RP is rejected for having some feature (or lacking some feature) that SP has (or lacks) as well.[12] The way that Alston answers these latter objections again demonstrates the methodology of strong particularism. We begin by assuming that perceptual knowledge and justified belief are possible in the empirical realm. On this basis, we can safely conclude that SP's having (or lacking) some feature does not have skeptical consequences. But then RP's having (or lacking) the same feature cannot have skeptical consequences for religious belief either.

12 Alston, *Perceiving God*, p. 249.

Of course, this line of reasoning does not establish that RP *is* an epistemically efficacious practice, even when granted the assumption that SP is. No matter how many features RP and SP share, there might be some further, relevant feature that the practices do not share, and in such a way that RP ends up being epistemically subpar. But the methodology that both Alston and Plantinga adopt sets up an interesting and difficult dialectic for the skeptic about the rationality of religious belief: When raising objections to the rationality of religious belief, such a skeptic must be careful not to issue in a more general, unacceptable skepticism. That is, the religious skeptic must be careful not to issue in a skepticism that is unacceptable even to *himself*. Avoiding this pitfall ends up being far more difficult than one might first expect, as the discussions by Alston and Plantinga testify.[13]

II. Moral Epistemology

We have seen that one major motivation for thinking of perception as non-inferential is to avoid skepticism. If perceptual knowledge requires some good inference from a relevant kind of experience to the relevant kind of reality, then skepticism about perceptual knowledge is correct. This is because there are unanswerable skeptical arguments which show that such an inference is impossible. However, we have also seen that thinking of perception as non-inferential poses a different kind of problem. Specifically, it would seem that our perceptions are theoretically loaded, in the sense that they seem to depend on background beliefs, prior assumptions, expectations, special training, and the like. The problem, then, is this: How can we account for the theoretical character of perception, if perceptual beliefs are not inferred from other beliefs that act as their evidence? This problem is nowhere more pronounced than in the case of moral perception. Even in cases that are plausibly described

---

13 This same dialectic is also manifested in recent discussions of the problem of evil. See, e.g., various essays in Howard-Snyder, *The Evidential Argument from Evil*, cited in n. 5. For yet other instances of the same dialectic, see Nicholas Wolterstorff, "Can Belief in God Be Rational Even If It Has No Foundation?", in Plantinga and Wolterstorff (1983); Wolterstorff, "Epistemology of Religion," in Greco and Sosa (1999); and various works by John Hick, esp. *An Interpretation of Religion: Human Responses to the Transcendent* (New Haven: Yale University Press, 1989). Some relevant selections from this work are reprinted in "The Rationality of Religious Belief," in R. Douglas Geivett and Brenden Sweetman, eds., *Contemporary Perspectives on Religious Epistemology* (Oxford: Oxford University Press, 1992).

as "seeing" that some action is wrong or "feeling" that some action is right, it would be hard to deny that such moral experiences are shaped by prior moral judgments, background assumptions, and so forth.

Perhaps this kind of consideration more than any other has made theories of moral perception unpopular. Nevertheless, in Part II of the chapter I want to argue that an adequate theory of empirical perception opens up the possibility of moral perception. Such a theory helps us to address exactly the present concern about the theory-laden character of perception in general. It also helps us to answer some other objections that have traditionally been raised against moral perception. Before we can turn to that argument, however, it will be necessary to engage in some preliminaries. In particular, I want to say a bit more about what I mean by moral perception.

1. THREE KINDS OF MORAL EPISTEMOLOGY

Theories in moral epistemology can be divided into three kinds. Since the publication of John Rawls' *A Theory of Justice*, the most prominent position in moral epistemology has been evidentialism.[14] According to this position, a moral belief is justified (or perhaps amounts to knowledge) only if it is supported by adequate evidence. Such evidence is construed as other justified beliefs or knowledge, and the general shape of the position is usually coherentist. That is, most evidentialists think that *all* justified moral beliefs require other moral beliefs for their evidence, and so to avoid a regress of justification they adopt the position that moral beliefs can lend each other mutual support. A second position in moral epistemology, now less popular than it once was, is intuitionism. Sometimes intuitionism is characterized as any position which holds that moral beliefs can be non-inferentially justified. Similarly, the term "moral sense" has often been used as a synonym for "moral intuition." But it seems to me that this terminology is inadequate, for it fails to distinguish between two very different ways that a belief might be non-inferentially justified. We may see this by considering four distinctions:

---

14 John Rawls, *A Theory of Justice* (Cambridge, MA: Harvard University Press, 1971). Rawls' book has had a tremendous influence on moral epistemology, despite the fact that it is not a work in the epistemology of moral belief. Rawls' account of "reflective equilibrium" concerns criteria for moral theory construction, rather than criteria for justification or knowledge. For a persuasive argument that this is the case, together with an excellent discussion of relevant issues, see Michael DePaul, "Reflective Equilibrium and Foundationalism," *American Philosophical Quarterly* 23 (1986): 59–69, and *Balance and Refinement: Beyond Coherence Methods of Moral Inquiry* (London: Routledge, 1993).

a. A belief is *non-inferential* if and only if it is not inferred from other beliefs.
   A belief is *inferential* if and only if it is inferred from other beliefs.
b. A belief is *a priori* if and only if it does not depend on experience for its evidence.
   A belief is *a posteriori* if and only if it does depend on experience for its evidence.
c. A belief is *necessary* if and only if it is logically impossible that it is false.
   A belief is *contingent* if and only if it is logically possible that it is false and it is logically possible that it is true.
d. A belief is *general* if and only if it does not refer to any particular existing thing.
   A belief is *particular* if and only if it does refer to a particular existing thing.

The first distinction is psychological; it concerns how a belief is formed. The second is epistemological; it concerns the kind of evidence that a belief has. The third and fourth distinctions are logical; they refer to the logical properties of a belief's content. Now it seems to me that intuitions are properly understood as non-inferential, *a priori*, necessary and general. This accords with the idea that simple mathematical truths and simple logical truths are paradigm cases of contents for possible intuitions. It also accords with the common understanding that intuited truths are self-evident, in the sense that understanding them is sufficient for being justified in believing them, or knowing them. On the other hand, perceptual beliefs are properly understood as non-inferential, *a posteriori*, contingent, and particular. When one perceives that something is the case, this involves some sort of experience as one's evidence, and it concerns some contingent matter of fact about a particular existing thing or things.

One might think about moral knowledge on either of these very different models. One might hold that there are moral intuitions, and cash this out on an analogy with mathematical and logical intuitions, or one might hold that there are moral perceptions, and cash this out on an analogy with empirical perceptions.[15] In the remainder of this chapter I want to pursue the latter alternative. What I mean by "moral perception," then, is a process by which moral beliefs concerning contingent truths about particular existing things are formed directly (i.e., non-inferentially) on the basis of moral experience. Moreover, in moral perception such experience serves as the evidential grounds of the moral

---

15 One might also hold both views, characterizing the foundations of moral knowledge as including both moral intuitions and moral perceptions.

beliefs it produces, thereby giving rise to justification or even knowledge.[16] An example of moral perception, on this model, would be seeing that a particular action – for example, some boys torturing a cat – is wrong. Such a belief is particular rather than general, in that it refers to particular existing things; in this case the boys, the cat, and the action they are involved in. The belief also expresses a contingent truth rather than a necessary one, in that its content is that *this* individual action is wrong, and it is only a contingent truth that this action took place at all. Finally, I will argue that such a belief can be formed directly on the basis of a moral experience of the action, and that the belief can be thereby justified, or can even amount to knowledge.

One reason for pursuing this kind of position is that it seems to be the most adequate phenomenologically. Seeing that an action is wrong, or that a man is trustworthy, or that a child is innocent seems to be an adequate description of a fairly common sort of occurrence. On the other hand, it seems to be phenomenologically *in*adequate to characterize many moral judgments in terms of an inference from evidence. At least in a broad range of cases, we precisely do *not* infer that some action is wrong from a general rule. What would such a rule be, and who but a philosopher even thinks in terms of such rules? Neither do we typically judge that some person is trustworthy by means of an implicit theory about what trustworthy persons look like, which we then use to infer that this particular person, who looks so and so, must be trustworthy. Rather, a person often "strikes" us as trustworthy; she has a certain look to her, which we probably could not articulate, on the basis of which we form our beliefs and act. Or perhaps a voice sounds insincere, or caring, or threatening. But who among us, except perhaps the odd phenomenologist or stage actor, has beliefs about what such a look or

---

16 Intuitionism in moral epistemology has recently been defended by Robert Audi in a number of places. Audi's work also contains an excellent treatment of a broad range of relevant issues in moral epistemology. E.g., much of what he says in defense of intuitionism goes toward a defense of non-inferential moral knowledge in general. See his "Intuitionism, Pluralism, and the Foundations of Ethics," in Walter Sinnott-Armstrong and Mark Timmons, eds., *Moral Knowledge?* (Oxford: Oxford University Press, 1996); and "Moral Knowledge and Ethical Pluralism" in Greco and Sosa (1999). For some recent defenses of moral perception views, see Michael DePaul, "Argument and Perception: The Role of Literature in Moral Inquiry," *Journal of Philosophy* 85 (1988): 552–565, and *Balance and Refinement*; John McDowell, "Values and Secondary Qualities," in Ted Honderich, ed., *Morality and Objectivity* (London: Routledge and Kegan Paul, 1985); and William Tolhurst, "On the Epistemic Value of Moral Experience," *Southern Journal of Philosophy* 29, supplement (1990):67–87.

sound amounts to, or believes that such and such an experience is a reliable indication of such and such a moral property?

A theory of moral perception, on which some moral beliefs are formed directly on the basis of experience, seems to offer a better description of the psychology of moral belief formation. What we would like is a theory that also gives us a plausible account of the epistemology of such beliefs. In other words, we want a theory that shows how beliefs so formed can be epistemically respectable.

My strategy for defending such a theory involves three stages. In Section II.2, I review some of our conclusions regarding empirical perception from previous chapters, and I put forward a positive account of empirical perception, perceptual justification, and perceptual knowledge. The account I defend makes use of some recent work in the psychology of perception. In particular, this work helps us to answer the problem posed earlier, regarding how perception can be both non-inferential and theoretically loaded. In Section II.3, I use this account of empirical perception to put forward a theory of moral perception. I argue that once we have an account of empirical perception that is both epistemically and psychologically adequate, an analogous account of moral perception suggests itself rather straightforwardly. Finally, in Section II.4, I address some traditional objections to the possibility of moral perception. My purpose in doing so is not to give a full-blown defense of moral perception. Rather, it is to further the case that strong particularism allows progress in moral epistemology. Once we have a theory of empirical perception that is immune to skeptical objections, we can see why some traditional objections to moral perception are unsound.

2. A THEORY OF EMPIRICAL PERCEPTION

We already know that empirical perception should be understood non-inferentially. We form beliefs about material objects immediately on the basis of sensory experience, without anything like an inference from a general rule, or knowledge about the character of the experience, or knowledge that experience with such and such a character is a reliable indication of such and such a material object.

How should we think about the sensory experience that is involved in such a process? First, it is clear that sensory experience involves a phenomenal content. When we see a material object, it has a certain look to it phenomenally. Alternatively, an object can have a particular sound, or smell, or taste, or feel to it. It seems to me, however, that in the typical case sensory experience also has a conceptual or representational content. To use a now familiar phrase, seeing is (at least often) "seeing as." This can be generalized to the other sensory modalities as well. At least in the typical case, hearing is "hearing as," smelling is "smelling as," and so forth. To illustrate this idea we may consider some atypical cases in which we do not experience a thing as what it is. We can then contrast these with more typical cases.

First, consider a case where you smell something vaguely familiar but cannot quite say what the thing is that you are smelling. You might concentrate carefully on the quality of the odor, trying to figure out for some time what the source of it is. Contrast this with walking into the house and smelling tomatoes and garlic cooking on the stove. In this case there is no awareness of the experience as an isolated aspect of your thinking – you simply smell the tomatoes and garlic cooking as tomatoes and garlic cooking.[17]

Consider next the case of hearing a sound coming from outside and trying to determine its source. Again, one attends to the quality of the experience so as to figure out whether it is from a car, a truck, a motorcycle, or something else. Compare this with hearing the voice of your spouse or your child. Here again there is nothing like an isolated experience, separated off from other aspects of one's thought. One hears the voice as the voice of the loved one. Even more likely, one simply hears the voice *as the person*, and does not even think of the voice as a voice.

Based on this kind of investigation into the phenomenology of perception, I assume that when one sees a tree (or smells her dinner, or hears his child) the sensory experience involved in this has a conceptual as well as a phenomenal content. To perceive that there is a tree bearing apples by the brook, for example, is to be appeared to phenomenally in a particular way, and to take this phenomenal appearance as that of a tree bearing apples by the brook. One then forms a perceptual belief with this content immediately on that basis. On this way of thinking, the psychological and evidential grounds of empirical perceptual beliefs is thick experience rather than thin, and it is the experience itself rather than beliefs about the experience.

This way of thinking about perception has distinct advantages over inferential and simple causal accounts. Over inferential accounts, it

---

17   In the example I am assuming that you are Italian, or at least sufficiently familiar with Italian cooking. If not, substitute your own example.

shows how phenomenal experience can be involved in the evidential grounds of perceptual beliefs, but not by figuring into some premise that must now be used in an inference. Over simple causal accounts, it allows that phenomenal experience really does play an evidential role in perception, and is not merely a causal antecedent. Rather, we may think of the relation as broadly semiotic, as opposed to either inferential or merely causal. Sensory appearings are meaningful signs, giving rise immediately to perceptual beliefs with the same contents. These meaningful signs can be analyzed into phenomenal content and conceptual content, but *qua* evidential grounds they are always already meaningful. Again, this explains why bare phenomenal *qualia* cannot serve as evidence alone, but it also gives them more than a merely causal role in perception.

Together with the results of Chapters 2 through 8, these considerations suggest the following account of empirical perception, perceptual justification, and perceptual knowledge.

(P) S perceives X as F if and only if (a) X is F, (b) X appears phenomenally to S as X normally would if X were F, and (c) S takes this phenomenal appearing as an appearing of X as F.

(PB) S perceives that X is F if and only if (a) S perceives X as F and (b) S believes that X is F on this basis.

(PJB) S has a justified perceptual belief that X is F if and only if (a) S perceives that X is F and (b) S's perceiving that X is F is a result of the cognitive dispositions that S manifests when S is thinking conscientiously.

(PK) S has perceptual knowledge that X is F only if (a) S has a justified perceptual belief that X is F and (b) the cognitive dispositions that S manifests in believing that X is F are objectively reliable in S's environment.

A few comments are in order. First, I am leaving unanalyzed the somewhat awkward locution "S takes this phenomenal appearing as an appearing of X as F." However, something can be said by way of clarification. Most importantly, such "takings" or "seemings" are intended to somehow involve representational or conceptual content, namely the content that X is F. Thus the intentional object of a perceptual taking is the object being perceived, and not the appearance of the object being perceived. As I have noted repeatedly, in the typical case people do not think about appearances, or the way things appear, at all.

Second, the present account treats "perceives" and its cognates as success terms: when we say that one perceives that something is the case, for example, this implies that what one perceives really is the case. If we use "perceives" in this way, then cases of perceptual illusion are not cases of perception. We have to say, for example, that one seems to perceive (but does not) that there is a pink elephant in the room.

Third, the account allows that there is a phenomenal aspect of perception, but it conceives of that in terms of normality. In other words, it is not assumed that there is any intrinsic feature of a phenomenal appearing that makes that appearing, say, the appearance of a tree. What makes a phenomenal appearance the appearance of a tree is just the fact that this is how a tree would normally appear phenomenally, relative to the cognitive agent in question. By means of this same feature, the account disallows that just any phenomenal appearing can ground a perception, just so long as the agent takes it a certain way. Rather, the appearing must be tied into the normal perceptual dispositions of the agent.

Another feature of the account is that it places no restrictions on what kinds of things can be perceived. Specifically, there is no implication that only colors, sounds, smells, and other traditional "perceptual qualities" can be perceived. It leaves it open, for example, that one can see that his friend is amused or hear that one of the pistons is not firing. It seems to me that this is as it should be, since it is pre-theoretically plausible that we can perceive such things.

The account of justified perceptual belief adds the requirement that the representational aspect of the perception must also be tied into the cognitive dispositions of the agent. Moreover, the dispositions that are relevant are the ones that S manifests when properly motivated toward the truth. This ensures that not just any perception can ground a justified perceptual belief, and it makes the account consistent with the general account of subjective justification defended in Chapter 7. Finally, it should be noted that the account of perceptual knowledge states only necessary conditions rather than necessary and sufficient ones. This is in order to avoid making claims about the adequacy of the account with regard to Gettier cases. I take it that Gettier cases raise an entire range of issues which, for present purposes, can and should be set aside.[18]

---

18 I discuss the relationship between agent reliabilism and Gettier problems in Part III of this chapter.

On the present account perception is conceptually loaded. This is because perceptual takings involve conceptual as well as phenomenal content. But to say that perception is conceptually loaded is different from saying that it is theoretically loaded. The latter claim is that perception is influenced by prior assumptions, background beliefs, expectations, special training, and the like. So, for example, perceiving that some tree is an elm might depend not only on one's sensory experience having a certain conceptual or representational content, but also on one's prior beliefs about trees or one's expectations about where elms can be found. We still have not addressed this problem for a non-inferential theory of perception. That is, how can prior beliefs, expectations, and the like influence perception, even if perceptual beliefs are not inferred from these?

One way that I have already suggested is through counter-evidence. In order for our perception to be both reliable and subjectively justified, cognitive beings like ourselves must be sensitive to evidence that contradicts the way things appear perceptually, and must be able to adjudicate conflicts appropriately. Accordingly, the production of perceptual justification and knowledge, at least for beings like us, must involve other beliefs that function in this way. A second suggestion that has already been made is that background beliefs and the like "shape" our perceptual dispositions; they function as causal antecedents to perception, influencing us to discriminate some objects rather than others, to pick out salient information, to filter out the unimportant. But how this is all supposed to work was left overly vague. If it could work only by having the sorts of beliefs and inferences that we have deemed to be psychologically implausible, then saying that the theoretical background shapes perceptual dispositions does not do the job it is supposed to do. What we need is a model for how perception can be thus theoretically loaded, and yet not in a way that invokes psychologically implausible beliefs and inferences.

Recent work in empirical psychology provides us with just such a model. In what follows I will not argue that the model is correct, since I do not have the expertise to adjudicate competing empirical theories of perception. Instead, I will argue for a more cautious thesis: that *if* the model is correct, then it shows how perception can be non-inferential, and at the same time be the product of prior assumptions, theory, background beliefs, special training, and the like. Even if the model is not correct about how perception actually works, it at least demonstrates the possibility of non-inferential, theory-laden perception; it demonstrates that this idea is not incoherent or impossible, even if it does not show how such perception actually works in us.

The main idea of Schema Theory in empirical psychology is that our cognition involves "scripts" and "personae" through which information such as sensory appearances is processed. The dispositions of perception that result are loaded, to be sure. But they are best understood, I want to argue, as being non-inferential; they ground a process very different from inferring conclusions from premises. In the following passages Richard Nisbett and Lee Ross describe how scripts and personae are supposed to work:

To understand the social world, the layperson makes heavy use of a variety of knowledge structures normally not expressed in propositional terms and possibly not stored in a form even analogous to propositional statements. In describing these cognitive structures we shall use the generic designation "schema" and will comment in detail about only two types of schema – event-schemas, or "scripts," and person-schemas, or "personae."

A script is a type of schema in which the related elements are social objects and events involving the individual as actor and observer. Unlike most schemas, scripts generally are event sequences extended over time, and the relationships have a distinctly causal flavor, that is, early events in the sequence produce or at least "enable" the occurrence of later events. A script can be compared to a cartoon strip with two or more captioned "scenes," each of which summarizes some basic actions that can be executed in a range of possible manners and contexts (for instance, the "restaurant script" with its "entering," "ordering," "eating," and "exiting" scenes).

Social judgements and expectations often are mediated by a class of schemas which we shall term "personae," that is, cognitive structures representing the personal characteristics and typical behaviors of particular "stock characters." Some personae are the unique products of one's own personal experience (good old Aunt Mary, Coach Whiplash). Others are shared within the culture or subculture (the sexpot, the earth-mother, the girl-next-door, the redneck, the schlemiel, the rebel-without-a-cause). . . . In each instance the persona constitutes a knowledge structure which, when evoked, influences social judgements and behaviors. Once the principal features or behaviors of a given individual suggest a particular persona, subsequent expectations of and responses to that individual are apt to be dictated in part by the characteristics of the persona.[19]

19 Richard Nisbett and Lee Ross, "Judgmental Heuristics and Knowledge Structures," in Kornblith, *Naturalizing Epistemology*, p. 278, p. 280, and pp. 281–282.

The application to perception is straightforward. When we are seated at the restaurant table and a man approaches, we perceive that the waiter is coming. According to schema theory, this perception is not based on an inference from other things we believe – for example, that waiters typically dress in such and such a manner, that there appears to be a man dressed this way, and that therefore this must be the waiter. In other words, we do not mount an inference from premises about the way the man appears visually to a conclusion regarding who he is. Rather, we are operating with a script that disposes us to expect a waiter in the present time and place, and that invokes an immediate (i.e. non-inferential) interpretation of present sensory cues. Or again, suppose that we are working with the persona of the surly waiter. We will be apt to interpret a tone of voice as impatient or a facial expression as sarcastic. On the present proposal, such perceptions are not grounded in anything like premises about vocal tone or facial expression, together with theories about what these usually signify. And rightly so, since we would be hard-pressed to find such premises or theories in the typical restaurant-goer. Rather, sensory information is processed in such a way that we make these interpretations more immediately, aided by some relevant, currently evoked schema.

If this is right, then perception is non-inferential. As was explained earlier, scripts and personae are not thought of as beliefs or assumptions, as premises for inferences would have to be. They are not, for example, judgments, that serve to entail or probabilify other judgments. Nevertheless, perception is theoretically loaded on this view. As was also explained earlier, scripts and personae can be part of our cultural inheritance, the result of special training, or gleaned from previous life experience.

3. A THEORY OF MORAL PERCEPTION

The present account of empirical perception opens up the possibility of moral perception straightforwardly. That is, it opens up the possibility that we can sometimes see (quite literally) that an action is wrong, that a child is innocent, or that a man is dishonest. The basic idea is that we are equipped with moral scripts and moral personae. If all perception involves schema-governed interpretation, then moral perception involving this kind of interpretation would be just another kind of perception. For example, the moral perception that some man is dishonest would not be essentially different from the empirical perception that some man is a waiter.

We may pursue this idea further by considering the nature of moral experience. Some moral epistemologists have thought of moral experience as moral emotions. On this view, affective reactions such as indignation, empathy, revulsion, and attraction ground appropriate moral judgments about the objects of such emotions. For example, a feeling of revulsion toward some action might ground a moral judgment that the action is wrong.[20] Other philosophers have thought of moral experience as moral seemings. Upon witnessing an action or meeting a person, the object of one's experience appears morally a certain way. For example, an action strikes one as tragic, or a person strikes one as kind and good. On this view events and things can have a kind of "moral color" or "moral feel" to them, and such experience can epistemically ground moral judgments about the relevant objects.[21]

Finally, some philosophers have identified the experience involved in moral perception with sensory experience. On this view moral properties supervene in some way on the natural properties of events and things, and for this reason it is possible to experience their moral properties by experiencing their natural properties. For example, suppose, for the sake of argument, that utilitarianism is correct, and that anything that is pleasurable thereby has moral value. Given the requisite theoretical background, one could then perceive that something is morally valuable by perceiving that it is pleasurable.[22]

Without arguing against other possibilities, I want to defend a conception of moral experience that combines features of the last two suggestions. Staying close to the analogy with empirical perception, I suggest that moral experience involves both phenomenal and representational content. The phenomenal content is the same: it involves the same sensory modalities that are normal for empirical perception. What makes the experience distinctively moral is its representational content. On this view, to morally perceive that something has some moral property is to perceive the thing empirically, but to take the phenomenal appearing involved in a moral way as well. For example, to morally

---

20 This kind of view is defended by Tolhurst in "On the Epistemic Value of Moral Experience" and by DePaul in *Balance and Refinement*.
21 At times Tolhurst and DePaul characterize moral experience this way.
22 This view of moral experience is suggested but not defended in Audi, "Moral Knowledge and Ethical Pluralism," Section 3.

perceive that a man is dishonest is to be appeared to phenomenally in a particular way (a way in which dishonest men normally appear phenomenally), and to take that phenomenal appearing to be of a dishonest man. To morally perceive that some action is tragic is to be appeared to phenomenally in a particular way (a way in which tragic actions normally appear phenomenally), and to take the phenomenal appearing involved to be the appearing of something tragic.

On this account moral experience is conceptually loaded. As was already suggested, schema theory provides a way in which moral perception might be theoretically loaded a well. Again, the main idea is that we have moral scripts and personae. In our cast of characters there is the shifty lawyer, the cop on the take, the schoolyard bully, the vicious drug dealer, the petty neighbor, and the greedy doctor. There is also the selfless mother, the devoted teacher, the kind doctor, the courageous cop, and the crusading lawyer. The list goes on and on. There are also countless moral scripts. As with personae, many of these are highly specific to time, place, and culture. Others are more universal, perhaps showing up in the great literature of several distinct cultures. For example: courageous boy meets innocent girl, boy and girl fall in virtuous love, boy and girl are separated by immoral parents (or appointed guardian), boy and girl are reunited as the result of selfless devotion to each other. This is a big picture painted in broad strokes. But scripts can be loaded with moral details and subtleties as well. Consider the Shakespearean tragedy or the Austenian novel.

We have seen that according to schema theory perceptual processing can involve scripts and personae. Some feature of a situation activates a relevant schema, and as a result we are disposed to see or hear things a particular way. The present suggestion is that these might be moral ways as well as empirical ways. Moral schema might influence one to see a movement as aggressive, to hear a voice as threatening, or to feel a touch as reassuring. If this is indeed the case, then the influences that moral schema have on cognition are epistemically relevant. Certainly some schema amount to no more than stereotypes and myths. In such cases their influence would undermine the reliability of our moral judgments, thereby having a negative epistemic effect. But it is also possible that more apt schema contribute positively to the reliability of moral judgments, helping us to see or hear or feel what is actually the case, to perceive what we otherwise would miss. Again, whether or not moral schema do function in this way is largely an empirical question. But if they do, then this explains how moral perception can be theoretically loaded and yet non-inferential. And even if they do not, the present discussion at least demonstrates that the idea in not incoherent.

If all of this is right, then moral perception is possible. Aside from its subject matter, moral perception would have little to distinguish it from perception in general, working pretty much the same way that empirical perception does. Accordingly, the present account of moral perception allows us to adopt without qualification the accounts of perception, perceptual justification and perceptual knowledge that were put forward in Section II.2. To say that S morally perceives that something is the case is just to say that S perceives that X is F, where F is a moral property. As in the empirical case, this will involve a sensory phenomenal appearing, but the relevant perceptual taking will involve a moral representational content, namely that the thing perceived has (moral property) F. The accounts of perceptual justification and perceptual knowledge can then be carried over without qualification. They do no more than add requirements placing the source of S's perception in S's relevant cognitive character. But there is no reason why moral perceptions, as characterized above, could not be grounded in S's character in these ways.

4. SOME TRADITIONAL OBJECTIONS TO MORAL PERCEPTION

If the theory of perception presented here is correct then a number of traditional objections to moral perception are removed. I will end this section by looking at some of these, focusing on ones where it is especially useful to pursue the analogy with empirical perception.

First, many philosophers have thought that moral perception requires an occult faculty – a mysterious moral sense, or some kind of moral intuition. But again, if perception in general is understood along the lines I have suggested, then no *special* moral faculty is required. Moral perception would be just like all perception, being distinguished only by the conceptual content of the judgments it produces, rather than by the mechanism by which it produces them.

A second objection to moral perception is that moral judgments are always culturally mediated. We never make moral judgments immediately, it is argued, but always in the thick context of our cultural inheritance. This objection is easily answered in the present context, for it is merely a version of the more general idea that moral perceptions would have to be theoretically loaded. But if all perception, including that of the empirical variety, involves the kind of theoretical background invoked by the objection, then this cannot count against the possibility of moral perception. Moreover, we have seen at least one way in which perception can be theoretically loaded and yet satisfy the conditions on knowledge regarding subjective justification and objective reliability. Cultural influence is not incompatible with epistemic respectability.

A third objection claims that moral perception is impossible because it is impossible to perceive high-level dispositional properties, as moral properties are properly understood to be. Thus to say that someone is honest, or kind, or selfish is to attribute a range of dispositional properties that cannot manifest themselves in a moment's experience. On the current account of perception, however, it is in principle possible to perceive high-level, dispositional properties. What properties can be perceived is a matter of empirical fact, concerning the extent of our cognitive powers. This is as it should be, I have suggested, since it is pre-theoretically plausible that we can perceive any number of things. For example, any one of us can see that a given vehicle is a firetruck. Some of us can hear that the brakes need replacing or smell that the carburetor needs tuning. Since all of these are high-level, dispositional properties, it cannot count against the possibility of moral perception that moral properties are as well.

The current objection might be pressed, however. It might be claimed that, unlike in the empirical case, it is implausible that we have the requisite background knowledge to perceive moral properties. The idea is that the nature of moral properties is highly controversial. Even if such properties are reliably tied to particular phenomenal cues, no one understands in what ways this is so, and so no one is in a position to employ such cues in moral perception. This way of stating the objection, however, misunderstands how perception in general is supposed to work. In no case does perception operate by noting the phenomenal character of one's experience and by using general rules to infer dispositional properties. We have already seen that empirical perception cannot work this way, for lack of the requisite knowledge of one's experience, as well as of the required general rules. There is no reason to think that moral perception would have to work this way either.

Let us try one more version of the objection. In empirical perception, it is claimed, the perception of high-level properties such as being a firetruck or needing brakes is acquired. Moreover, the acquired perception of high-level properties depends on the perception of low-level properties of the object that are reliable indications of the high-level ones. Perhaps this works by perceiving the low-level properties on which the high-level ones supervene. In the moral case, however, no one has the required knowledge regarding which lower-level properties are a reliable indication of which higher-level properties. Presumably, some perceivable natural properties are reliable indications of the higher-level moral properties which are related to them, but not even moral philosophers have a good idea of what these relations are.

This objection depends on the assumption that one must have knowledge of relevant relations, perhaps supervenience relations, in order to perceive higher-level properties. But that assumption is implausible regarding empirical perception. It would seem that people can perceive firetrucks, elm trees, computers, dogs, and much else without having any knowledge whatsoever about what lower-level perceivable properties are related to these higher-level ones. At least this is so if we are talking about propositional knowledge. Of course, people do have the required *procedural* knowledge. This simply means that they know how to make reliable perceptual judgments on the basis of the relevant perceptual cues. But there is no reason to think that people cannot have such procedural knowledge in the moral case as well. It would seem that some people *can* reliably judge that a person is kind by the way that he sounds, and most people know that some things are wrong when they see them.

The final objection against moral perception that I will consider trades on the existence of widespread disagreement among moral judgments. If moral perception were a reality, it is argued, there would not be so much moral disagreement. This objection assumes, however, that perception must be innate, or at least very widely shared. It thinks of perception as a natural faculty that, if possessed at all, will be possessed by more or less everyone and more or less equally. On the theory of perception that I have proposed, however, even empirical perception can be the result of highly specialized training and other particularities of one's circumstances. Perception is not a natural ability to merely "read off" the properties of the world. Rather, it is at least often an acquired ability to interpret the way things appear phenomenally. Consider that we have no more a natural ability to see that someone is a waiter, or to perceive that he is being sarcastic, than we have to see that someone is dangerous, or dishonest, or kind.

Therefore, our perceptual powers need not be widely shared nor equally effective. Such a position is in fact required by the idea of expert perception. Consider that not everyone can see what experts see. This is a generally acknowledged fact for which a good theory of perception ought to account. The current theory does well with it by allowing us to think of moral perception as a kind of acquired, expert perception. Not everyone is a reliable moral perceiver. But this does not entail that no one is, or that some people are not more reliable than others.

Schema theory in empirical psychology again provides suggestions for how this might be so. Specifically, those with the best scripts and personae will be in a position to make the most reliable perceptions. For example, consider the different schemas available to the tourist and the seasoned New Yorker. Walking in the city, the tourist is ill equipped with personae and scripts derived largely from movies and sensationalist news reports. Accordingly, she might see a particular look as aggressive, or a particular gesture as threatening, where the native New Yorker would make no such moral interpretation. There are stories of tourists being approached for directions or the time of day, and clutching their purse.

Or consider an unusually affectionate child – one who runs up to hug and kiss strangers with little or no caution or discrimination. Many people will see this behavior as carefree and innocent. But it can have another moral color for a psychologist or social worker, for whom medical evidence or testimony has evoked the persona of a sexually abused child. The same actions, now understood as manifesting an absence of normal boundaries, will present themselves as tragic, even horrifying. In moral cases as in others, the fact that the expert disagrees with non-experts, or sees differently than they do, does not count against the knowledge of the expert.

What makes the expert's schemas better than those of the non-expert? One answer is that the expert's scripts more accurately portray series of events that we are likely to observe or be involved in, and her personae more accurately portray characters we are likely to encounter. Another possibility is that experts tend to have more schemas, and these enable them to make finer discriminations among types of events and characters. Someone with more available schemas is less restricted by her expectations than someone operating with fewer. Finally, individual scripts and personae of experts might be richer, again allowing for finer discriminations, this time within an invoked script or persona.

But however moral perception works, the important point is that moral disagreement does not count against the possibility of moral perception, or against the possibility that such perception gives rise to justified belief and knowledge in the moral realm. This is because perceptual powers in general need not be widely shared and need not be equally effective. Just as there can be acquired, expert empirical perception, this might be the case regarding moral perception as well.

III. General Conclusions

I will be very brief in drawing some general conclusions from the foregoing study. First, I have been arguing that the analysis of skeptical arguments deserves pride of place in the methodology of epistemology. Specifically, skeptical arguments repay analysis by highlighting plausible but mistaken assumptions about the nature of knowledge and evidence. As I said earlier, I have been intending this thesis both descriptively and prescriptively; I have been arguing that this is how many contemporary epistemologists actually employ skeptical arguments, and that this is what epistemologists ought to do.

Second, I have been arguing that taking skeptical arguments seriously pushes us toward agent reliabilism. That theory explains why various plausible assumptions of skeptical arguments are in fact mistaken. But unlike other forms of reliabilism, it also preserves our persisting intuitions that knowledge requires both (a) non-accidental reliability and (b) subjective justification. The broad picture of knowledge and evidence that results is an externalist, contextualist foundationalism, which is also a version of virtue epistemology. According to agent reliabilism, epistemic notions such as justification, knowledge, and evidence are to be understood in terms of virtuous cognitive character, rather than the other way around. For example, we do not first define a notion of good evidence, perhaps in terms of its logical or quasi-logical relations to evidenced belief, and then define virtuous character in terms of a disposition to form one's beliefs on that kind of evidence. Rather, good evidence is to be understood in terms of reliable and properly motivated character; it is the evidence that a person with virtuous cognitive character would use to form her beliefs. By reversing the direction of analysis in this way, an agent-centered reliabilism is able to explain the kind of non-accidentality required for knowledge, define a relevant sense of subjective justification, and do so in a way that avoids skeptical consequences.

Third, in defending agent reliabilism I have not been claiming to defend a fully detailed theory of knowledge and evidence. Rather, I have been arguing for a general direction in epistemology, or a general framework within which a fully detailed epistemology must work. Accordingly, agent reliabilism is capable of different versions and varieties. I have already mentioned Alston's social practice view, Plantinga's proper functionalism, Sosa's perspectivism, and Zagzebski's neo-Aristotelian approach, and there are other possibilities as well. All of these positions are versions of agent reliabilism, in that they agree that knowledge and justified belief are grounded in the reliable dispositions that make up the knower's intellectual character. Where they differ is on the next level of analysis down, concerning the nature of those dispositions. Another way to put the point is as follows: each of these authors makes his or her position stronger by adding conditions on what counts as virtuous character and, therefore, on what kind of agent reliability is involved in knowledge.

The specific features of these more detailed positions might be necessary to address other important epistemological issues. For example, aspects of Alston's social practice view might be needed to more fully explain the ways in which knowledge is social. Another possibility, however, is that by strengthening the conditions for knowledge these authors make those conditions too strong. In other words, it is possible that the conditions for knowledge and justification that I have been defending, and that all of these authors either already share or could easily endorse, are already sufficient to capture the ways in which knowledge must be objectively reliable and subjectively appropriate. We have already seen that this is a plausible conclusion regarding Sosa's theory. In Chapter 7 we noted that Sosa's notion of a perspective on one's faculties is ambiguous between (a) a set of dispositional beliefs about one's faculties and (b) a set of dispositions which can be identified with one's faculties. There I argued that requiring a perspective in the former sense was too strong, because typically we have no such perspective. But requiring a perspective in the second sense does not add anything to agent reliabilism, since the requirement of a perspective then amounts to no more than the requirement of a reliable character.[23]

A similar dialectic plays out with respect to Alston's and Plantinga's theories. As we have seen, Alston claims that knowledge and justified belief must be grounded in reliable social practices. But as with the first interpretation of Sosa's perspectivism, this seems too strong. Why should

---

23 Sosa's account does add that the perspective must be formed in a reliable way, but again, it is not clear that this requirement can be cashed out in such a way that it both (a) adds something to the requirements already laid down by agent reliabilism and (b) remains a plausible condition on justified belief and knowledge.

we deny knowledge to cognitive agents who are not part of a social group, and who therefore do not engage in *social* practices at all? If such an agent is nevertheless reliable, and if her beliefs are subjectively appropriate in the relevant ways defined, what motivation is there for denying that she has knowledge among her true beliefs? At one point Alston considers this kind of objection. He writes,

> Why not take *all* practices to be prima facie acceptable, not just socially established ones? Why this prejudice against the idiosyncratic? ... It is a reasonable supposition that a practice would not have persisted over large segments of the population unless it was putting people into effective touch with some aspect(s) of reality and proving itself as such by its fruits. But there are no such grounds for presumption in the case of idiosyncratic practices.[24]

It is not clear that Alston's supposition is warranted, nor is it clear why one could not have similar grounds for accepting an idiosyncratic practice. But putting these issues aside, Alston's rationale for distinguishing social and non-social practices makes sense only in the context of his discussion of *practical* rationality. Regarding epistemic justification and knowledge, Alston embraces a reliabilist account; what matters for justification and knowledge is that one's belief-forming practices are in fact reliable. In this context Alston explicitly rejects, and quite rightly, any requirement that one have reasons for believing one's practices are reliable.

We might conclude, therefore, that the social aspect of social practices does no work, and as such has no motivation, in Alston's conditions for epistemic justification and knowledge. Quite the contrary: including a social aspect in these conditions threatens to make them too strong, entailing that individuals who do not engage in group practices cannot have knowledge or epistemically justified belief. On the other hand, by taking the "social" out of social practices, we effectively remove any sense in which Alston's conditions add something to agent reliabilism as I have characterized that position. As we have already seen, to say that an agent engages in reliable practices is just to say that she manifests reliable dispositions in forming her beliefs – that is, it is to say that she displays a reliable cognitive character.

Finally, consider Plantinga's claim that knowledge is grounded in properly functioning faculties, and that proper function is to be understood in terms of functioning according to a design plan. Once again the

---

24 *Perceiving God*, pp. 169–170.

added conditions seem too strong, and so once again there is pressure to weaken what one means by them. As it turns out, Plantinga allows that cognitive faculties might be "designed" by evolution, or by other non-intelligent forces. But this effectively reduces proper function to reliable function, and so effectively reduces Plantinga's position to agent reliabilism *simpliciter*.[25] All of this suggests that agent reliabilism already lays down conditions that are sufficient for objective reliability and subjective appropriateness. It is possible that different versions of the position do less by trying to do more.

Even if this is so, however, it remains the case that the position I have been defending does not constitute a complete epistemology. This is because there are important issues regarding the nature of knowledge and evidence that the position does not address. In closing I will consider two of these.

First, the conditions for justified belief and knowledge laid down in Chapters 7 and 8 are not adequate for addressing Gettier problems. For this reason, I have been careful to characterize the account of knowledge only in terms of necessary conditions rather than sufficient ones. To see why the conditions are not adequate, consider the following Gettier-type example from Zagzebski:

> Suppose that Mary has very good eyesight, but it is not perfect. It is good enough to allow her to identify her husband sitting in his usual chair in the living room from a distance of fifteen feet in somewhat dim light. . . . Of course, her faculties may not be functioning perfectly, but they are functioning well enough that if she goes on to form the belief *My husband is sitting in the living room*, her belief has enough warrant to constitute knowledge when true and we can assume it is almost always true. . . . Suppose Mary simply misidentifies the chair sitter, who is, we'll suppose, her husband's brother, who looks very much like him. . . . We can now easily amend the case as a Gettier example. Mary's husband could be sitting on the other side of the room, unseen by her.[26]

Of course the point is that Mary does not have knowledge in the case, even though her belief is true and is also reliably formed and subjectively appropriate. Accordingly, the conditions that agent reliabilism sets down

---

25 *Warrant and Proper Function*, pp. 13–14. In truth, the issue with regard to Plantinga is more complicated than I have presented it. This is because Plantinga argues that the notion of proper function cannot be given a naturalistic analysis. See esp. Ch. 11.
26 Zagzebski, *Virtues of the Mind*, pp. 285–287. Zagzebski is discussing Plantinga's proper function view, but the example is potentially a problem for any version of agent reliabilism.

as necessary for knowledge are not also sufficient for knowledge; something else must be added.

As far as I can see, there are three ways that agent reliabilism might handle such cases. First, it is possible that the conditions for objective reliability and subjective appropriateness laid down by the position can be interpreted in a particular manner, thereby making them sufficient for addressing this kind of case and other Gettier-type problems. This strategy is represented by Sosa, who goes on to analyze agent reliability in a way that is designed to do just this. The main idea is that reliability is to be understood, at least partly, in terms of a special kind of tracking. So understood, Sosa argues, we get a solution to standard sorts of Gettier problems.[27] A second possibility is that an adequate answer to Gettier problems must add to the conditions for justification and knowledge already laid down by agent reliabilism, but can do so by continuing to draw on the special resources of virtue epistemology. This strategy is represented by Zagzebski, who attempts to address Gettier problems by means of the notion of an act of intellectual virtue. The main idea is this: in cases where one's belief results from an act of intellectual virtue, one believes the truth *because* one's belief is both reliably formed and properly motivated. Placing this sort of condition on knowledge, Zagzebski argues, solves the problem concerning Mary, as well as other Gettier-type problems.[28] Finally, a third possibility is that an adequate answer to Gettier problems is independent of both agent reliabilism and virtue epistemology. Any number of solutions proposed over the past four decades fall into this category.

A second issue that is not fully addressed in the preceding chapters concerns the various ways in which justified belief and knowledge are sensitive to context. We have already seen that agent reliabilism is consistent with contextualism. Indeed, it would be incredible if agent reliability, and therefore justified belief and knowledge, are not partly a function of contextual features. However, there remain substantive issues concerning *how* knowledge is affected by context. For example, there are questions about which social factors affect reliability, and how, and on what subject matters. Very little of what has been said in the preceding chapters bears directly on these important issues.

27 See Sosa, "Postscript to 'Proper Functionalism and Virtue Epistemology,'" in Jonathan Kvanvig, ed., *Warrant in Contemporary Epistemology* (Lanham, MD: Rowman and Littlefield, 1996).
28 See Linda Zagzebski, *Virtues of the Mind*, and Zagzebski, "What Is Knowledge?", in Greco and Sosa (1999).

Moreover, recent authors have argued that knowledge (or knowledge attribution) is sensitive to context in a different sense.[29] Specifically, it has been argued that the *standards* for knowledge depend on context, and so whether a knowledge-claim is true is relative to the context in which the claim is made. It follows from this position that a sentence of the form "S knows p" can be true when uttered by one person in her context, and at the same time false when uttered by a different person in a different context. For example, suppose that I make the claim that traffic is light on the parkway right now. In a context where it does not matter greatly whether I am right, the standards for knowledge are low. Accordingly, you might truthfully say that I know what I claim about the traffic. But suppose that another person is trying to decide what route to take to the hospital, and that it is essential that she take the best one. In this context the standards for knowledge are raised, and the person might truthfully judge that I do not know what I claim.

Agent reliabilism is at least consistent with this sort of position. One way to accommodate it is to say that the *degree* of reliability required for knowledge changes with context. But another way is to say that the *range* of reliability required for knowledge changes. It will be remembered that, in Chapter 8, I defined a cognitive ability in terms of success across close possible worlds. It is plausible that context affects how far out into relevant possible worlds one's reliability must extend.[30] This kind of consideration has been put forward to answer a certain type of skeptical argument. Namely, we noted in Chapter 2 that the skeptical argument from Descartes could be interpreted in the following way:

(D6)   1. A person can know that p is true only if she knows that every possibility inconsistent with p is false.
2. The skeptical dream hypotheses are inconsistent with my beliefs about the world, and I do not know that the skeptical dream hypotheses are false.
3. Therefore, I do not know anything about the world.

I said in Chapter 2 that interpreting Descartes' argument this way made it implausible. More specifically, I said that premise (2) of the argument was implausible, because it seems that I do know that I am not a brain in a vat, for example. But for those who do find (2) plausible, the

---

29 For example, Cohen, "How To Be a Fallibilist," and DeRose, "Solving the Skeptical Problem." My discussion of contextualism in the rest of this section is indebted to both of these authors.
30 A somewhat similar idea is put forward by DeRose in "Solving the Skeptical Problem."

contextualist has an answer. Namely, premise (2) is *true* in contexts where the skeptical argument is being considered, and argument (D6) is therefore sound. This is because that context drives the standards of knowledge high. For example, the context requires that our cognitive abilities extend all the way out to far-off worlds where the skeptical hypotheses are true. But in non-philosophical contexts where knowledge-claims are usually made, the standards for knowledge are not nearly so high. The result is that we do know many things about the world in those contexts, and even if it is also true that in "philosophical" contexts we do not.

Agent reliabilism, therefore, is at least consistent with contextualism of various sorts. But which versions of contextualism are true, and how we are to understand the details, depend on a variety of complex issues, both in the sociology of knowledge and the philosophy of language. Addressing these and other important issues would require a more complete epistemology than the one I have defended here. This being the case, however, agent reliabilism nevertheless constitutes the framework within which such further investigations should take place. This is because, first, rejecting a number of powerful skeptical arguments requires that we adopt some form of reliabilism. Second, the most plausible version of reliabilism is agent reliabilism. Further details in our epistemology, I conclude, should take into account these two results.

Bibliography

Alston, William. "Has Foundationalism Been Refuted?" *Philosophical Studies* 29 (1976): 287–305.
"Level Confusions in Epistemology." *Midwest Studies in Philosophy* 5 (1980): 135–150.
"Christian Experience and Christian Belief." In Plantinga and Wolterstorff (1983).
"A 'Doxastic Practice' Approach to Epistemology." In Clay and Lehrer (1989).
Perceiving God. Ithaca: Cornell University Press, 1991.
Anderson, John. *The Architecture of Cognition*. Cambridge, MA: Harvard University Press, 1983.
Annis, David. "A Contextualist Theory of Epistemic Justification." *American Philosophical Quarterly* 15 (1978): 213–219. Reprinted in Moser (1986).
Aristotle. *The Nicomachean Ethics*. Trans. David Ross. Oxford: Oxford University Press, 1980.
Posterior Analytics. Trans. Jonathan Barnes, 2nd ed. Oxford: Clarendon Press, 1994.
Audi, Robert. *The Structure of Justification*. Cambridge: Cambridge University Press, 1993.
"Dispositional Beliefs and Dispositions to Believe." *NOÛS* 28 (1994): 419–434.
"Intuitionism, Pluralism, and the Foundations of Ethics." In Walter Sinnott-Armstrong and Mark Timmons, eds., *Moral Knowledge?* Oxford: Oxford University Press, 1996.
"Moral Knowledge and Ethical Pluralism." In Greco and Sosa (1999).
Austin, J. L. *Sense and Sensibilia*. Oxford: Oxford University Press, 1962.
Ayer, A. J. *Language, Truth and Logic*. New York: Dover, 1952.
The Problem of Knowledge. Harmondsworth: Pelican, 1956.
Beauchamp, T. L. and Rosenberg, A. *Hume and the Problem of Causation*. Oxford: Oxford University Press, 1981.
Bechtel, William. "Connectionism and the Philosophy of Mind: An Overview." In William Lycan, ed., *Mind and Cognition*. Oxford: Blackwell, 1990.
Bender, John, ed. *The Current State of the Coherence Theory*. Dordrecht: Kluwer, 1989.
Berkeley, George. *A Treatise concerning the Principles of Human Knowledge*. LaSalle: Open Court, 1986.

Bogen, James. "Coherentist Theories of Knowledge Don't Apply to Enough Outside of Science and Don't Give the Right Results." In Bender (1989).
BonJour, Laurence. "The Coherence Theory of Empirical Knowledge." *Philosophical Studies* 30 (1976): 281–312. Reprinted in Moser (1986).
"Can Empirical Knowledge Have a Foundation?" *American Philosophical Quarterly* 15 (1978): 1–13. Reprinted in Moser (1986).
The Structure of Empirical Knowledge. Cambridge, MA: Harvard University Press, 1985.
Carnap, Rudolf. *Logical Foundations of Probability*. Chicago: University of Chicago Press, 1950.
Cavell, Stanley. *The Claims of Reason*. Oxford: Oxford University Press, 1979.
Cherniak, Christopher. "Rationality and the Structure of Human Memory." *Synthese* 57 (1985): 163–186.
Chisholm, Roderick. *Perceiving: A Philosophical Study*. Ithaca: Cornell University Press, 1957.
The Theory of Knowledge. 2nd ed. Englewood Cliffs, NJ: Prentice Hall, 1977.
"Comments and Replies." *Philosophia* 7 (1978): 597–636.
The Foundations of Knowing. Minneapolis: University of Minnesota Press, 1982.
Clay, Marjorie and Lehrer, Keith, eds. *Knowledge and Skepticism*. Boulder: Westview, 1989.
Cohen, Stewart. "How To Be a Fallibilist." *Philosophical Perspectives* 2 (1988): 91–123.
Davidson, Donald. "The Method of Truth in Metaphysics." In P. A. French, T. E. Ueling, Jr., and H. K Wettstein, eds. *Midwest Studies in Philosophy 2: Studies in the Philosophy of Language*. Morris: University of Minnesota Press, 1977.
Inquiries into Truth and Interpretation. Oxford: Clarendon Press, 1985.
"A Coherence Theory of Truth and Knowledge." In Ernest LePore, ed., *Truth and Interpretation: Perspectives on the Philosophy of Donald Davidson*. Oxford: Blackwell, 1992.
Davis, Wayne and Bender, John, "Fundamental Troubles with the Coherence Theory." In Bender (1989).
DePaul, Michael. "Reflective Equilibrium and Foundationalism." *American Philosophical Quarterly* 23 (1986): 59–69.
"Argument and Perception: The Role of Literature in Moral Inquiry." *Journal of Philosophy* 85 (1988): 552–565.
Balance and Refinement: Beyond Coherence Methods of Moral Inquiry. London: Routledge, 1993.
DeRose, Keith. "Solving the Skeptical Problem." *Philosophical Review* 104 (1995): 1–52.
"Contextualism: An Explanation and Defense." In Greco and Sosa (1999).
Descartes, René. *Philosophical Works*. Vol. 1. Trans. Elizabeth S. Haldane and G. R. T. Ross. Cambridge: Cambridge University Press, 1979.
Dewey, John. *The Quest for Certainty*. New York: Minton, Balch, 1929.
Reconstruction in Philosophy. Boston: Beacon Press, 1948.
Dretske, Fred. "Epistemic Operators." *Journal of Philosophy* 67 (1970): 1007–1023.
Dreyfus, Hubert L. *Being-in-the-World*. Cambridge, MA: MIT Press, 1991.
Edwards, Paul. "Bertrand Russell's Doubts about Induction." In Flew (1951).

Fodor, Jerry and Pylyshyn, Zenon. "Connectionism and Cognitive Architecture: A Critical Analysis." In Brian Beakley and Peter Ludlow, eds., *The Philosophy of Mind*. Cambridge, MA: MIT Press, 1992.

Fogelin, Robert. *Pyrrhonian Reflections on Knowledge and Justification*. Oxford: Oxford University Press, 1994.

Foley, Richard. "The Epistemology of Sosa." In Enrique Villanueva, ed., *Philosophical Issues 5: Truth and Rationality*. Atascadero, CA: Ridgeview, 1994.

Flew, Anthony. *Logic and Language, First Series*. Oxford: Blackwell, 1951.

—— *David Hume*. Oxford: Blackwell, 1986.

Fumerton, Richard. *Metaepistemology and Skepticism*. Lanham, MD: Rowman and Littlefield, 1995.

Ginet, Carl. *Knowledge, Perception and Memory*. Dordrecht: Reidel, 1975.

Goldman, Alvin. "Discrimination and Perceptual Knowledge." *Journal of Philosophy* 73 (1976): 771–791. Reprinted in Pappas and Swain (1978).

—— "What Is Justified Belief?" In Pappas (1979). Reprinted in Moser (1986).

—— *Epistemology and Cognition*. Cambridge, MA: Harvard University Press, 1986.

—— "BonJour's *The Structure of Empirical Knowledge*." In Bender (1989).

—— *Liaisons: Philosophy Meets the Cognitive and Social Sciences*. Cambridge, MA: MIT Press, 1992.

Greco, John. "Internalism and Epistemically Responsible Belief." *Synthese* 85 (1990): 245–277.

—— "Virtues and Vices of Virtue Epistemology." *Canadian Journal of Philosophy* 23 (1993): 413–432.

—— "Virtue Epistemology and the Relevant of 'Relevant Possibility.'" *Southern Journal of Philosophy* 32 (1994): 61–77.

—— "Modern Ontology and the Problems of Epistemology." *American Philosophical Quarterly* 32 (1995): 241–251.

—— "Reid's Critique of Berkeley and Hume: What's the Big Idea?" *Philosophy and Phenomenological Research* 55 (1995): 279–296.

—— "The Force of Hume's Skepticism about Unobserved Matters of Fact." *Journal of Philosophical Research* 23 (1998): 289–306.

—— "Perception as Interpretation." In Michael Baur, ed., *Texts and Their Interpretation*, Proceedings of the American Catholic Philosophical Association. New York: American Catholic Philosophical Association, 1999.

—— "Two Kinds of Intellectual Virtue." *Philosophy and Phenomenological Research*. Forthcoming.

Greco, John and Sosa, Ernest, eds. *The Blackwell Guide to Epistemology*. Oxford: Blackwell, 1999.

Hacking, Ian. *The Emergence of Probability*. Cambridge: Cambridge University Press, 1975.

Heidegger, Martin. *Being and Time*. New York: Harper and Row, 1962.

Henrich, D. ed., *Kant oder Hegel*. Stuttgart: Klett-Cotta, 1983.

Hick, John. *An Interpretation of Religion: Human Responses to the Transcendent* (New Haven: Yale University Press, 1989.

—— "The Rationality of Religious Belief." In R. Douglas Geivett and Brenden Sweetman, eds., *Contemporary Perspectives on Religious Epistemology*. Oxford: Oxford University Press, 1992.

Holland, John, Holyoak, Keith, Nisbett, Richard, et al. "Learning Inferential Rules." In Kornblith (1994).

Horwich, Paul. *Probability and Evidence*. Cambridge: Cambridge University Press, 1982.

Howard-Snyder, Daniel, ed. *The Evidential Argument from Evil*. Bloomington: Indiana University Press, 1996.

Hume, David. *Enquiries concerning Human Understanding and concerning the Principles of Morals*. Ed. L. A. Selby-Bigge, 3rd ed. Oxford: Clarendon Press, 1975.

  A Treatise of Human Nature. Ed. L. A. Selby-Bigge, 2nd ed. Oxford: Clarendon Press, 1978.

Klein, Peter. *Certainty: A Refutation of Scepticism*. Minneapolis: University of Minnesota Press, 1981.

Kornblith, Hilary. "The Unattainability of Coherence." In Bender (1989).

  Inductive Inference and Its Natural Ground. Cambridge, MA: MIT Press, 1993.

Kornblith, Hilary, ed. *Naturalizing Epistemology*. 2nd ed. Cambridge, MA: MIT Press, 1994.

Kvanvig, Jonathan. *The Intellectual Virtues and the Life of the Mind*. Savage, MD: Rowman and Littlefield, 1992.

Lehrer, Keith. "The Coherence Theory of Knowledge." *Philosophical Topics* 14 (1986): 5–25.

  "Coherence and the Truth Connection: A Reply to My Critics." In Bender (1989).

Lehrer, Keith and Paxson, Thomas. "Knowledge: Undefeated Justified True Belief." *The Journal of Philosophy* 66 (1969): 225–237. Reprinted in Pappas and Swain (1978).

Locke, John. *An Essay Concerning Human Understanding*. Ed. Peter Nidditch. Oxford: Oxford University Press, 1975.

McClelland, James, Rumelhart, David and Hinton, Geoffrey. "The Appeal of Parallel Distributed Processing." In Brian Beakley and Peter Ludlow, eds., *The Philosophy of Mind*. Cambridge, MA: MIT Press, 1992. Reprinted from James Rumelhart, David McClelland and the PDP Research Group, *Parallel Distributed Processing: Explorations in the Microstructure of Cognition*, vol. 1. Cambridge, MA: MIT Press, 1986.

McDowell, John. "Values and Secondary Qualities." In Ted Honderich, ed., *Morality and Objectivity*. London: Routledge and Kegan Paul, 1985.

  Mind and World. Cambridge, MA: Harvard University Press, 1996.

McGinn, Marie. *Sense and Certainty*. Oxford: Blackwell, 1989.

Moore, G. E. "Four Forms of Scepticism." In *Philosophical Papers*. London: Allen and Unwin, 1959.

Moser, Paul, ed. *Empirical Knowledge*. Totowa, NJ: Rowman and Littlefield, 1986.

Nisbett, Richard and Ross, Lee. "Judgmental Heuristics and Knowledge Structures." In Kornblith (1994).

Nozick, Robert. *Philosophical Explanations*. Cambridge, MA: Harvard University Press, 1981.

Pappas, George. "Some Forms of Epistemological Scepticism." In Pappas and Swain (1978).

Pappas, George, ed. *Justification and Knowledge*. Dordrecht: Reidel, 1979.

Pappas, George and Swain, Marshall, eds. *Essays on Knowledge and Justification*. Ithaca: Cornell University Press, 1978.

Plantinga, Alvin. "Reason and Belief in God." In Plantinga and Wolterstorff (1983).

"Epistemic Probability and Evil." *Archivio di Filosofia* 56 (1988): 557–584. Reprinted in Howard-Snyder (1996).

"Positive Epistemic Status and Proper Function." In James E. Tomberlin, ed., *Philosophical Perspectives 2: Epistemology, 1988*. Atascadero, CA: Ridgeview, 1988.

Warrant: The Current Debate. Oxford: Oxford University Press, 1993.

Warrant and Proper Function. Oxford: Oxford University Press, 1993.

Plantinga, Alvin and Wolterstorff, Nicholas, eds. *Faith and Rationality*. Notre Dame: University of Notre Dame Press, 1983.

Plato. *Dialogues*. Trans. B. Jowett. Vol. 3. Oxford: Clarendon Press, 1953.

Pollock, John. *Contemporary Theories of Knowledge*. Totowa, NJ: Rowman and Littlefield, 1986.

Potter, Vincent G. *On Understanding Understanding*. New York: Fordham University Press, 1994.

Prichard, H. A. *Knowledge and Perception*. Oxford: Clarendon Press, 1950.

Putnam, Hilary. *Reason, Truth and History*. Cambridge: Cambridge University Press, 1981.

Rawls, John. *A Theory of Justice*. Cambridge, MA: Harvard University Press, 1971.

Reicher, G. "Perceptual Recognition as a Function of Meaningfulness of Stimulus Material." *Journal of Experimental Psychology* 81 (1969): 275–280.

Reid, Thomas. *Philosophical Works*. Ed. H. M. Bracken. 2 vols. Hildesheim: Georg Olms, 1983.

Rescher, Nicholas. *Scepticism: A Critical Reappraisal*. Totowa, NJ: Rowman and Littlefield, 1980.

Rorty, Richard. *Philosophy and the Mirror of Nature*. Princeton: Princeton University Press, 1979.

Schmitt, Frederick. *Knowledge and Belief*. London: Routledge, 1992.

Sellars, Wilfred. "Empiricism and the Philosophy of Mind." In *Science, Perception and Reality*. London: Routledge, 1963.

Sextus Empiricus. *Selections from the Major Writings on Scepticism, Man, and God*. Ed. Philip P. Hallie, trans. Sanford G. Ethridge. Indianapolis: Hackett, 1985.

Sosa, Ernest. "The Raft and the Pyramid: Coherence versus Foundations in the Theory of Knowledge." *Midwest Studies in Philosophy* 5 (1980): 3–25. Reprinted in Sosa (1991).

"Knowledge in Context, Skepticism in Doubt." In James Tomberlin, ed., *Philosophical Perspectives 2: Epistemology*. Atascadero, CA: Ridgeview, 1988.

Knowledge in Perspective. Cambridge: Cambridge University Press, 1991.

"Philosophical Scepticism and Epistemic Circularity." *Proceedings of the Aristotelean Society* (1994): 263–290.

"Virtue Perspectivism: A Response to Foley and Fumerton." In Enrique Villanueva, ed., *Philosophical Issues 5: Truth and Rationality*. Atascadero, CA: Ridgeview, 1994.

"Postscript to 'Proper Functionalism and Virtue Epistemology.'" In Jonathan Kvanvig, ed., *Warrant in Contemporary Epistemology*. Lanham, MD: Rowman and Littlefield, 1996.

Stove, D. C. *Probability and Hume's Deductive Scepticism*. Oxford: Clarendon Press, 1973.

Stroud, Barry. *Hume*. London: Routledge and Kegan Paul, 1977.

The Significance of Philosophical Scepticism. Oxford: Clarendon Press, 1984.

"Understanding Human Knowledge in General." In Clay and Lehrer (1989).

"Scepticism, 'Externalism,' and the Goal of Epistemology." *Proceedings of the Aristotelean Society* (1994): 291–307.

Strawson, P. F. *Introduction to Logical Theory*. London: Methuen, 1952.

Stump, Eleonore. "Aquinas on the Foundations of Knowledge." *Canadian Journal of Philosophy*, supplementary volume 17 (1992): 125–158.

Tolhurst, William. "On the Epistemic Value of Moral Experience." *Southern Journal of Philosophy*, 29, supplement (1990): 67–87.

Tulving, E., Mandler, G. and Baumal, R. "Interaction of Two Sources of Information in Tachistoscopic Word Recognition." *Canadian Journal of Psychology* 18 (1964): 62–71.

Van Cleve, James. "Foundationalism, Epistemic Principles, and the Cartesian Circle." *Philosophical Review* 88 (1979): 55–91.

"Reliability, Justification, and the Problem of Induction." *Midwest Studies in Philosophy* 9 (1984): 555–567.

"Epistemic Supervenience and the Circle of Belief." *Monist* 68 (1985): 90–104.

Wheeler, D. D. "Processes in Word Recognition." *Cognitive Psychology* 1 (1970): 59–85.

Williams, Michael. *Unnatural Doubts*. Princeton: Princeton University Press, 1996.

"Skepticism." In Greco and Sosa (1999).

Wittgenstein, Ludwig. *On Certainty*. Oxford: Blackwell, 1969.

Wolterstorff, Nicholas. "Can Belief in God Be Rational Even If It Has No Foundation?" In Plantinga and Wolterstorff (1983).

"Epistemology of Religion." In Greco and Sosa (1999).

Zagzebski, Linda. "Religious Knowledge and the Virtues of the Mind." In Zagzebski (1993).

"Intellectual Virtue in Religious Epistemology." In Elizabeth Radcliffe, and Carol White, eds., *Faith in Theory and Practice: Essays on Justifying Religious Belief*. La Salle: Open Court, 1993.

Virtues of the Mind. Cambridge: Cambridge University Press, 1996.

"What Is Knowledge?" In Greco and Sosa (1999).

Zagzebski, Linda, ed. *Rational Faith: Catholic Responses to Reformed Epistemology*. Notre Dame: University of Notre Dame Press, 1993.

Index

agent reliabilism, 1, 4–6, 50–1, 177–8
  and contextualism, 252–4
  and Gettier problems, 251–2
  historical roots of, 6n
  and problem of strange and fleeting processes, 174–80
  and relevant possibilities, 207, 217–19
  and subjective justification, 180–1, 190–2, 202
  versions of, 248–9
Agrippa, 108
Alston, W., 14, 120n, 178–9, 183n, 226–31, 249–50
American pragmatism, 77
analytic epistemology, 21, 77–8, 179, 181
Anderson, J., 20n
Annis, D., 114, 123–4
appearance–reality distinction (*see also* sensory appearances), 85–6
Aquinas, 6n, 44, 179
Aristotle, 6n, 7, 44, 109–10, 113, 179, 200–1
Audi, R., 96n, 120n, 160–1, 189n, 234n, 242n
Austin, J., 39, 77–8, 81
Ayer, A. J., 50, 96n

Baumal, R., 170n
Bayesianism, 96n, 156n
Bechtel, W., 194n
Bender, J., 132–3
Berkeley, G., 77–8, 81–3, 89, 105–6
blindsight, 171n
Bogen, J., 115n
BonJour, L., 20n, 113–15, 120n, 128–30, 160n, 168n, 181–4, 200n

Calvin, J., 224
Carnap, R., 156n
case of absurd reasoner, 175
case of epistemically serendipitous lesion, 175
case of helpful demon, 175–6
Cavell, S., 39
certainty, 3, 69, 111, 120, 145–6
Cherniac, C., 20n
Chisholm, R., 20–3, 85–7, 113, 116–17, 182n, 200n, 224
Cohen, S., 53n, 253n
coherentism, 19, 20, 126–35
connectionism, 194–8
consequentialist approach to evidence, 99–101
contextualism
  regarding cognitive abilities or virtues, 213–15
  and foundationalism, 124–6
  regarding knowledge attribution, 253–4

contextualism (*cont.*)
  regarding knowledge conditions, 47, 68–9, 252–4
  regarding regress argument, 121–6
Continental philosophy, 77–9

Davidson, D., 72–3, 75, 168n
Davis, W., 132–3
debate with skeptic, 22, 39–40, 43, 65–7, 115–16, 210
deduction, *see* induction
deontological approach to evidence, 99–101
DePaul, M., 232n, 234n, 242n
DeRose, K., 18n, 53n, 186n, 253n
Derrida, J., 168n
Descartes' project, 34–6
Descartes, R.
  argument for skepticism about world, 7, 34–8, 54–60, 253
  as a contextualist, 126
Dewey, J., 69n, 79, 81, 141–3, 145n
Dretske, F., 206n
Dreyfus, H., 79n, 91n

Edwards, P., 146n
epistemic circularity, 229–30
epistemic norms, 100, 192–200
epistemic responsibility, 200–2
epistemology's project, 22, 43–4, 66–9, 120
externalism, 1, 181–2

Flew, A., 146n
Fodor, J., 196n, 197
Fogelin, R., 2n, 16–17, 116–17, 108n
Foley, R., 189n
Foucault, M., 168n
foundationalism, 118–21, 170–1
  classical, 222–3
  and contextualism, 124–6
Fumerton, R., 157n, 160n, 161n

Gadamer, H., 168n
Gettier problems, 251–2
Gilson, E., 77
Ginet, C., 182n, 200n

Goldman, A., 6n, 20n, 54n, 100n, 114–16, 166–7, 170n, 179n, 206n, 209n

Habermas, J., 168n
Hacking, I., 150n, 156n
Heidegger, M., 72–3, 77–9, 81, 90–1, 168n
hermeneutical school, 168
Hick, J., 231n
Hinton, G., 194–7
Holland, J., 199n
Holyoak, K., 199n
Horwich, P., 156n
Hume, D.
  argument for skepticism about future, 27–8
  argument for skepticism about unobserved matters of facts, 7, 138–41, 145, 154
  argument for skepticism about world, 7, 25–34
  and deductivism, 146–8

induction
  inductive and deductive support, 58–60, 149–55, 159–63
  as merely contingently reliable, 172–4
  problem of, 137
inference from appearance to reality, 86–8, 95–101, 169–70, 173–4, 239–41
infinite regress of reasons, skeptical argument from (IR), 7, 110–11

Jeffreys, H., 150n
justification, subjective, 5, 180–1, 190–2, 198–200, 202, 226n

Kant, I., 72–3, 78–9, 200
Keynes, J., 150n
Klein, P., 2n
knowledge (*see also* agent reliabilism, contextualism, Gettier problems)
  account of, 218
  knowing that one knows, 180–4

understanding that one knows, 184–7
Kornblith, H., 115n, 172n
Kvanvig, J., 179n

Lehrer, K., 130–3, 208n
Locke, J., 64
logical space of reasons, 4, 33–4

McClelland, J., 194–7
McDowell, J., 33n, 234n
McGinn, M., 122–3
Mandler, G., 170n
Moore, G. E., 17, 20, 43
moral epistemology, 232–5
moral perception, *see* perception

Nagel, T., 66
naturalized epistemology, 43
Nisbett, R., 199n, 240
no good inference argument (NGI), 84
Nozick, R., 53n

Pappas, G., 62n
particularism, Chisholm's (*see also* strong particularism), 20–3, 224
Paxson, T., 208n
Peirce, C. S., 145n, 146n, 156n
perception (*see also* inference from appearance to reality, sensory appearances)
  elements of, 97–9
  empirical, 235–41
  expert, 246–8
  as merely contingently reliable, 173–4
  moral, 231–4, 241–8
  as non-inferential, 95–101, 239–41
  religious, 225, 226–31
Plantinga, A., 6n, 14, 171n, 172n, 175n, 179n, 226, 231, 250–1
Plato, 44, 67, 109, 113, 177
Pollock, J., 101n, 128–9, 192–3, 193n
post-modernism, 77, 79–80, 90–1
Potter, V., 62n, 63n
Prichard, H. A., 182n

project of epistemology, *see* epistemology's project
proprioception, 93
Putnam, H., 32n, 72–3
Pylyshyn, Z., 196n, 197
Pyrrho, 108

question begging against the skeptic (*see also* debate with skeptic), 39–40, 67, 115–16
Quine, W. V. O., 43–4

Randall, J., 77
rationalism, 69, 126, 148
Rawls, J., 232
regularity principle, 27, 139, 152–6, 159–62, 173
Reicher, G., 170n
Reid, T., 6n, 19–20, 64–5, 105–6, 146n, 179
relevant possibilities approach to skepticism, 56–8, 204–10, 217–19
reliabilism (*see also* agent reliabilism)
  as answer to skepticism, 167–74
  evidence, 5–6, 178
  generic or simple, 1, 4–6, 68, 165–7
  method, 5–6, 178
  objections against, 174–80
  process, 5–6
  social practice, 178–9
religious perception, *see* perception
representationalism, 4, 90–4, 103–6, 141–5
Rescher, N., 62n, 63n, 69n, 145n
Rorty, R., 77, 80–1, 90–1, 124, 168n
Ross, L., 240
Rumelhart, D., 194–7
Russell, B., 17

schema theory, 240–1, 243–4, 247–8
Schmitt, F., 37n
Sellars, W., 33n
sensory appearances (*see also* perception, representationalism)
  as evidence, 95–101

sensory appearances (*cont.*)
  theories of, 85–6
  thin *versus* thick conceptions of, 30–4, 97–9, 135, 174, 236–7
sensus divinitatus, 225
Sextus Empiricus, 108–9
skepticism
  as existential problem, 22, 66, 107
  as theoretical problem, 22, 107
Sosa, E., 6n, 122n, 124n, 134–5, 167n, 168n, 176–7, 187–90, 192, 206n, 216n, 249, 252
Steup, M., 202n
Stove, D., 146–8
Strawson, P., 66, 146n, 153n
strong particularism, 21–4, 108–18, 198, 220–2, 226, 230–1, 235
Stroud, B., 2n, 37n, 39, 41–4, 53–4, 66, 146, 184–7

Stump, E., 110n
Swain, M., 206n

theory of ideas (*see also* representationalism), 4, 141–5
Tolhurst, W., 234n, 242n
Tulving, W., 170n

Van Cleve, J., 169n, 172, 184n
virtue epistemology, 1, 4–6, 177, 191–2, 248, 252
virtues, intellectual, 5–6, 96–7, 176–7, 191–2, 216–17

Wheeler, D., 170n
Williams, M., 2n, 36, 44–51, 96n, 125, 168n
Wittgenstein, L., 39, 121–3
Wolterstorff, N., 231n

Zagzebski, L., 179n, 251–2

For EU product safety concerns, contact us at Calle de José Abascal, 56–1°,
28003 Madrid, Spain or eugpsr@cambridge.org.

www.ingramcontent.com/pod-product-compliance
Ingram Content Group UK Ltd.
Pitfield, Milton Keynes, MK11 3LW, UK
UKHW012212030426
469672UK00010B/219